Radical Wellness

By

The Viking Buddha

Copyright © 2025 by The Viking Buddha

ISBN: 9781917601931

All rights reserved. No part of this book may be reproduced or used in any manner without written permission of the copyright owner except for the use of quotations in a book review. For more information, your details for contact here.

Acknowledgements

I would like to dedicate this book to my best friend, my brother from another mother, who sadly passed away in December 2024, Micky Miller. We had so many plans with the businesses going forward, and he was an important part in the retreats and workshops planned. Both myself, and the kids miss you daily my friend. Until we meet again, Love you always my brother.

I would also like to say a few thanks to a few people who have made this book possible. To my Mum who is always there, for myself and the kids, and is so important to myself and her grandkids. To my dad, who passed away in 2010, who was my hero, and after he passed away took me on this journey to where I am today, questioning many things that were just not right about both medicine and the health world.

The biggest thanks go out to my five children. My eldest two, Shane and Shannon, who I am so proud of, and especially the three not so little ones now, Cheyenne, Cheroken and Cielo, who are my constants, my rocks and the three people who are always there for me. Thank you all for being there.

Also, many thanks to the many people throughout my life who have brought me to this point in my life, Some have been good, and some bad, but all have been lessons which I have learned so much from to become the person I am today.

As in my last book 'The Awakening', thanks go out every day to the amazing people who make up nurses, health care assistants, and support workers, who work hard every day, to help people who need that help in hospitals and care facilities, and to the staff I have worked with over the years including Blackpool Hospital on Ward 12, CIU and also at the Harbour Blackpool.

My last acknowledgement is where my heart goes out to all the people in Los Angeles, who lost their homes and possessions in the fires of January 2024. Myself, Cheyenne, Cheroken, and Cielo, were lucky to be out there just before the fires happened. Los Angeles, is an incredible place, full of wonderful people, and for me like no other place on earth, and our hearts go out to every single person affected by the fires in the Beautiful City of LA.

DISCLAIMER

ABOUT THE AUTHOR

The Viking Buddha, aka, David Bentley, started his interest in the mind, and therapy, whilst studying Psychology, In 2003 he qualified in Clinical Hypnotherapy, and then did further training in 2004 to become a Remedial hypnotist and master hypnotist with some of the best hypnotists. He also qualified as a stress Management Consultant around the same time.

He then added Holistic therapies and clinical reflexology to his qualifications in 2005. He continued more studying into the mind and expanding his knowledge in hypnosis, EMDR, and other forms of Mind therapies.

In 2010, after his father passed away, he started learning more about cancer, and the Natural Cancer Protocol, and has since added many different qualifications to his resume. He is a trained CBT/DBT/REBT/NLP practitioner, Mental Health Therapist, psychodynamic Psychotherapist, and trauma Specialist.

Over the last five years, he has expanded that knowledge to where he is today with a broad knowledge of Precision Health and Functional Medicine, Lifestyle Medicine, The Natural Cancer Protocol, and has further studied into the Autoimmune solution, adrenal fatigue, menopause, the gut brain axis, hormone and thyroid imbalances and diabetes reversal. His desire to finally become a complete mind, and body therapist where he can try and help as many people turn their lives around and help them health themselves is finally here, and this book is the start of something he homes will help so many people in the world.

David has a particular interest in Epigenetics, Quantum Physics and Neuroplasticity, and this knowledge he hopes to share with as many people as he can in this book.

Contents

Acknowledgements

Disclaimer

About the Author

Introduction	1
Chapter 1 Epigenetics	4
Chapter 2 Neuroplasticity	17
Chapter 3: Quantum Embodiment	24
Chapter 4: Mental Health	30
Chapter 5: Substance Abuse	77
Chapter 6: Stress	90
Chapter 7: Cancer	98
Chapter 8: Trauma	121
Chapter 9: Gut-Brain Axis	127
Chapter 10: Hormone Rollercoaster	164
Chapter 11: Obesity & Insulin Resistance	169
Chapter 12: Diabetes Reversal	184
Chapter 13: Autoimmune Disorders	205
Chapter 14: Adrenal Fatigue	243
Chapter 15: Thyroid Imbalances	249
Chapter 16: Immune System & Inflammation	265
Chapter 17: Functional Medicine	278

Chapter 18: Skin Problems 289

Chapter 19: Menopause 293

Chapter 20: Forgiveness & Ho'oponopono 306

Chapter 21: Food as Medicine 314

Chapter 22: Herbalism & Superfoods 329

Chapter 23: Lifestyle Medicine 336

Chapter 24: Hypnosis 344

Chapter 25: Regenerative Medicine 349

Conclusion 353

INTRODUCTION

Namaste, Aloha and welcome to my second book. Following on from first book 'The Awakening', which was a more generic book about various different topics such as Epigenetics, stress, Mental Health, and law of Attraction, to name but a few.

My new Book, which you have in front of you right now, is about 'Radical Wellness'. What I wanted to do with this book is hopefully change lives. I have spent many years training as both a mind and body therapist, and studying about epigenetics, the world we live in and quantum embodiment, and many thousands of hours studying about the human mind, trauma, mental health and how to help people, and over the last few years looking into cancer, the human body, inflammation, the immune system and what causes dis-ease, and how to help people to get their lives back on track.

This book is an alternative medicine book about how things like changing your diet, getting rid of toxins, healing our trauma and past issues and getting rid of your stress, can and will change your lives and it can heal you and your health problems.

I want to say before carrying on, having worked for the NHS for 10 years in general medicine and then worked for last few years in Mental Health, I have nothing but the utmost respect for doctors, nurses, Health Care Assistants and any other person who works in the health and care industry. And the people who work in emergency departments and surgeons demand the highest respect for everything they do

But the one thing I have found is that conventional medicine doesn't heal anyone, it doesn't cure most people, it puts plasters over ailments, diseases and health conditions. Unfortunately, the conventional orthodox medicine fraternity is run by Pharmaceutical companies, making trillions off people being ill, and there have been many doctors and nurses who have come away from conventional medicine to alternative medicine.

If you take for instance, someone who has an headache, a doctor will prescribe pain medication to block out the neuro receptors, not to heal the person, but dampen down the symptom, to put a plaster on.

Someone who has asthma, and wheezy, is given a spray to alleviate or relieve the problem. Does it cure the asthma? Have we found out what is causing those symptoms of being out of breath? Could the person have allergies, food sensitivities, overweight, or other causes of the symptoms? Instead, the plaster is put on, and of course medication for life.

Unfortunately, millions of women are suffering with menopausal symptoms around the whole world, with varying symptoms and debilitating problems. Now Menopause is a significant area where most doctors have no clue how to deal with lessening those symptoms, and for many women the plaster of HRT doesn't even cover the symptom wound. But when you look closer at the symptoms, and the ever-decreasing estrogen levels, the thyroid imbalances, the very probable adrenal fatigue, insulin resistance and gut microbiome problems which ay be at play, you find that there may well be a natural way women can heal their own symptoms and get their life back.

Type 1 diabetes is an autoimmune disease, the pancreas doesn't produce insulin, but type 2 diabetes is a totally different problem, It is basically an insulin resistance problem, where most of the time the pancreas is still producing insulin. Think of your insulin as a special key, which opens the door to the cells, where the glucose which has been made by the carbohydrates you have eaten, should go to give you energy, but it doesn't because it can't get in there, because you are insulin resistant. So why would someone pump more insulin into your body, when the problem isn't actually with the insulin in the first place, and with lifestyle changes type 2 diabetes can be reversed or at the very least managed very effectively.

My last example is cancer, and after watching my father pass away and seen so many friends who have passed away, I have done so much extensive research into cancer. Cancer again is not a disease; it is your body crying out to be healed from the toxic overload and toxicity in the body. Cancer cannot kill you. Chemotherapy does kill! Cancer is formed due to abnormal mutated cells, a toxic overload in the body. When you have 'cancer' it lives off your acidic body, and also feeds off sugar, and this would make me laugh if it didn't make me so sad. Why the hell are they still feeding cancer patients with sugar, acidic food, bread, and other cancer feeding food in hospitals? Cancer cannot survive in an alkaline environment, and it cannot survive without things like the sugars it loves to feed off. I go much deeper into cancer in the cancer chapter, and I really do hope that this starts to open the eyes of people, and they start to heal themselves and their bodies.

I invite you to go on a journey of self-discovery, and a journey of learning about what makes your body go out of a state of homeostasis and your body goes into a state of dis-ease, and how you have the power to regain your health, and take back your life and be healthy again. You have that power! Your health is in your hands, if you only start to listen to it, and learn what you are doing wrong.

I firmly believe that conventional and alternative medicine have a place side by side, where both sides can actually heal people and make people well, but until we actually stop trying to treat the symptoms and put plasters on them, and actually deal with the actual reasons why illness and dis-ease are making people sick, then we are just making an increasingly sick world, and that is so sad, because every single one of us has the ability to take charge of their own lives, and live the healthy disease free life they were meant to have,

I hope you enjoy the book
Namaste
The Viking Buddha

Chapter 1
Epigenetics

Did you know that we all have the ability to change the expression of our genes?

Your DNA and Chromatin regulate the expression of your genes, they can be altered by either external – environmental, or internal-mental and emotional signals without altering the gene sequence itself.

The food you eat, the lifestyle you maintain, the stress, the dramas, the emotional experience, and the quality of the thoughts that you think, and also the relationships that you have, each send signals at different vibrational levels that either support cellular growth, optimal functioning, or predispose you to illness and disease.

Genes are NOT your destiny, as they can be switched on or off. What you need to understand, is that with your thoughts and actions you can build and reinforce new neural networks in your brain, which then send this information to your endocrine system, which in turn send new signals to the receptors on the cells. The receptors on the cells absorb the quality of the vibration being received. We distribute and produce billions of volts of energy every single second. This is circulated through the body and through the space creating intersecting fields.

Joining us at birth, we have an amazing partner in our existence, our microbiome. These are micro-organisms such as bacteria, fungi and viruses that cover our skin, and are in our mouth, fill out stomach and other body parts, sharing their DNA and interacting with ours.

You can heal all of your chronic, emotional, mental and physical illnesses and disorders by learning how to redirect your genes, and to shift your DNA's expression, and to optimize your health and wellness, and improve your existence and the way that you feel, whilst learning how to control your body's biochemical production.

You can become an active participant in your own healing, your emotional and spiritual growth, and prevention of future illnesses. The genes in each cell's DNA respond to the signals that they receive from the environment, externally and internally. You can turn the expressions of your genes on or off.

The food you eat, the company you keep, the TV you watch, the books you read, each of them changes your chemistry and determines the wellness that you experience. Every experience and interaction you have, good or bad, send coded messages to your brain, your cells, to either feel safe and relaxed, or to feel stressed. This establishes your emotional state, which is them expressed through your thoughts, which in turn creates an environment where you either feel safe or unsafe.

The thoughts that you have, send electrical impulses about the way you are perceiving and evaluating the world, and those signals send codes of the judgements that you have about your environment, through your nervous system. All of this produces the results you experience, and this triggers the biological response and emotional response, and this happens thousands of times every day on a subconscious level.

Your beliefs build your ego identity, and this influences your gene expression. Your thoughts and your actions direct your cells on how to respond, the receptors receive these signals and send these signals to the nucleus within each cell and then based on the vibrational energy, it produces the bio chemicals to maintain survival.

It is you who chooses how you look at life, and each choice influences your health. Whether your thoughts and actions are good or bad, they impact your brains receptors, this changes your DNA and cells.

Every single moment you are receiving signals from around you, and from inside yourself and your thoughts. These are either positive or negative, which influence you. It is so vitally important to send the positive vibrations to your DNA and cells.

We need to learn how to switch on the vibrations, thoughts and feelings which bring you empowerment, and joy, which recode your cells and DNA, instead of negatives, which bring on illness and disease.

The roots of any condition you may be suffering from are buried in the unconscious mind and body. Any weakness, or pain which we feel physically has a mental or emotional history which needs to be looked at and dealt with. Your body is giving you messages from the depth of your being, to pay attention and do something about what is causing these issues.

You need to deal with past hurt, past trauma, and you need to go past the walls which have been built in your life, which are saying avoid, don't deal with me, and you need to look within, and deal with them right now. Whatever has happened in the past is over, but until you deal with it, it is still deeply ingrained in you, and your unconscious mind, and is holding you back and making you sick.

Why are you still carrying around the fear, the trauma, the hurt, the pain? Because if you are holding onto all of this negative energy and blockages, that can, and most probably is, the cause of your cancer, your heart disease, your diabetes, and of any other type of imbalance in your endocrine system, because that part of your unconscious mind and body is still holding onto all of these negative emotions and causing blockages in your body, which along with other lifestyle choices eventually cause dis-ease.

The Chinese and eastern medicine looks at illness as an interference of circulation. All of the hormones, the neurotransmitters, are being interfered with and creates blockages and back up in your body, and these need unblocking by facing these problems, and dealing with problems of the past. Anger and stress deposits that we make throughout our lives are put in a bank account, and if they aren't withdrawn, this becomes the build-up of blockages and rage within our body that eventually erupt into symptoms within the body. What we repress inside and are unwilling to look at within our minds, are the things that eventually make us sick and harm us.

If you ever want to get deeper into the subject of epigenetics, I would suggest watching videos or buying books written by the absolutely brilliant Bruce Lipton. Here are a few quotes from him about epigenetics.

"I will show you the science of how the cells actually work, and you will have more knowledge than most doctors in the world today, because they still believe in the genes" Bruce Lipton
"What can cause dis-ease?, either the protein is bad, or the signal is bad. People with bad proteins got them from birth defects, because if you were born with defective genes, and the genes make the protein, then the protein is defective. But less than 5% of the world population has birth defects. That means 95% of the people should have a healthy existence, but if you are one of the healthy people and now you are sick, what would cause the problem?

There are only 3 ways to mess up the signal – 1. Trauma... 2. Toxin's... both of these interfere with the propagation of the signal... and 3. Thoughts – the mind... there is nothing wrong with the body, it is just sending the wrong signal at the wrong time, so if you change your thought and your mind, you can change the biology" Dr Bruce Lipton

"the mind is the primary cause of illness on our planet today. Perception is name of the switch that controls your biology. It is you and how you see the world that controls the biology" Dr Bruce Lipton

Your genes don't make the decisions! A gene is just a blueprint. The gene has no control. The gene is never off or on. What controls the signal? Perception. Your thoughts.

"you are not the victim of your genes, because you control your genes. One gene blueprint using epigenetic control, can make 30,000 different proteins from one blueprint. So you can come with good genes, and then through epigenetic control create cancer, diabetes, heart disease, and it has nothing to do with the genes, but epigenetic control, it returns responsibility for your health to YOU" Dr Bruce Lipton

"95% of cancer is not because of mutant genes, but because of epigenetic control. And it can be passed from parent to child-like genes, but the difference is you can change your epigenetics at any time... if you change your perception, your thoughts, you change the reading of your genes" Dr Bruce Lipton

If a doctor tells you that you have a disease, and you believe that, then you can create the disease.

"The function of the brain is perception, and from that creates the mind. The placebo effect is when you have a very positive thought, that something can heal you, even if it is a sugar pill, but you believe that it is real medicine, then you can heal yourself, The pill didn't heal you, it was the thought that healed you" Dr Bruce Lipton

Statistics show that 33.3% of all medical healings including surgery are from the placebo effect.

"negative effect is called the 'nocebo effect' and in the same power that positive thinking can heal you, negative thinking can kill you. The point is that negative thinking can create all the effects of chemotherapy. If a doctor tells you that you have a disease, or the doctors tells you that you are going to die, and YOU believe the doctor because he is a professional, the belief will give you a disease and can cause you to die, so belief becomes an important part of medicine" Dr. Bruce Lipton

One of the most important reasons we get sick is due to stress.

"the functions of the stress hormones is to take the energy of the body and get it all to run and fight, so the stress hormones will shut off the functions of things that will not be needed in fight or flight. One of the most important uses of energy in the body is the immune system. Stress hormones shut off the immune system, and the significance is, that every one of you right now is infected with almost all of the disease germs that humans have. You all have viruses, bacteria and parasites in your body right now. If your immune system is working properly, it will suppress these parasites, germs, viruses etc, but the moment you start to shut off the immune system then these organisms begin to start growing again" Bruce Lipton

So, it is NOT true that you catch a disease, you already have the disease.

"The medical people call these germs and parasites opportunistic organisms, so if you are under stress and you shut off the immune system, then you give these organisms the opportunity to them make the disease"

Dr Bruce Lipton

You need to start changing your perception and thoughts. You can heal yourself from any dis-ease or condition by changing your thoughts to positive ones and thus changing your cells instructions and blueprint inside your body.

It doesn't matter if you have diabetes, heart disease or stage 4 cancer, you can change your life and regain your health at any time you want to, by changing your thoughts, perception, and thinking positive thoughts and most importantly not getting stressed. You need to deal with trauma, and learn how to not get stressed over things, and learn to change your thoughts and perceptions to renew your cells into new healthy cells and a new healthy blueprint inside your mind and body.

So, when we talk about genetics, our genes are what we inherit from our parents. We get one set of chromosomes from our mother, and the other set from our father. These chromosomes live in the nucleus, which is the centre of every cell. They are made up of one molecule of DNA, and one molecule of protein.

Chromosomes are made up of genes, and they carry DNA in the centre of every cell. The DNA is responsible for building and maintaining your structure. The genes are segments of your DNA which give you the physical characteristics that make you unique. Our genes carry certain coding, and these coding's are what determine things like our blood type, our hair colour, the colour of our eyes, and things like whether we are colourblind or not.

Our genes are what determine many of our physical characteristics, and they are also what can predispose us to certain health conditions such as cancer, diabetes, or coeliac disease as well as many other conditions. Until recently, it was believed that it as our genes that predisposed us to disease, and that as luck that determined whether you suffered from that disease or not. Many people still believe this, and it is simply NOT true. How many people do you hear say 'their parents were both overweight, so it is inevitable that they are going to be overweight. Or some people believe they are going to suffer the same fate of their parents, because they believe they are going to inherit the disease. It is simply NOT true.

Just because we may have inherited a predisposition to a disease, does NOT mean we are going to develop it. It doesn't even mean we are likely to develop it. If you think about genes as a start and finish line for our health destiny is a wrong approach, and it is not true. Genes are not capable of switching themselves on and off. It is something else which is responsible for activating or deactivating these genes.

In 1990 a team of scientists from all around the world, formed an experiment called the Human Genome Project, where they set out to map our genetic material. By 2003, the scientists had identified over 25,000 genes in humans. The main thing that did uncover was something called the epigenome.

DNA contains the instructions for creating every cell in your body. The DNA in our bodies is wrapped around proteins called Histones. Both the DNA and histones are covered with chemical tags. These chemical tags are what are referred to as the epigenome. Your DNA code is fixed for life, BUT the epigenome is flexible. This is because the epigenetic tags respond to the outside world. So, whether a gene is read or unread, or switched on or off, it is completely down to the environmental input.

So, Epigenetics is the science on how environmental signals regulate your gene activity, which in turn shapes your biology. The environmental signals relate to everything from what you eat and drink, the air you breathe, the things you touch, your emotions, how you feel and how you think. What this list above should do, is empower you to think that your health truly is in your hands, because it is a choice. You CAN hack your genes via epigenetics. We are no longer doomed by the genes that we were born with. Our lifestyle choices, the foods we eat, our exposure to pollutants and the air we breathe, our stress levels, toxins, and exercising, all have a direct impact on how our genes are expressed. Which basically means that all of these factors have an ability to switch certain genes on and off.

"Your genes are like a deck of cards, and how you play them is epigenetics, and determines whether you win the game of having an healthy life" Deepak Chopra

How disease develops

Inflammation is a process where the body is trying to protect itself from pathogens and traumas. When inflammation is occurring internally, we have no idea it is happening until it has escalated to such a level that it is causing us obvious outward signs, which often goes hand in hand with a disease diagnosis. Inflammation is implicated in most if not all disease. All disease starts with cellular inflammation, and this inflammation leads to either early cell death, or irregular cell activity. If cells of a particular organ or gland are continually dying at a more rapid speed than they renew, that causes disease of that organ or gland. If cells are activating with irregularity and are left unchecked by the immune system, that fuels cancer cell growth, which leads to tumours.

So, how can we cure disease by looking at the disease itself, when the disease is actually the end point? We need to look at the start point, which is what is happening inside the cells. The cells are constantly reacting to their environment. We need to change the environment to allow healing to occur.

All cells need four basic elements to survive, water, oxygen, food coming in, and waste products going out. If there is a breakdown of any of these four elements, that is when inflammation occurs. We have the power to dampen down inflammation.

Our body is constantly being oxidised, just by breathing, or exercising, or ingesting food. In this process, 1% of cells get damaged, and it is these cells that turn into free radicals.

Free radicals are molecules with unpaired electrons, and each atom in the centre and protons on the outside. These electrons when in pairs, create stable atoms and molecules. When the electrons are unpaired, the atom or molecule loses its stability. It is this instability that makes it a free radical.

The free radicals are desperate to find another electron to pair with, so they will steal from anywhere, and in doing so they kill the healthy cell they stole it from. The problem is that in killing the cell, the free radicals damage the DNA. When the cell's DNA changes, the cell becomes mutated, and mutated cells divide and grow rapidly. The cells that reproduce with mutated DNA will lead to more imperfect copies of themselves, which leads to health issues.

Did you know that by the time you have finished reading this sentence, 50 million of your cells have died and have been replaced by new ones. Our body is constantly being oxidized, just by breathing, The problem is that the free radicals damage the DNA, and when the cells DNA changes, the cell becomes mutated. When the cells are mutated, the divide and grow rapidly, and a cell that reproduces with mutated DNA will lead to more imperfect copies of itself which inevitably leads to health issues, including cancer.

Hacking your genes

Unfortunately, we are exposed to many toxins on a daily basis. Pesticides, and herbicides sprayed on our food crops, which if you didn't know are what was used as nerve gas in World War 2. Another example of toxins every day, are the heavy metals and hormones from HRT and the contraceptive pill, which are in the water supply. Alcohol, smoking, recreational drugs, prescription drugs are all toxins.

The air that we breathe is full of toxins, and stress emotional issues, the job are all toxic to our health and leave an imprint on our body.

The armour in our battle is something called antioxidants. Antioxidants inhibit the oxidation of vital molecules within our cells., and without them we wouldn't last very long. The ore antioxidants you take into your system, the healthier you will be. So, antioxidants are molecules that can safely interact with free radicals and terminate the chain reaction, which alters further DNA damage. How they do this is by donating one of their electrons to the free radical, thereby making it a stable molecule again, what we need to do is make sure that our antioxidant status in our body to outweigh the oxidation in the body.

You need to understand that alcohol, cigarettes, air pollution, UV rays, processed foods and even non-processed foods with heavy metals and pesticides all create additional oxidation in the body. So, the more toxin exposure, the freer radical formation, which in turn means the more free radical formation the greater the need for antioxidants.

Toxicity test

ok, I want you to be honest and take this test about toxin exposure, score 1 point for each question you say yes to, here we go...

		Yes	No
1	Are you overweight?		
2	Do you consider yourself to be unfit?		
3	Do you feel exhausted (as opposed to energised) after physical exertion?		
4	Do you exercise excessively without giving your body rest?		
5	Do you experience regular fatigue with no known cause?		
6	Do you work a shift pattern or have irregular sleep patterns?		
7	Are you often exposed to strong sunlight?		
8	Do you work or live in a polluted city/town or near a busy road?		
9	Do you spend 2 or more hours in traffic on most days?		
10	Do you smoke/ or regularly spend time in a smoky atmosphere?		
11	Do you smoke 10 or more cigarettes a day?		
12	Have you previously smoked regularly & given up less than 5 years ago		
13	Do you find it difficult to recover from infections (lingering symptoms)		
14	Do you tend to bruise easily?		

15	Have you ever suffered from arthritis, cancer, diabetes, gingivitis, heart disease, hypertension, infertility, macular degeneration, or measles?		
16	Have your parents suffered from two or ore of these diseases collectively		
17	Do you suffer from acne, eczema, dry skin, excessive wrinkles for age?		
18	Does your skin take a long time to heal?		
19	Do you suffer from infections regularly (cough or cold more than twice a year) or suffer from reoccurring infections (cystitis etc)		
20	Do you eat processed foods every day (anything out of a tin/packet/jar not in its normal state		
21	Do you eat less than 2 servings of raw or fresh vegetables every day?		
22	Do you eat less than 2 pieces of fruit every day?		
23	Do you eat beans, pulses, lentils, nuts and seeds less than 3 times a week		
24	Do you rarely eat foods rich in Vitamin C?		
25	Do you rarely eat foods rich in Vitamin E		
26	Do you rarely eat foods rich in Vitamin A		
27	Do you eat smoked or barbecued food (including grilled cheese)		

28	Do you eat processed meat (sausages, bacon, ham, salami)?		
29	Do you regularly drink alcohol more than once a week?		
30	Do you drink alcohol every day?		

Score:
1-4: - well done keep up the good work
5-10: - there is clear room for improvement
11-20: - immediate attention is needed
20+: - serious attention is need and drastic lifestyle changes

Antioxidant values and food sources

Antioxidants in food are measured using a scale called the Oxygen radical absorbance capacity (ORAC). The body's main antioxidants are Vitamin C, Vitamin E, beta carotene, which is a form of Vitamin A, and Selenium. These cannot be manufactured in our body, so we need to consume them every single day.

Food sources of vitamin C: - bell peppers, Broccoli, Watercress, Cabbage, cauliflower, Kiwis, Oranges, lemons and strawberries

Food sources of Vitamin E: - sunflower seeds, Sesame Seeds, peas, beans, salmon, sardines, tuna

Food sources for Vitamin A: - carrots, pumpkin, squash, sweet potatoes, melon, watercress, mangoes, beef liver,

Food sources for selenium: - Brazil nuts tuna, sardines, turkey, chicken, cottage cheese, brown rice, eggs, baked beans.

Antioxidant food groups

Phytochemicals help repair human DNA, which in turn helps us avoid disease. The more you eat the more protected you are. You should eat 5 portions of fruit and vegetables per day.

Flavonoids: - Blackberries, Blueberries, cranberries, cherries, elderberries, red and purple grapes, strawberries, grapefruit, lemons, limes, oranges, bananas, carrots, onions, parsley, celery, hot peppers, green tea, dark chocolate (flavan-3ols)

Polyphenols:- blueberries, strawberries, blackberries, cherries, plums, apples, blackcurrants, grapes, pears, peaches, nectarines, apricots, red onions, red chicory, artichoke heads, olives, spinach, nettles, chestnuts, almonds, pecans, hazelnuts, turmeric, cloves, cinnamon, ginger, cumin, oregano, thyme, rosemary, dark chocolate, cocoa powder, black tea, green tea, ginger tea, extra virgin olive oil, red wine, linseed

Phytoestrogens: -apples, berries, grapes, peaches, pears, plus, barley, oats, coffee, beer, olive oil, red wine, tea, flax seeds, sesame seeds, cruciferous vegetables, tofu, tempeh.

Phytochemicals: - carrots, Broccoli, Berries, apples, soybeans, onions, green tea, basil, oregano, parsley, sage, thyme, turmeric, garlic, ginger, nuts, pears, turnips, celery, spinach.

How we live, ie, the lifestyle factors are epigenetically responsible for expressing our genes. Changing your life, your health problems, any ailments you do have is down to you. You can change your life by changing your nutrition, what you eat, your stress, your beliefs and your mindset. You control your future, you control your cells, and you control whether you are healthy and living your best life, or unhealthy, full of disease, and have a short unhappy life. It really is down to you. Epigenetics, Neuroplasticity and Quantum Physics are the way forward to realising your true potential and realising that you control your destiny, and you are not bound to your genes or predisposition from ancestors. You have the power to be healthy or unhealthy, disease free or full of ailments and disease.

Throughout this book you are going to learn more about how you can turn around almost any illness or disease and take back your life.

Chapter 2

Neuroplasticity

How does it work?

Every task requires Neurons. A neuron is a specialized cell that transmits nerve impulses. We have these in our brain, and even the smallest task requires a vast number of interconnected neurons. More complexed tasks require more neurons.
"Neurons that fire together, wire together"
Donald Hebb
We form new neural pathways through repetition. So, by doing things again and again, our neurons connect.
It is kind of like a dance... it takes constant repetition for neuroplasticity to work. Through repetition, they are slowly becoming connected together.
When you repeat actions, neurons wire together, and fire together. You need to keep repeating these actions.

Stage 1: - Chemical changes
When do chemical changes happen? Chemical changes include the following: -
- Neurons which carry signals to the brain are destroyed
- Signals transmitted between brain cells, carried between synapses by neurotransmitters are interrupted.
- The connections between nerve cells of the brain become interrupted.

The chemical changes are only temporary, they do not last forever. What you need to do in the short term is to repeat actions to experience chemical changes.

Stage 2: - Structural changes
Structural changes last longer. The brain structure can change as we learn and form new habits. When the neurons bind together the wire together, and there is a change in the brain structure. The brain structure also changes as we age. We notice certain degenerative factors occur when we get older.

In order to change your brain structure, you need constant repetition that often takes years of practice. By training your brain on a constant basis, you can improve brain structure and cognition.

Your brain structures around your lifestyle.

Stage 3: - Functional changes.
This means the brain has changed. The brain functions are optimized. Now there are different abilities that were not present before, which have now been acquired, and there is a huge increase in neurological performance.

So, if you want to use neuroplasticity to strengthen things that are weak within your mind, such as your memory, or physical co-ordination, you need to alter your brain and form these new connections. You can literally change anything in your life, by forming these new connections.

You need to self-audit yourself and figure out the things you don't do very well. You need to discover your strengths, but also your weaknesses. Then find specific activities and exercises for those weaknesses.

Improve overall memory
Repeat things constantly for long term memory. You need to learn how to move things from your short-term memory to your long-term memory. And this is done by repetition.

If you have a few things that you need to remember, make a story about the things you want to remember.

The grey matter in your brain contains most of the brain's neuronal cell bodies. The grey matter includes regions of the brain involved in muscle control, and sensory perception such as seeing and hearing, memory, emotions, speech decision making and self-control.

The proportion of grey matter can change, and synapses may strengthen or weaken over time.

Until the end of the 20th century scientists assumed that grey matter could never increase in adults, but now recent research has found that this is not true.

Elderly people do show decreased grey matter in the brain, but when it comes to neuroplasticity, we look at things in a different way. Every single person can change their brain, and neural structure through the concept of plasticity.

So, research has shown that a lot of different aspects of the brain can be altered even through adulthood, and neuroplasticity can be observed from multiple scales, from microscopic changes in individual neurons, to larger scale changes such as cortical remapping in response to injury.

"Neurons that fire together, wire together... Neurons that fire out of sync, fail to link"

Each time we learn a new dance step, it reflects a change in our physical brains, new wires (neural pathways) that give instructions to our bodies on how to perform the step.

When you stop exercising, it reflects changes in our physical brain as well, old wires that give instructions related to physical activities weaken or disappear.

If you start a new hobby, and you stop every week, only to get back to doing it after 2 weeks, and you repeat, you will most likely never wire it properly in your brain.

There is a misconception that childhood and young adulthood are the peak periods for brain growth, and in older adulthood, it is considered as a period of cognitive decline. This is not true. Recent research has shown that under the right circumstances, the power of brain plasticity can help adult minds grow.

Neuroplasticity enables people to recover from many things such as strokes, injury, birth abnormalities, and can improve symptoms of autism, ADHD, learning disabilities and other brain deficits.

It can also help with depression, addictions and reverse obsessive compulsive patterns.

The brain has the ability to change, adapt and adjust, both physically, functionally, and chemically, by stimulation from your environment, behaviour, thinking, emotions, habits, and other physical elements.

Neural chains and connections are not fixed at all. When we practice one activity on a consistent basis, neuronal circuits are being formed, leading to better ability to form the practical task with less waste of energy. Once we stop practicing a certain activity, the brain will redirect those neuronal circuits through a much known 'use it or lose it' principle.

You, have the ability to rewire your brain, we aren't just talking about thoughts, we are talking about changing the actual chemistry and physical state of your brain.

Neuroplasticity and Mental Health

How much can neuroplasticity affect our mental health?

Schizophrenia, Bipolar disorder, depression, OCD, and phobic behaviours, epilepsy, occur because of neuroplasticity changes in the brain.

The Mental illnesses are due to a chemical change, and as a result, mental illnesses are part of neuroplasticity., because of these behaviours, your brain is changing its chemistry, and the more this behaviour is repeated, the more it is going to become wired in your brain, and the more it will be hard for you to get over it.

If there is a behaviour that is related to mental health illnesses, that is not treated properly or is not met by an equivalent that can actually reduce its impact, it will become stronger and stronger every single day.

What we want to achieve, is to build something else in your brain, to use your brains plasticity to build another system that can work on lowering the impact of a certain mental health illness that you have.

It can even get to a point that you have full control over it, by just having some triggers and cues that you use, then you can get yourself out of this mental health state at any time.

It is possible to overcome a mental health condition such as depression, schizophrenia, bipolar, addiction, by driving a brain back towards normal operation through neuroplastic change.

Here is what you can do...

- Introspection: - become aware of the problems, how they occur, their effect on you and your surroundings
- Exercises: - practices and exercises to help you overcome the problem by finding a fix for it
- Repetition: - neuroplasticity is all about repetition. make sure that you repeat the exercises daily and regularly to change and help heal your mental health issues.

Every day your brain is like an old tape recorder, playing your problems the moment you wake up, which are connected to certain memories, which in turn are connected to certain people, places and things. So this is the record of the past, and when you start your day like this, you are already thinking and living in the past.

Our memories are emotions which are the outcome and product of past experiences. When you recall your problems, you feel sad, unhappy, and pain, and this creates your state of being, and if you start your day with your past, then sooner or later that past and thoughts will become your future.

Every one of your thoughts, have something to do with your destiny. Think negative thoughts and that is what your future looks like, think positive thoughts, then your future will be more positive. If you keep thinking in the past, you are going to keep creating the same life for yourself.

This normally happens because every day we do the same things, the same procedures, we get out of bed, we look at our phones and social media, watch the news on TV, coffee in same cup, take a shower, and do everything the same way nearly every day.

When you get to work you see the same people, and some of them will irritate you, and push the same buttons every single day, and in the evening, you go back home, and have the same routine nearly every single night, and the repeat, and it becomes your routine. And then it becomes a subconscious program.

By the time we are 35 years old, 95% of who we are is a memorized set of behaviours, emotional reactions, unconscious habits, perceptions, beliefs and attitudes that are hardwired that are just like a program.

With the other 5% of your conscious mind, you might be saying I want to be happy, healthy, wealthy, etc., but unfortunately your body is run by the subconscious minds 95%.

Most people spend around 70% of their lives in survival mode just going along with their safe lives and waiting for something to happen, and all they do is choose the negative things instead of the infinite possibilities available to them in the quantum field.

Your brain produces the same chemistry each, and every time you recall negative events and experiences as if it is happening again. You are sending these same signals to your body about these negative events, and your body thinks it is happening right now, and that is why people are constantly reliving their negative states because they are constantly thinking about them.

Unfortunately, your body becomes programmed to this negative programming, and even though you want to change, the body does not like this, as this is stepping into the unknown, and this is why the body would rather feel suffering, guilt and hurt because it feels familiar and safe, and it can predict it.

The best ways to bypass this negative programming, is by meditation, imagery and visualization. hypnosis, affirmations etc. it is about repetition, and teaching the mind to accept change, and allow your body to feel emotions of your thoughts, and this is where you can download your new programming, and new future life.

On average each person has about 60,000 to 70,000 thoughts in one day. 90% of those thoughts are the same thoughts as the day before. Just because you have a thought it doesn't mean that it is true.

You have the power to change your life anytime you want, you can change your brains neuroplasticity and change it to whatever you want in life.

Chapter 3

Quantum Embodiment

FACT: - Everything you see around you is made up of space (atoms) and time. Space and matter is made up of atoms.

Did you know there are 7 billion billion atoms per person, that's 7,000,000,000,000,000,000 per person, and those atoms are not as solid as we think they are.

Actually, each atom is mostly empty space. All matter is simply a collection of atoms. Everything is made of atoms, and all atoms are made of energy pockets. Matter is energy. Every single thing is made of energy, and these strings of energy all vibrate at different frequencies.

"I*nside atoms there are even tinier bits of matter, including protons and neutrons, which are made of smaller particles called quarks, but physicists realize that this might not quite be the end of the line, and these subatomic bits might be actually made up of something even smaller. Tiny vibrating strands, or loops of energy called strings. Everything that exists is made up of this one kind of ingredient. Strings can take on different properties depending on how they vibrate, creating many kinds of particles"*. Brian Greene

Energy can be in more than one place at a time. Energy appears in response to thought, to mind. It is YOUR mind that chooses to see a thing, and in response to that intent or thought, the energy of that thing, turns up where your mind decides to see it.

Energy is a wave that exists across spacetime, and when your mind chooses to see a thing at a particular place and time, that wave collapses into a particle. Once the mind withdraws, the particle becomes a wave once again.

"In the quantum world, there is a sense in which things don't like to be tied down to just one location, or to follow just one path. It's almost as if things were in more than one place at a time. And what you do there, can have an immediate effect somewhere else, even if there is nobody there" Brain Greene

Everything already exists as a probability when spread across space and time. When you choose to observe it, you then cause it to be a definite thing. Energy is both a wave and a particle. Energy pulses in and out of existence an estimated 50 billion times a second. This is what enables change to happen, when you think about the Law of Attraction.

It seems that energy rearranges or arranges itself according to the information that is filled around. Once the information changes, the arrangement changes.

Think of information as thoughts or beliefs. In essence, you have 50 billion chances per second, to change who you are, or to change the circumstances in your life. The minute you change your mind, the universe changes to that degree.

Thought shapes energy, therefore thought literally shapes matter.

"Every possibility happens, but in an alternate reality. Some physicists believe that all of the possibilities that exist in the quantum world, they never go away. But, Instead, each and every possible outcome actually happens, only most of them happen in other universes, parallel to our own"

Physical reality is a hologram, a projection, an illusion.

In reality, we see less than $1/50^{th}$ of 1% of what is out there, but we believe that what we see is all that is real, we discount what we don't see. In other words, we are given 100 billion bits per second, but we reject all but 2000 bits per second – the same 2000 over, and over again, due to our beliefs and attachments.

Time is also an illusion. All moments of time already exist simultaneously. The only reality is now!

So, what does quantum energy have to do with money and anything else? Consciousness + thought = reality experience.

Quantum physics shows how we are all connected, and how we are all one being, that perpetuates an illusion of separate individual beings.

Your body is made up cells, these cells are in turn made up of molecules, which are in turn made up of atoms, which in turn are made up subatomic particles such as electrons – this is the world of quantum physics.

Quantum energy is NOT 3 dimensional, not linear, not mechanical. It is multi-dimensional, uncountable and unbound by space and time.

So, what is your body made of? Tissues and organs. What are tissues and organs made up of? Cells. What are cells made of? Molecules. What are molecules made of? Atoms. What are atoms made up of? Subatomic particles. What are subatomic particles made up of? ENERGY. They are energy.

Things appear "solid" because that is how human senses and density is built. - but really nothing is solid.

No solid object is solid. It is made up of rapidly flashing packets of energy, billions and trillions of packets of energy, which flash in, and flash out of that space where the object is

"So why does a human body or a car look like a solid continuous object? It is actually a rapidly flashing field of energy. The world is a rapid flash that causes an illusion of being solid and continuous. No matter is a wholly independent existence, independent of the observer. As some scientists say, if everyone, and everything in the universe stopped looking at the moon, and thinking about it, it would not be a physical moon anymore, it would be a probability of existence. The act of observation makes the probability become a definite thing, and all other probabilities of it being elsewhere in the same world a non-existence. Continuous attention keeps it that way, producing the illusion of a solid continuous existence"

David Gikandi

Quantum energy is intelligent, it isn't dead, it is living. Quantum particles make decisions, they are powered by intelligence, and not only that but they also know instantly what decisions are being made by other particles anywhere else in the universe.

This synchronicity across space and time is instantaneous, they communicate without taking any time.

You are the cause for everything around you. Nothing you observe can exist without your observation. All you need to do is choose what you wish to observe, choose it with certainty, and with consistency, and this will cause it to materialize over time.

Your perception is just an optical illusion. Our perception creates our reality based on how we judge and process the events in our lives.

"People only see what they are prepared to see"
Ralph Waldo Emerson

The world as we perceive it, is constantly shifting and constantly changing according to our beliefs and the decisions that we make, not only about the world, but about ourselves.

Whatever environment we have come from, whatever family we have come from, and whatever experiences we have had, we view from those lenses, so everything becomes a reality based on from where we have come from the past.

Whatever you are perceiving, is creating your reality.

In the experiencing of many of our lives, this is a Newtonian experience, because we may all be made of quantum particles, but in this experiencing, at this moment, they are very densely packed, and car running into you will HURT, if you step out in front of it.

Your perception gives you the experience you are having, you are living your reality through your thoughts.

"We don't see things as they are. We see them as we are" Anais Nin

"The reality that you perceive right here is an outward projection of your internal state" Joe Vitale

The world is not being done to you, it is being done by you. It is not coming at you, it is coming FROM you

"Atoms are not things, they are only tendencies"
Werner Heisenberg

"You are not here to create something outside of you, you are here to find who you are, and express that outside of you". Amir Zoghi

"We are slowed down sound and light waves, a walking bundle of frequencies turned into the music of the cosmos, we are souls dressed up in sacred biochemical garments, and our bodies are the instruments through which our souls play their music"
Albert Einstein

Read this again and again... We are energy. Yes, our body is made up of matter, tissues, organs, which are made up of cells, which in turn are made up of atoms, which in turn are protons, neutrons and electrons, which broken down to its smallest is a quark. If you were to look at this it is nearly all just energy, we are energy. When you start to realise this, then you realise you can change your lives, you can get rid of illness, disease, you can manifest anything you want in your life.

You need to beware of your thoughts, as every thought, every action creates vibrations through this infinite field of consciousness. Be mindful of your thoughts and emotions for their effects are far more potent than you realise. When you are able to awaken to the truth that you are life force energy in a human suit, everything in your life transforms, your perceptions shift, your purpose becomes clear, and your connection to the universe deepens.

Everything you do is based on the choices that YOU make. It's not your parents, your past relationships, your job, your genes, the economy, the weather, an argument or your age that is to blame. You and only you are responsible for every decision and choice you make. Period.

Once you understand that your life is in your hands, and your future is in YOUR hands, then it is down to you what your future is going to be. And this goes to your physical body, as to what you put into your body, and how you treat your physical body, with the food, the toxins, stress and the damage you do to your body.

Over the rest of this book, we are going to go from the epigenetics and the quantum physics of what you are spiritually and your soul and energy, to your vessel in this life, and your human body. It's time to look at your spirit, mind and body, and start to reclaim your life in every way,

Only you can decide what your future brings, and in what state your body is in now and what your body will look like 12 months or 5 years from now. Where do you want to be. Let's go on a journey to heal your body!

Chapter 4

Mental Health

The first aspect of your physical health i want to look at is your mental health, and how this can affect you and loved ones around you, and how you can change your mental health around and become the best you can be,
Definition
- A state of well-being in which the individual realises his or her abilities, can cope with normal stresses of life, can work productively and fruitfully, and is able to make contribution to his or her community (WHO 2001)
- Professor Langeveld (1970) suggested 6 criteria against which mental health could be measured: - responsibility, competence and willingness to carry out tasks, self-correction, self-knowledge, common sense, self-reliance

Other definitions
- Autonomy: - any person should be able to manage his own affairs and tasks without necessary reliance on others and should be depended on to meet obligations. Should also be able to discharge responsibilities appropriate to his occupation, social circumstances and interests
- Accurate self-perception: - realisation of our limitations. Everything should be approached within our capabilities
- Mental illness is behaviour, feelings or thinking which interfere grossly with a person's ability to work, to get along with other people or to enjoy life. The concept has the same as mental disorder.
- What are mental disorders: - psychiatry disturbances in perception, beliefs, thought processes and mood (psychosis). Disturbances in mood, concentration, irritability fatigue

Causes of mental ill health
- Bio psychosocial causes of mental health
- Social: - life events, e.g., bereavement, unemployment, chronic adversity eg poverty, domestic violence, lack of social support
- Physical: - genetic, endocrine, nutrition, infection
- Psychological: - learned helplessness, pessimistic cognitive approaches, unhelpful learned patterns of behaviour

Consequences of mental illness
- Suffering, stigma, disability, mortality (suicide, physical illness), unemployment, low productivity, poverty, stress on carer, marital breakdown, intellectual and emotional damage to children, cycle of disadvantage across generations, reduces access to and success of physical health programmes.

Signs and symptoms of minor mental illness
- Depression, anxiety, panic disorder, excessive concern about bodily symptoms (headaches, backaches)
- Loss of enjoyment, low mood, crying, anxiety, panic, fatigue, poor concentration, impaired sleep, impaired appetite and weight loss, irritability, low libido, obsessional thoughts and actions,

Common mental disorders
- Acute psychosis, schizophrenia, bipolar.

Management of mental illness
- History taking: - this is a core skill essential to mental health practice, it has a number of stages
- Assessment: - identifying information (particulars) name, age, sex, address.
- Assessment: - history of current complaint (nature, duration, severity, and impact on person's life, brief systematic review. Are medicines (or other treatments) being taken? The person's belief about the illness, what the person feels the illness is and why it has happened.

- Assessment: - previous history, social circumstances, social support, forensic, personality, mental status examination.
- An orderly and systematic procedure of examining the client's status of cognitive feeling, and behaviour, making an accurate interpretation of findings to assist in diagnosis.
- Differential diagnosis: - possible alternative diagnosis of the condition, carry out investigations.
- Purpose of investigations: - confirm causes, confirm diagnosis and rule out alternatives, assess change and monitor progress in response to treatment.
- Types of investigations: - physical and social investigations

Principles in managing mental health illnesses
- Treat with respect and dignity, whole person approach, proper diagnosis, comprehensive management.

Phases of treatment
- Acute phase : - stabilise acute symptoms, relieve symptoms, and restore previous function.
- Continuation: - maintain stabilisation, prevent return of acute symptoms, continue treatment for the duration of the episode
- Maintenance: - ensure against relapse

Counselling
- A process through which one person helps another through purposeful conversation in an understanding atmosphere
- Its basic purpose is to assist the individual to make his own decision from among the choices available to him.

Hopson (1978) identifies 4 types of helping strategy
- Direct action: - taking action yourself to provide for someone else's needs

- Giving advice: - making suggestions about courses of action another person can and possibly should take, looking at it from your position
- Teaching – helping someone acquire knowledge and skills that you think they need
- Counselling: - helping someone to explore a problem so that he or she can decide what to do about it

Mental health counsellor
- The mental health counsellor works with individuals who are dealing with problems such as drug and alcohol abuse
- Family conflicts, suicidal thoughts and feelings, stress management, problems with self-esteem, issues associated with ageing, job and career concerns, educational decisions, issues of mental and emotional health.

Rehabilitation counsellors
- The rehab counsellor helps people deal with the personal, social and vocational effects of their disabilities.
- Disabilities may be social, mental, emotional, or physical, calling for the services of counselling, evaluation, medical care, occupational training, and job placement.

Rehabilitation
- The process of helping people find ways of returning to the normal life they led before the illness started (learning and retraining)
- The minimisation of the disabilities and impairments resulting from illnesses and disorders
- Abnormal behaviour can make the person isolated from others
- To improve quality of life for person and family and reduce both the stress and stigma associated with mental illness
- To reduce and prevent disability, complications and handicap

- To avoid / prevent acute relapses and enable people with mental illness to live satisfactory lives in the community

Schizophrenia

- Distortion of thinking and perception, detachment from reality, lack of insight, delusions, hallucinations
- Presenting problems: - hearing voices when no one is around, strange beliefs, failure to manage daily activities e.g. cooking washing, strange beliefs, distance with concentration and thinking, failure to manage social interactions.
- Diagnosis of schizophrenia: - client may show signs and symptoms for 1 month. E.g. hallucinations, delusions, thought interference, and disorientated thinking. Differential diagnosis to exclude organic factors.

Stages of schizophrenia

1. Prodromal stage: - general loss of interest, avoidance of social interaction, odd behaviour, over sensitive, odd belief, avoidance of work and study
2. Active phase: - delusions, hallucinations, odd behaviours, strong effects of anxiety and distress
3. Residual phase: - blunted affect, impairment of role function,

Information to patients and family for schizophrenia

- Symptoms may come and go over time
- Medication will reduce the current difficulties and prevent relapse
- Stable living conditions are important for effective recovery (housing, support of family)
- Support of relatives is essential for compliance with treatment and effective rehabilitation
- Advice and support to patient and family: - discuss the treatment with family, explain benefits of medication, encourage patient to be productive, minimise stress and stimulation, keep patient under review.

Management of acute episode of schizophrenia
- Reduce symptoms of psychosis and disturbed behaviour
- Maximise safety of the individual and others
- Think bio psychosocial level
- Build a therapeutic relationship with individual and family
- Reduce symptoms and disturbed behaviour (anti-psychotic medications (chlorpromazine, fluphenazine diaconate
- Long term management: - structured problem solving, communication skills, physical health, lifestyle, community support, rehabilitation, adherence to medication, self-help groups, follow up visits.

Introduction to abnormal psychology
- Abnormal psychology focuses on the patterns of emotions, thought and behaviour, that can be signs of a mental health condition.
- If a behaviour is creating problems in a person's life or disruptive to other people, then this would be an abnormal behaviour.
- Abnormal psychology is the scientific study of abnormal behaviour and mental disorders, in order to describe, predict, explain, and change abnormal patterns of functioning
- Research in abnormal psychology include investigation of the causes and treatment of psycho pathological conditions
- Clinical psychology is the profession and academic discipline that is concerned with the application of psychological science to the assessment and treatment of mental disorders.
- Abnormal behaviour can become pathological and has led to the scientific study of psychological disorders, or psychopathology.
- Mental disorders are characterised by psychological dysfunction, which causes physical, and pr psychological distress or impaired functioning.

How do we determine what abnormal behaviour is?
- Although no definition can capture all aspects of the range of disorders contained in the DSM-5, certain aspects are required, known as the Four D's, Dysfunction, distress, deviance, dangerousness
- Dysfunction: - includes clinically significant disturbance in an individual's cognition, emotion regulation or behaviour that reflects a dysfunction in the psychological, biological, or developmental processes underlying mental functioning.
- Distress- the person experiences a disabling condition in social, occupational or other important activities. It can take the form of psychological or physical pain, or both concurrently.
- Deviance: - closer examination of the word abnormal indicates a move away from what is normal, or the mean, and so is behaviour that infrequently occurs.
- Dangerousness: - when behaviour represents a threat to the safety of the person or others. It is important to note that having a mental disorder does not imply a person is automatically dangerous.
- Ethnocentric concerns: -most definitions of psychological abnormality are devised by white middle-class men. It has been suggested that this may lead to disproportionate numbers of people from certain groups being diagnosed as 'abnormal'. For example, in the UK depression is more commonly identified in women, and black people are more likely than their white counterparts to be diagnosed with schizophrenia.
- Abnormal psychology is the scientific study of abnormal behaviour, with the intent to be able to predict reliably, explain, diagnose, identify the causes of, and treat maladaptive behaviour.

How abnormality was viewed and treated in the past
- Deviant behaviour was seen as a battle of 'good v evil. Deviant behaviour was believed to be caused by demonic possession, witchcraft, sorcery. Mass hysteria and the church, treatments included exorcism, snake pits, beatings, and crude surgeries.

The saw the movement of the moon and stars as a cause of deviant behaviour. They viewed the body and mind as a battleground. The treatment for severe abnormality was to force the demons from the body through trephination and exorcism.

Depression
- Depression is a complex multifaceted mental health condition that affects individuals of all ages, backgrounds and genders.
- It is characterised by persistent feelings of sadness, hopelessness and a loss of interest or pleasure in activities once enjoyed. Depression is more than just feeling down or going through a rough patch, it is a chronic condition that can significantly impact on an individual's daily functioning, relationships, and overall quality of life.

Types of depression
- Major depressive disorder (MDD), also known as clinical depression is the most severe form of depression. Individuals with MDD experience a combination of symptoms that interfere with their ability to work, study, sleep, eat and enjoy life. These symptoms can include feelings of sadness, worthlessness and guilt, as well as changes in appetite, sleep patterns, energy levels, and concentration.
- Persistent depressive disorder (PDD) is a chronic form of depression characterised by a depressed mood that lasts for most of the day, more days than not, for at least 2 years. While the symptoms may not be as severe as those of major depressive disorder, they can still significantly impact an individual's daily functioning and quality of life.
- Seasonal affective disorder (SAD): - SAD is a type of depressive disorder that occurs in a cyclical pattern typically during the winter months when there is less natural sunlight. Individuals with SAD may experience symptoms like those of Major Depressive Disorder, such as low mood, fatigue, changes

in appetite, and difficulty concentrating, but these symptoms tend to subside during the spring and summer months.

Symptoms of depression
- Depression can manifest itself in various ways, and its symptoms can range from mild to severe. Some common symptoms of depression include
- (a) persistent sadness, emotional emptiness, individuals with depression often experience a pervasive feeling of sadness, melancholy or emotional emptiness that persists for an extended period.
- (b) loss of interest or pleasure. Depression can cause a significant loss of interest or pleasure in activities that were once enjoyable such as hobbies, social interactions or intimacy.
- (c) changes in appetite or weight. Depression can lead to significant changes in appetite resulting in either unintentional weight loss or weight gain.
- (d) sleep disturbances: - individuals with depression may experience insomnia or hypersomnia where they either struggle to fall asleep or sleep excessively.
- (e) fatigue and lack of energy: - depression can cause persistent feelings of fatigue and a lack of energy even after adequate rest or sleep.
- (f) difficulty concentrating: _ depression can impair cognitive functions making it challenging to concentrate, make decisions or remember things.
- (g) feelings of worthlessness or excessive guilt: - individuals with depression may experience overwhelming feelings of worthlessness, self-loathing, or excessive guilt, even when these feelings are not based on reality.
- (h) recurrent thoughts of death or suicide: - in severe cases depression can lead to recurrent thoughts of death or suicidal ideation, which require immediate professional intervention.

Causes of depression
- Depression is a complex condition with various contributing factors, including, biological, psychological and environmental influences. Some of the potential causes of depression include: -
- (a) genetic and biological factors: - research has shown that depression can have a genetic component and imbalances in certain neurotransmitters such as serotonin, dopamine, and norepinephrine can contribute to the development of depression
- (b) life events and stressors: - significant life events or stressors such as the loss of a loved one, relationship problems, financial difficulties or traumatic experiences can trigger or exacerbate depressive episodes.
- (c) medical conditions and medications: - certain medical conditions such as chronic illnesses, hormonal imbalances or neurological disorders can increase the risk of developing depression. Additionally, some medications such as certain blood pressure drugs or corticosteroids can have side effects that contribute to depressive symptoms
- (d) substance abuse: - the use of alcohol, recreational drugs or the abuse of prescription medications can contribute to the development of depression or worsen existing depressive symptoms.
- (e) personality traits: - certain personality traits such as low self-esteem, pessimism, or a tendency towards negative thinking patterns can increase an individual's vulnerability to depression.

Impact of depression
- Depression can have far reaching impacts on various aspects of individuals life including: -
- (a) interpersonal relationships: - depression can strain relationships with partners, family members and friends. Individuals with depression may withdraw socially, experience communication difficulties, or struggle maintain intimacy and emotional connections.

- (b) work or academic performance: - depression can significantly impair an individual's ability to concentrate, make decisions and perform at their full potential in work or academic settings. Absenteeism decreased productivity and difficulties meeting deadlines are common challenges faced by those with depression.
- (c) physical health: - depression can have a negative impact on physical health increasing the risk of developing or exacerbating certain medical conditions such as heart disease, chronic pain, or sleep disorders.
- (d) increased risk of substance abuse: - individuals with depression may turn to alcohol or drugs as a means of self-medicating their symptoms leading to an increased risk of substance abuse and addiction.
- (e) suicidal thoughts and behaviour: - in severe cases depression can lead to suicidal ideation or attempts, making it a potentially life-threatening condition that requires immediate professional intervention and support

Breaking the chains of depression
- Depression is a treatable condition, and various therapeutic approaches can be employed to manage symptoms and improve overall wellbeing. Some common treatment options for depression include
- Psychotherapy: - such as cognitive behavioural therapy, interpersonal therapy, or psychodynamic therapy can help individuals with depression. Identify and modify negative thought patterns, develop coping strategies and address underlying emotional issues.
- Anti- depressant medications such as Selective serotonin reuptake inhibitors (SSRIs), Serotonin-Norepinephrine reuptake inhibitors (SNRIs) or tricyclic antidepressants can help regulate neurotransmitter levels and alleviate depressive symptoms.
- Incorporating lifestyle changes such as regular exercise, a balanced diet, stress management techniques and adequate sleep can help alleviate depressive symptoms and overall wellbeing.

- In cases of treatment resistant depression, brain stimulation therapies such as electroconvulsive therapy (ECT) or transcranial magnetic stimulation (TMS) maybe recommended as alternative treatment options.
- Despite its prevalence depression is often surrounded by stigma and misconceptions that can hinder individuals from seeking the help and support that they need.

Some common misconceptions about depression include.

- "Depression is a sign of weakness or a personal flaw" – depression is a legitimate mental health condition that is influence by various biological, psychological and environmental factors, it is not a character flaw or a sign of personal weakness....
- "People with depression should just snap out of it" ... depression is not something that can be easily overcome by sheer willpower or positive thinking alone, it is a complex condition that often requires professional treatment and support....
- "Depression only affects certain types of people" ... depression can affect individuals of any age, gender, ethnicity, socioeconomic status or profession. It is a widespread mental health condition that does not discriminate....
- "Talking about depression or suicidal thoughts will make things worse" ... openly discussing depression and suicidal thoughts with a trusted individual or mental health professional can be an important step in seeking help and support. Silence and isolation can exacerbate depressive symptoms

Psychosis
- Psychosis is a mental state characterised by a loss of contact with reality. Symptoms may include hallucinations, delusions, disorganised thinking, and impaired perception. For example, a person experiencing psychosis may hear voices that others cannot hear or believe that they have special powers or are being persecuted.

- Causes and risk factors: - Psychosis can be a symptom of various mental health disorders such as schizophrenia, bipolar disorder, or severe depression. Other potential causes include substance abuse, brain trauma, or certain medical conditions.
- Genetic and environmental factors may also play a role in the development of psychotic disorders
- Substance induces psychosis such as methamphetamines, LSD, or high doses of cannabis can trigger psychotic episodes in some individuals. Example a person using methamphetamines may experience paranoid delusions, believing they are being watched or followed.
- Psychosis in bipolar disorder: - during manic episodes of bipolar disorder, individuals may experience psychotic symptoms such as grandiose delusions or hallucinations. Example a person in a manic state, may believe they have special powers, or an important mission, leading to impulsive and reckless behaviour.

Schizophrenia
- Schizophrenia is a chronic and severe mental disorder characterised by a range of symptoms including psychosis, disorganised thinking, impaired cognition, and negative symptoms. Symptoms are typically divided into positive symptoms, negative symptoms, and cognitive impairments.
- A person with schizophrenia may experience auditory hallucinations believing that voices are commenting on their actions, or communicating messages

1. Paranoid schizophrenia
- Paranoid schizophrenia: - This is characterised by a sense of paranoia. Heightened anxiety, worrying that someone is watching them, somebody is following them. This often involves delusions and hallucinations. Paranoid delusions, and paranoid hallucinations. The difference between a delusion and an hallucination, is that a delusion focuses on our thinking. Hallucinations refer to us hearing voices or seeing things that are not there, that nobody else sees. They may have auditory

hallucinations or visual hallucinations. They might see a whole load of spies following them.
- Paranoid behaviour is often associated with paranoid schizophrenia, and it is often characterised by feelings of persecution. they are worried about somebody talking about them and planning to do harm to them. The person could try to run away from the voices.
- Paranoid schizophrenia symptoms are associated with very high levels of fear and anxiety, and sometimes anger and hostility. Where the person feels genuinely persecuted and in fear of their lives, they will often lash out a fight other who they see as being involved in this persecution. it can be very frightening for the individual experiencing paranoid schizophrenia like symptoms.
- For paranoid schizophrenia, the interpretation of the environment around us, the interpretation of people laughing on the train when they are on the train, takes on a more sinister role very often, and for the person who is paranoid, they can feel very threatened by that.

2. Disorganised schizophrenia
- this is often characterised by disorganised speech, and disorganised bizarre behaviours. So very often the person with disorganised schizophrenia will talk a language that nobody understands. It doesn't seem to make sense. The sentences, sentence structure, the words are incoherent. They will often be repetitive, and they will talk in a kind of babbling way and grunts, noises and squeaks. Catatonic schizophrenia, Residual schizophrenia, undifferentiated schizophrenia
- they also tend to exhibit inappropriate emotions. For individuals displaying these kinds of symptoms, their emotional reaction to the world around them, is often very different and is not easily understood by the rest of us.
- There is different emotional content, and a different emotional reaction to stimuli or to the world around them. With this type of schizophrenia, as with other types of schizophrenia, often daily regimens and schedules of personal hygiene, eating,

drinking, going to work etc, are often disrupted in disorganised schizophrenia. The person's life becomes very disorganised. It is very difficult for them, and for others to make sense of what is going on.

    3.   Catatonic schizophrenia
- Their behaviour is often associated with disturbances of movement. The person might be motionless, and sit very still, or stand very still and motionless for several minutes, and in some cases several hours, then all of a sudden, they can start to move, and can move very erratically and unpredictably, and outside expectations of 'normal' movement.

- They can often make bizarre noises, and they may often repeat what you say to them.
- These individuals are particularly vulnerable, because they often neglect their personal needs, an often unable to take of themselves adequately.

    4.   Undifferentiated schizophrenia
- This is where the symptoms that are being experienced by the individual do fall under the general umbrella of schizophrenia, but the symptoms might fall under several different types of schizophrenia.

    5.   Residual schizophrenia
- With residual schizophrenia, we refer to the individual who has been diagnosed with schizophrenia in the past, they have been unwell with various symptoms associated with schizophrenia, but at this current point in time they are not displaying any schizophrenia like symptoms.
- Some professionals prefer to refer to this as schizophrenia in remission.

Schizophrenia in children
- The peak age for the onset of symptoms is usually between 16 and 25. Schizophrenia in children is actually very rare. Around 1 in 40,000 children, experience inset of schizophrenia before the age of 14.
- Some children develop childhood psychosis, and experience brief psychotic episodes, especially if they have undergone a lot of traumas during their childhood.

Causes of schizophrenia
- The exact cause of schizophrenia is not fully understood, but it is believed to result from a combination of genetic and environmental factors. Risk factors may include family history, exposure to viruses, or malnutrition before birth, and brain chemistry imbalances.
- Think about this…. what if schizophrenia is 'A sane person's reaction to an insane world?' a famous person argued that 'it's not the individual with schizophrenia that has lost his/her sanity, but that person is reacting in totally normal ways to a world around them that is insane, that is enough to drive any of us crazy'
- Genetics: - one idea is that sometimes we inherit the schizophrenia gene from one or more of our parents. Or grandparents. It is passed down in the genetic history.
- Environment of the individual: - perhaps stressors in the environment, kind of upbringing, racism, discrimination, poverty, poor housing, violence, religious violence.
- Chemistry of the brain: - the brain is the nerve centre of who we are and what we feel. Could schizophrenia is due to abnormal brain chemistry. Imbalance in chemistry
- History of abuse and neglect: -abuse, neglect, trauma. We do know from research that people who develop schizophrenia between the ages of 16 and 25, are more likely to have suffered a deprived childhood, trauma, abuse, traumatic experiences.

Symptoms of schizophrenia.
- Very often with schizophrenia the person doesn't appear to be unwell. Other people around the individual might just feel something isn't quite right. Behaving slightly different, thinking and feeling somehow not quite right. But they are not displaying the full symptoms, the psychosis, the delusions, the hallucinations for example.
- As the illness progresses, the symptoms become more prevalent, more severe, more frequent.
- Social withdrawal, feeling persecuted, experiencing paranoia, high levels of anxiety and worry.
- Anxiety often works alongside psychosis and feed each other.
- Delusions of grandeur, hallucinations, delusions (believe people are out to get them),
- With hearing voices, auditory hallucinations can often be one person, like a running commentary about the individual. Or the voice can talk directly to the individual and tell them what to do. We can that command hallucinations. The voice is telling the individual to do something.
- Voices can also come where there is a conversation going on between several people in the background.
- With hallucinations, sometimes the individual can feel like there are insects crawling all over them, or on the walls, or scratching away at their face.
- They can experience paranoid feelings, or feelings of persecution. and that persecution can come from many different quarters.
- Often in schizophrenia there is a neglect on individual's needs, eating, drinking, sleeping, resting, personal hygiene. The individual can lose confidence in maintaining those friendships and relationships around them.

Positive and negative symptoms of schizophrenia
- Positive: - these are added to the person, that the rest of us don't experience. In addition. Example, delusions, hallucinations, disorganised speech and behaviour.

Dysfunctional thinking, delusional aspects of thinking. Catatonic behaviour.
- Negative: - somehow taken away from individual. Difficult to socialise with other people, social withdrawal, flat effect, lack of feeling, difficulty in expressing their emotions, lack of self-care, the taking away of pleasures, the inability to feel pleasure.

Cognitive symptoms of schizophrenia
- Thinking can be quite chaotic, and the individual with frightening thoughts and the persecution might often not want to tell the clinician about these, so can be quite difficult.
- Paranoid type thoughts on daily basis, difficult to process information, difficulty focusing and concentrating, making decisions, paying attention, confusion when they are hearing lots of voices.

Affect: - the mood component of schizophrenia
- People with schizophrenia often have very high levels of anxiety. The feel paranoid. They often have overlapping depression, suicidal thoughts.
- Sometimes these voices tell the individual that they are worthless, and there is no point in continuing.

More about symptoms of schizophrenia
- Thought broadcasting: - feel their thoughts are being broadcast to the whole world, or to other people.
- Thought insertion: - may feel that other individuals or groups of people are inserting thoughts into that individuals mind. Thoughts been out there by FBI or other people.
- Thought withdrawal: - this is where individual feels thoughts are being stolen from their minds. Somebody is raining their thoughts away, taking their thoughts out of their mind.
- Being controlled: - this is where the individual feels that perhaps aliens etc are controlling their thoughts, feelings and behaviour.

- Loose association: - this is where the individual associate's various words together with no logical meaning for them to be associated.
- Neologisms: - this is where the individual with schizophrenia invents their own kind of language or their own words, these words are just not understood by anybody else, they just don't make any sense to anybody else.
- Concrete thinking: - this is where the individual has very fixed cognitions, very fixed thoughts and ideas on a subject, and stubborn about changes those, or renewing ideas.
- Echolalia: - this is where the individual repeats word for word what somebody else has said. Almost like a parrot.
- Clang association: - this is where the individual will associate words together possibly because they sound alike, but they have no connection otherwise and it doesn't make sense to associate them together just based on how they sound
- Word salad: - this is where the individual uses lots of different jumbled up words that are quite mixed, and the whole sentence structure is quite incoherent, and hard to make sense of what they are trying to communicate to you

Assessment and diagnosis of schizophrenia
- This is based on whole range of factors. First, there is the interview, where the psychiatrist will meet the individual who has been experiencing schizophrenia type symptoms.
- We have the clinical interview where lots of questions are asked about the symptoms, when did they begin, how frequently do they occur, when do they occur, how do they occur, what are the voices you hear, what are the accents of the voices, who do you associate with these voices, do you hear one voice or a whole conversation, do the voices tell you to do things, are the voices condemning you, threatening you, are they helpful and supportive to you.
- In terms of the delusions, the professional wants to get a full understanding of what these delusions are, what is it that the person is thinking about, what are the nature of those thoughts, full story of those thoughts and how they emerged, how

frequently are they thinking in this way and having those delusions.
• Drug testing, alcohol testing, brain scans, blood tests. To rule out other explanations for symptoms
• Ask friends and family about their perception of the individual's behaviour, how does that differ from normal, how has it changed. When did it change.

Assessing and making the initial diagnosis
• Psychiatric evaluation: - a doctor or mental health professional checks mental status by observing appearance, demeanour, and asking about thoughts, moods, and awareness. A person may be diagnosed if they have at least 2 of the following symptoms usually over a month: - delusions, hallucinations, disorganised behaviour, disorganised speech and thought processes, catatonic behaviour presenting as strong daze or hyperactivity, negative symptoms, impaired normal function.

Diagnostic and Statistical manual of mental disorders-schizophrenia (DSM-IV)
• Positive symptoms for > one month, either at least two of elusions, hallucinations, disorganised speech, catatonic behaviour, negative symptoms, OR one of bizarre delusions, commentary or discussing voices
• Markedly impaired functioning
• Continuous signs of disturbance for > 6 months positive or negative symptoms

International classification of Diseases (ICD-10) schizophrenia
• Individual must have at least one of these following symptoms. Thought echo, thought insertion, thought withdrawal, thought broadcasting, delusions of control, commentary voices, bizarre delusions
• OR at least two of: - hallucinations, thought disorder, catatonic behaviour, negative symptoms

- Present for > one month

Electro-Convulsive Therapy (ECT)
- With ECT a rubber gumshield is placed in the individual's mouth, little pads are placed on the temples and hooked up to a machine that gives small but constant electrical charge, kind of electric shock. The brain is being shocked. Used with patients such as schizophrenia with no response to prescribed medication. Some of indications for ECT in schizophrenia are catatonic stupor, acute symptoms, high risk of suicide and self-harm, danger to themselves or others.

Treatment options
- Antipsychotic medications are the primary treatment managing psychotic symptoms and preventing relapses in schizophrenia. Examples include risperidone, olanzapine, and clozapine which help regulate neurotransmitters like dopamine and serotonin.
- Psychosocial interventions: - psychotherapy, CBT, family therapy, can help individuals cope with symptoms and cope with functioning. Social skills training and vocational rehabilitation programs can aid in developing daily living skills and maintaining employment.
- Supportive services, case management, supported housing and assertive community treatment programs provide comprehensive support and assistance with daily living and activities.
- A person with schizophrenia may believe that others can read their thoughts or that they are being controlled by outside forces. They may experience visual hallucinations such as seeing people or objects that are not present, or auditory hallucinations such as hearing voices. Negative symptoms like social withdrawal and lack of motivation can make it challenging to maintain relationships and pursue goals.

Schizo Affective Disorder

Schizoaffective disorder is a complex mental health condition which combines the features of both schizophrenia and mood disorders, such as bipolar or major depression. It is a relatively rare diagnosis, affecting approximately 0.3% of the population. Despite its rarity, schizoaffective disorder can have a significant impact on those who experience it, leading to challenges in daily functioning, relationships and overall quality of life.

Individuals with schizoaffective disorder often experience a combination of psychotic symptoms, such as hallucinations, delusions, disorganised thinking, and mood symptoms, including mania, depression, or a mix of both. It is very difficult to diagnose and treat effectively due to the range of symptoms. People with this disorder may also exhibit symptoms of anxiety, impaired cognition, social withdrawal, and difficulty with self-care.

The symptoms of the disorder can interfere with relationships, work or school performance, and the ability to engage in daily activities. Individuals with schizoaffective disorder may also be at increased risk of substance abuse, self-harm and suicide. The chronic nature of the disorder can contribute to a sense of isolation and hopelessness if not adequately managed.

There are two main subtypes of schizoaffective disorder: - bipolar type and depressive type. In the bipolar type, individuals experience episodes of mania or hypomania in addition to psychotic symptoms. In the depressive type, psychotic symptoms occur alongside major depressive episodes.

While schizoaffective disorder shares some characteristics with schizophrenia, such as psychotic symptoms, it is distinguished by the presence of prominent mood symptoms. In schizophrenia, mood symptoms are generally less pronounced or absent, focusing primarily on psychosis and cognitive deficits.

Treatment for schizoaffective disorder normally involves a combination of medication, psychotherapy, and psychological interventions. Antipsychotic medications are often described to manage psychotic symptoms, while mood stabilisers or antidepressants may be used to address mood symptoms. Psychotherapy, such as CBT, or supportive therapy, can help individuals cope with symptoms, improve insight, and develop coping strategies. Hypnosis can be a huge help with all mental health problems, and we discuss this subject later in the book.

Emotionally Unstable Personality Disorder (EUPD)

Emotionally Unstable Personality Disorder, which is also known as borderline personality disorder (BPD), is a mental health condition characterised by pervasive instability in mood, behaviour, self-image, and interpersonal relationships. Individuals with EUPD often struggle with intense emotions, impulsivity, fear of abandonment, and difficulty regulating their emotions. /

With EUPD there can be intense and unstable emotions, and this may include rapidly shifting emotions, such as anger, anxiety, and sadness. They may have difficulty regulating these emotions, leading to frequent mood swings and emotional dysregulation. They may also show impulsive behaviour, which can manifest in various ways, including reckless driving, substance abuse, binge eating, self-harm, or risky sexual behaviour. Impulsive actions are often driven by a desire to alleviate emotional distress or seek immediate gratification.

People with EUPD often have a pervasive fear of abandonment or rejection, leading to clingy or dependent behaviour in relationships. They may go to great lengths to avoid real or perceived abandonment, which can strain relationships and contribute to emotional instability. They may also have a distorted or unstable sense of self, where they have difficulty forming a coherent identity, leading to feelings of emptiness, confusion, or identity disturbance.

Their interpersonal relationships can be tumultuous, and they may experience intense and stormy relationships characterised by idealisation and devaluation of others. Fear of abandonment and emotional reactivity can lead to conflict and difficulties maintaining stable relationships.

There can be many effects from suffering with EUPD, including relationship instability, occupational impairment and problems at work, self-harm and suicidal behaviour, as they are at increased risk of engaging in self-harming behaviours such as cutting, burning, and other forms of self-injury, and are more at risk of suicidal ideation and suicide attempts.

Treatment for EUPD can be very effective with treatments such as medication, psychotherapy such as DBT, hypnosis and group therapy.

Bipolar disorder
- Psychosis in bipolar disorder: - during manic episodes of bipolar disorder, individuals may experience psychotic symptoms such as grandiose delusions or hallucinations. Example a person in a manic state, may believe they have special powers, or an important mission, leading to impulsive and reckless behaviour.
- Bipolar disorder can affect anyone in the world. There are approximately 51 million people in the world who have Bipolar. In the USA 1 in 7 approximately have Bipolar.

Understanding Bipolar
- Acute: - a short period of severe intensity, for example, an acute mood episode
- Mania: - madness or elatedness. During mania a person will go through a manic period, very high energy, very active, highly confident.
- Hyperthymic: - high energy, very active mentally and physically, highly confident and extroverted, wanting to take risks and not backing down.
- Hypomania: - milder form of mania with increased energy, does not impair daily function.
- Rapid cycling: - a stage in which the mood of the person rapidly shifts from depression and mania more than 4 times in 1 year.

What is bipolar disorder
- Bipolar disorder is a mental illness that brings high and low moods along with changes in sleep, energy, thinking and behaviour. People who have bipolar disorder can have periods in which they feel overly happy and energised, and other periods of

feeling very sad, hopeless and sluggish. In between those periods they usually feel normal.

Bipolar disorder 1
- This is diagnosed in patients who have at least 1 manic episode lasting at least a week. These patients also have multiple episodes of major depression. 30% of affected people cannot function efficiently at work causing them to be at a lower social-economic status due to negligence in treatment plan.

Bipolar disorder 2
- This form of bipolar has a milder form of mood elevation or mania called hypomania. This mania then converts into severe form of depression. Since hypomania is often mistaken for ordinary happiness, this form of bipolar is often misdiagnosed as depression alone.

Cyclothymic disorder
- This type of bipolar, has alternative periods of depression and mania, which do not generally last as long, and not as severe. Bipolar is an imbalance of chemicals in the brain.

Risk factors of developing bipolar
- Genetics: - there is a link between it running in families
- Abnormal brain structure: - PET and MRI scans can show if there are certain abnormalities in the brain that could lead to bipolar disorder. Changes in the hippocampus, amygdala, and the sub-genial prefrontal cortex are examples.
- Substance abuse: - this can affect the brain adversely
- Stress: - stressful environments such as losing a job, relationship issues, bereavement, can trigger the first episode of bipolar.
- Age: - people of ages 15-30 are at a higher risk
- Lack of sleep: - this is also an increased risk of developing bipolar disorder.

Signs and symptoms of bipolar disorder
- Unexpected periods of aggression or anger, overconfidence, frequent sadness, requiring less sleep to feel rested, moodiness, impulsiveness, confusion, melancholy.
- During a manic, or hypomanic episode, they are likely to be euphoric, upbeat, racing thoughts, relentless shopping sprees, sexual risks, very talkative.
- Depressive episode, little or no interest in life, sad, hopelessness, sleep too little or too much, show signs of low energy, fatigue, suicidal ideation.
- People with bipolar are usually not in control of their impulses. They live in the moment and mostly do not think of the consequences of their actions. They are often found indulged in activities that they shouldn't be doing in the first place. Most bipolars, fall easily in the trap of negative activities, because their brain does not know when to stop, whether it is binge eating, sex addiction, lying excessively, driving fast, alcohol an substance abuse,
- Serotonin plays a role in sleep, depression, appetite, and arousal
- Dopamine, controls behaviour, cognition, and emotion
- Norepinephrine: - controls stress response.
- Bipolar medication helps restore normal brain function by stabilising the chemical of the brain. There are 3 major classes of drugs used to treat bipolar.
- Anti-manics / mood stabilisers:- valproate, olanzapine, lithium.
- Anti-psychotics: - chlorpromazine, haloperidol.
- Anti-depressants: - fluoxetine,

Anxiety & Panic attacks
- Anxiety and panic attacks are common mental health issues that can have a significant impact on an individual's daily life, and overall well-being.

- Anxiety is a natural response to stress or perceived threats, characterised by excessive worry, apprehension, and physical symptoms such as muscles tension, breathlessness, and difficulty concentrating. Symptoms may include excessive sweating, rapid heartbeat, trembling, nausea, and feelings of fear or dread.
- Generalised anxiety disorder (GAD), the person may experience persistent and excessive worry about various aspects of life, such as work, relationships, or health, even in the absence of a specific threat.

General anxiety disorder (GAD)
- This is characterised by persistent and excessive worry about multiple areas of life.

Social Anxiety Disorder
- Intense fear and anxiety in social situations often due to a fear of being judged or embarrassed.

Panic Disorder
- Recurrent and unexpected panic attacks often accompanied by a persistent fear of having another attack

Specific phobias
- Excessive fear or anxiety triggered by specific objects or situations such as spiders, wasps, heights, enclosed spaces, flying.

Causes and risk factors
- Anxiety disorders can be caused by a combination of genetic, biological and environmental factors. Traumatic life events, chronic stress, substance abuse and certain medical conditions can increase the risk of developing anxiety disorders
- Brain chemistry imbalances, particularly involving neurotransmitters like serotonin and norepinephrine

Definition of panic attacks
- A panic attack is a sudden and intense episode of overwhelming fear or anxiety, often accompanied by physical symptoms such as chest pains, shortness of breath, dizziness, and a feeling of impending doom. Symptoms typically peak within 10 minutes and can be mistaken for a heart attack or other medical emergencies.

Causes and triggers of panic attacks
- Panic attacks can be caused by specific situations, thoughts or physical sensations, but they can also occur unexpectedly. Stress, trauma, substance abuse and underlying anxiety disorders can increase the risk of panic attacks. Certain medical conditions such as thyroid disorders or respiratory problems may also contribute to panic attacks.

Treatment options for panic attacks
(a) Psychotherapy, CBT, hypnotherapy, are all effective treatments for anxiety and panic disorders. Helping individuals identify and modify negative thought patterns and develop coping strategies. Exposure therapy can gradually desensitize individuals to the situation or stimuli that trigger their anxiety or panic attacks.
(b) Medication: - such as anti-depressants, SSRI's, SNRIs can help manage anxiety symptoms and prevent panic attacks. Benzodiazepines i.e., clonazepam, alprazolam may be prescribed for short term relief of severe anxiety or panic attacks, but they carry a risk of dependence and should be used cautiously.
(c) Lifestyle changes and complementary therapies: - regular exercise, stress management techniques, mindfulness, meditation, breathwork, and a balanced diet can help reduce anxiety and improve overall wellbeing.

Social anxiety disorder
- A person with social anxiety disorder may experience intense fear, and avoid social situations, public speaking, attending parties or meeting new people. They may avoid eye

contact, speak softly, become flushed and sweaty when interacting with others leading to significant stress and impairment in social and professional settings.
- Physical symptoms: - excessive sweating, trembling, rapid heartbeat, muscle tension, and nausea in social situations.
- Cognitive symptoms: - negative thoughts or beliefs about being judged, embarrassed or humiliated by others. Fear of being the centre of attention or scrutiny from others. Constantly worry about saying the wrong thing or appearing awkward during conversations. Leading to avoidance of social interactions.
- Behavioural symptoms: - avoidance of social situations or enduring them with intense anxiety and stress. Difficulty making eye contact, speaking softly, reserved in social interactions,
- Medication: - SSRIs such as paroxetine or sertraline can be effective in managing social anxiety symptoms. Beta blockers can be prescribed too.

Panic attacks
- A person experiencing a panic attack may feel an overwhelming sense of fear or dread, accompanied by physical symptoms such as chest pains, shortness of breath, and dizziness.

Generalised anxiety disorder
- A person with GAD may worry excessively about various aspects of their life such as work, finances, health or family, even when there is no apparent threat or reason for concern.

Eating disorders
Types of eating disorders
(a) Anorexia nervosa: - characterised by an intense fear of gaining weight, distorted body image, and severe restriction of food intake leading to significant weight loss. Symptoms may include extreme calories restriction, excessive exercise, denial of hunger, and an intense preoccupation of body weight and shape.

A person with anorexia nervosa may obsessively count calories, avoid social situations involving food and view themselves as overweight despite being underweight. Someone with anorexia nervosa may become preoccupied with counting calories, refuse to eat certain foods, and exercise excessively despite being underweight. They may deny the seriousness of their condition and resist treatment.

(b) Bulimia Nervosa: - characterised by recurrent episodes of binge eating followed by compensatory behaviours such as self-induced vomiting, laxative or diuretic abuse, excessive exercise. Symptoms may include a pre-occupation with body weight and shape, feelings of shame or guilt after binge episodes, and frequent fluctuations in weight. A person with bulimia nervosa may secretly consume large amounts of food in a short period and then purge through vomiting or laxative abuse to prevent weight gain. A person with bulimia nervosa may engage in cycles of binge eating large quantities of food, followed by purging through vomiting or laxative abuse. They may hide their behaviour and experience feelings of shame and guilt.

(c) Binge Eating disorder: - characterised by recurrent episodes of binge eating without compensatory behaviours, symptoms may include eating large amounts of food in a short period, feeling a lack of control during binges, and experiencing feelings of shame, guilt or distress afterwards. A person with BED may frequently consume large quantities of food in a short time, often in secret, and feel unable to stop eating despite feeling uncomfortably full.

Symptoms and warning signs

(a) Physical symptoms: - rapid or significant weight loss / gain, changes in menstrual cycles, dizziness, fatigue, hair loss, dry skin. Gastro-intestinal issues such as constipation, acid reflux, dental erosion,

(b) Behavioural symptoms: - pre-occupation with food, calories, and weight, ritualistic eating behaviours, avoidance of social situations involving food, hiding or disposing of food, excessive exercise, use of laxatives or diuretics, frequent trips to the bathroom after meals,

(c) Psychological symptoms: - distorted body image, low self-esteem, perfectionism, anxiety, depression, obsessive thoughts about food and weight,

causes and risk factors
(a) Biological factors: - genetic predisposition, brain chemistry and imbalances particularly in serotonin and dopamine levels, and hormonal factors may contribute to the development of eating disorders.
(b) Psychological factors: - low self-esteem, perfectionism, difficulty coping with emotions, preoccupation with body image and weight can increase the risk of developing an eating disorder.
(c) Environmental and social factors: - societal pressures and unrealistic beauty standards, exposure to weight stigma, bullying, traumatic life events and familial influences can play a role in the development of eating disorders.
(d) Treatment options: - hypnotherapy, psychotherapy, CBT, family based therapy. Nutritional counselling, medical monitoring. SSRIs May be prescribed for anxiety and depression.

Manic behaviour
Symptoms of manic episodes
(a) Elevated or euphoric mood: - feeling excessively happy, euphoric or high without a clear reason. A person in a manic episode may feel an intense sense of elation and excitement, even in ordinary situations. Increased energy and activity levels, engaging in excessive physical or mental activity often with little need for sleep. An individual in a manic state may exhibit restlessness, rapid speech, inability to sit still for extended periods, racing thoughts and distractibility.
(b) Experiencing a rapid flow of thoughts and ideas, often jumping from one topic to another. A person in a manic episode may struggle to focus on tasks or conversations, constantly shifting attention and being easily distracted
(c) Grandiose thinking and inflated self-esteem: - having an unrealistic sense of importance, power, or ability. An individual in a manic state will believe they have unique talents or abilities, or that they are destined for greatness.

(d) Risk taking behaviour: - engaging in impulsive, reckless, or risky behaviours without considering the consequences, a person in a manic episode may make impulsive financial decisions, engage in promiscuous behaviour or substance abuse.

Types of manic episodes
- Hypomania: - a milder form of mania, characterised by elevated mood, increased energy, and mild impairment in daily functioning. Individuals with hypomania may still be able to carry out their daily activities, although with some difficulty.
- Mania with psychotic features: - a severe form of mania accompanied by psychotic symptoms such as delusions, false beliefs, hallucinations. Sensory experiences not based in reality. A person in a manic episode with psychotic features may believe they have special powers, or that they are receiving messages from a higher being,

Causes and risk factors
- Biological factors: - imbalances in brain chemicals such as dopamine an serotonin may contribute to the development of manic episodes. Genetic factors also play a role as bipolar disorder tends to run in families.
- Environmental and life events: - stressful life events such as traumatic experiences or major life changes can trigger manic episodes in susceptible individuals. disruptions in sleep patterns and circadian rhythms may also precipitate manic episodes.
- Substance abuse: - the use of substances such as stimulants or hallucinogens can produce manic like symptoms or exacerbate existing manic episodes.

Treatment options
- Medication: - mood stabilisers such as lithium, valproate, or lamotrigine, are commonly prescribed to manage manic episodes and prevent future episodes. Olanzapine or risperidone may be used in combination with mood stabilisers to control acute manic symptoms.

Grandiose delusions
A person experiencing manic psychosis may believe they have special abilities or powers, such as the ability to control the weather, communicate with other beings, or possess extraordinary talents. Increased creativity, and productivity,

Self-harm
Definition and types
- This refers to intentional and non-suicidal intention of harm or injury to oneself. Common forms of self-harm include cutting, burning, scratching, hitting, hair- pulling, and interfering with wound healing.

Symptoms and warning signs
(a) Physical signs: - unexplained cuts, burns, bruises, scars, especially in areas that are easily concealed.
(b) Behavioural signs: - long sleeves or pants even in hot weather, withdrawing from social activities, acquiring sharp objects or potentially harmful items.
(c) Emotional signs: - expressing feelings of worthlessness, hopelessness, or desire to punish oneself.

Causes and risk factors
(a) Psychological factors: - self ham may serve as a coping mechanism for intense emotions such as anxiety, depression, or emotional numbness.
(b) Trauma and adverse life experiences: - individuals who have experienced abuse, neglect or traumatic events may be at higher risk for self-harm.
(c) Mental health conditions: - self harm is often associated with conditions like depression, anxiety disorders, borderline personality disorders, and PTSD.
(d) Social and environmental factors: - bulling, lack of social support, can contribute to self-harming behaviour.

Treatment and support
- Medication: - anti depressants or mood stabilisers

Examples
- Someone who has been bullied and has low self-esteem may resort to cutting their arms or legs as a way to cope with overwhelming emotions and a sense of numbness. She may wear long sleeves to conceal the cuts and isolate herself from friends and family.

Bereavement
Stages of grief
1. Denial: - initially individuals may experience the sense of disbelief or denial. The defence mechanism to protect themselves from the overwhelming emotions associated with the loss.
2. Anger: - as the reality of the loss sets in, individuals may experience intense feelings of anger, either directed at the deceased themselves or even towards others.
3. Bargaining: - in this stage individuals may engage in what if scenarios, or attempt to negotiate a way to undo the loss, often with a higher power or through irrational thoughts
4. Depression: - as the reality of the loss becomes more apparent, individuals may experience profound sadness, loneliness, and feelings of emptiness or despair.
5. Acceptance: - over time individuals may come to terms with the loss and find a way to incorporate it into their lives, allowing them to move forwards whilst still honouring the memory of their loved one.

Types of grief
1. Anticipatory grief: - this type of grief occurs before the actual loss, often experienced by the individuals caring for the terminally ill loved one or facing the impending loss of a relationship or way of life.
2. Complicated grief (also known as prolonged grief disorder): - this involves intense and persistent grief reactions that impair a person's ability to function and adapt to the loss.

3. Disenfranchised grief: - this refers to losses that are not socially recognised or validated such as the loss of a same sex partner, a miscarriage, or the loss of a pet.

Medications
- Generalised anxiety disorder: - SSRI's, benzodiazepines, tricyclic antidepressant or buspirone.
- PTSD: - SSRI's, SNRI's (prazosin is added to control nightmares)
- Delirium: - antipsychotics such as haloperidol
- Major depressive disorder: - first line SSRIs (citalopram, fluoxetine, paroxetine). Second line SNRIs such as atomoxetine, venlafaxine, duloxetine... third line: - TCAs such as amitriptyline, trimipramine, nortriptyline... MAO inhibitors such as isocarboxazid, phenelzine, selegiline.
- Bipolar: - Mood stabilisers such as lithium.
- Schizoaffective disorder: - lithium + antipsychotics.

Antidepressants
- Antidepressants: - two neurons are connected to other using a synapse. This is how one neuron communicates with another. The first neuron retakes or reuptakes the transmitters that have been sent. The medications simply block this action.
- SSRIs: - Selective serotonin reuptake inhibitor – side effects include agitation, feeling sick, indigestion, bowel habit changes, weight loss, blurry vision, and dryness in mouth.
- SNRIs: - serotonin-norepinephrine reuptake inhibitor – side effects include tiredness, constipation, insomnia, libido changes, appetite loss.
- DNRIs: - norepinephrine-dopamine reuptake inhibitor
- TCAs: - Tricyclic antidepressant, side effects include dry mouth, blurry vision, constipation, drowsiness, weight gain, excessive sweating
- Monoamine oxidase inhibitor: - side effects include dry mouth, constipation, headaches, drowsiness, insomnia, rashes.

Antipsychotics
- First line: - pine, done, zole. Eg, olanzapine, risperidone, aripiprazole
- Second line: - azine + haloperidol, eg thioridazine, fluphenazine
- Acute psychosis: - first line – LAZ – Lurasidone, Aripiprazole, Ziprasidone
- Acute psychosis: - second line – clozapine, olanzapine.
- Potency: - high potency but more side effects:- haloperidol, fluphenazine, Loxapine
- Agitated patients: - first line – lorazepam – injectable and rapid onset of action

Barbiturates
- Phenobarbital, Pentobarbital, Secobarbital, Thiopental
- Sedative, seizure control, induction of anaesthesia – thiopental

Benzodiazepines
- Diazepam, lorazepam, triazolam, chlordiazepoxide
- Mechanism of action: - allows chloride to flow into neurons by increasing the frequency that chloride channel is open. Chloride suppresses neurons. Receptor type (like barbiturates) is ligand-gated NOT G-protein coupled.
- Insomnia_ midazolam due to its short half-life - Seizure control:- 1st line for alcohol withdrawal seizures, night terrors, sleepwalking, anxiety

Depressants
- Opioids – MOA, Ca-channel close & K-channel opens – cell inactivated – decrease pain substances – treatment: - naloxone, naltrexone
- Alcohol: - MOA potentiates GABA and depresses multiple centres in the brain. Slurred speech – naltrexone. Labs- Raised GGT. …. Ataxia – disulfiram. Raised AST…. Disinhibition – acamprosate. Use benzodiazepines to avoid delirium tremens in case of alcohol withdrawal

Understanding mental health disorders

One of the first steps in supporting s loved one with mental health issues is to educate yourself about the various mental conditions and issues.

Understanding the symptoms, causes, and treatment options for various mental health disorders can help you provide better support and care for your loved one. It is essential to recognise that mental health issues are medical conditions that require proper diagnosis and treatment, just like physical illnesses.

A definition by the WHO in 2011 described mental health as 'A state of well-being in which the individual realises his or her abilities, can cope with normal stresses of life, can work productively and fruitfully, and is able to make contribution to his or her community'

In 1970, Professor Langeveld suggested 6 criteria against which mental health could be measured: - Responsibility, Competence and willingness to carry out tasks, self-correction, self-knowledge, common sense, and self-reliance.

Other definitions for mental health include autonomy, 'where any person should be able to manage his/her own affairs and tasks without necessary reliance on others and should be depended on to meet their obligations. They should also be able to discharge responsibilities appropriate to their occupation, social circumstances and interests'

Do I agree with all the above, no not necessarily, which I will cover in this book.

Mental illness can be described as certain behaviour, feelings, or thinking which interferes greatly with a person's ability to function properly, their ability to work, and get along with other people or to enjoy their life.

"It's difficult to describe depression to someone who's never been there because it's not sadness. Sadness is to cry and to feel. But it's that cold absence of feeling – that really hollowed out feeling" J.K. Rowling

Breaking stigma and promoting understanding

It is crucial to dispel myths and misconceptions surrounding mental health and reduce stigma associated with mental illness. By promoting awareness and understanding, you can create a supportive environment that encourages open dialogue and reduces barriers to seeking help. One of the hardest things for a person suffering with mental health conditions is having to hide their condition and how they are feeling.

Stigma is thinking negatively about people with menta health conditions, and mental health still has to a degree a stigma attached to it, even though it has got slightly better with media campaigns etc, but the stigma is still very much there.

There is also discrimination, where people with mental health get treated unfairly because of their condition, whether it be out in the world in general, or in the workplace.

There are some general factors in our society that shape the way that many people think about mental illness, and this can lead us to stigmatise those who have mental health conditions. One of these factors that can help to create this stigma about mental health, is how societies have dealt with people who had mental health in the past and historically.

So, I want you to imagine that you go to your GP and complain about a terrible sadness that you are feeling, you have felt this way for a month, and it is getting worse. Your doctor then tells you that he thinks this is caused by... evil spirits that are trapped in your skull... and the only solution, and that solution is to drill a hole through your skull to let the evil spirits to escape. Sounds like horrible fiction, right? But you would be wrong. This is one of the real procedures which was called trephination (also known as trepanning) which were performed on people who had mental health issues. Examination of prehistoric skulls and cave painting show that this procedure was actually used to try and cure people with mental and other illnesses. I think we can all agree that this probably didn't cure anyone who had mental health issues.

The idea that mental health had supernatural causes such as evil spirits which are inside you, continued to be believed, and some even believe this now can you believe. In the eleventh to the fifteenth centuries, supernatural explanations for mental health illness were very common. Many people saw a mental health condition as a punishment from God. To be able to cure it, you would have to attend religious worship, also confess and repent for all your sins.

In the fifteenth to seventeenth Centuries, if you had mental health issues, you were seen as a witch and was possessed by demons. The treatment for this was being hanged or burnt at the stake. They believed that being possessed could happen to anyone, and the only way for this evil spirit to be let from and exorcised was by causing the body physical pain. This amounted to torturing the patient.

In ancient Greece they thought that mental illness was caused by an imbalance of bodily fluids, which they called humours. The way they tried to cure people with mental illness was by bloodletting with the idea of readjusting the balance of bodily fluids.

In more modern times, the focus was to isolate people with mental health issues and hide them away from society. Mental asylums began to grow in the sixteenth century, which were used to put people with mental health conditions in away from the general society. The intentions for these institutions may have been to provide care, but they were more like a prison. People with mental health problems were often forced there against their will and lived in appalling conditions. A very common idea at this time would have been that the mental ill was just like animals, and it was fine to let them live like animals.

At the infamous Royal Bethlehem Hospital in London, also known as Bedlam, the conditions there were truly horrific, where they were left to live in their own filth, and some were chained to the wall. Patients were often left starving and sometimes had to beg staff for food.

In the twentieth century, treatments like Electroconvulsive therapy (ECT), where an electrical shock is used to treat mental illness, along with lobotomies, where a doctor would remove a small part of the brain via the eye socket. ECT does have some therapeutic value and is sometimes used now as a way of treating psychotic depression.

Blaming a person for their mental illness is something society has a history of doing, and it is a trend that sadly continues up to the present day. This is why mental health carries the stigma it does today, because we have a history of blaming people for being unwell.

The surprising fact is that it was only in the 1980s that the move away from asylums happened, and a more positive attitudes towards mental health. However, people with mental health problems are often stereotyped as unpredictable, unreliable and even dangerous. Many people with mental conditions still suffer prejudice and discrimination, and this must change.

Although it is better in many ways now, and things like the Ant and Dec mental health campaign on TV, and celebrities also coming out with their own mental health issues, it is still sometimes the case that mental health is often presented in the media in stereotypical ways. Mental health can often be sensationalised in the media, as a source of dangerous and irrational behaviour. When there is unbalanced negative coverage with regards to mental health, this often reinforces the negative stereotypical view of mental health.

Think of on-screen characters like Normal Bates (psycho), Hannibal Lecter (Silence of the Lambs), Malcolm Rivers (Identity), Martha Scott (Baby Reindeer), to name but a few. Seeing mental illness portrayed like these shapes how we think about mental health as a whole, and in many cases, people end up with a view of mental illness that isn't really in line with the reality of the situation. 77% of characters with schizophrenia were portrayed as being dangerous, whereas the figure is actually 3% (Corrigan and Watson, 2002).

The fact that some celebrities have been brave enough to come out and be open about their mental health problems has certainly helped to de-stigmatise mental health and it has helped raise awareness in society, the 'normalising' of mental health issues, and some of these celebrities have acted as good role models and giving others confidence to speak out. On the flip side of this, there may also be some negatives as there is a possibility that mental illness may become glamourised. Overall, I think it is so beneficial for people suffering with mental health issues, to see that they are not on their own, and mental health problems can happen to anyone.

If celebrities such as Stephen Fry, David Beckham, Prince Harry, JK Rowling can be open about their mental health issues, then it will hopefully encourage others to do the same.

I think how Tyson Fury the famous heavyweight boxer has been open and honest about his struggles with mental health and Bi-polar is actually quite inspiring, as he openly talks about his ups and downs, and has helped to make mental health more acceptable, and the fact that it can affect anyone.

"Honestly, you may not see mental health, but believe me, it's real. People may act happy, smiley, but inside they are hurting so bad. It takes a second to send a text to a loved one or friend to ask how they are. You are worth it. You are loved" Tyson Fury

"I fought back from thinking about suicide, mental health, depression and anxiety. I wanted more than anything to show the world it can be done. Anything is possible with the right mindset" Tyson Fury

Apart from being very brave coming out and talking about his own mental health problems, Tyson Fury has become kind of a mental health ambassador, and also shown how far a person can go in their lives even with mental health problems, depression etc, and that with the right help and right attitude you can go forward and get the most out of your life.

I want to share just a few more quotes from other celebrities who have struggled with mental health, which will hopefully show that you can turn your life around to whatever you want to be, and you can get through it with the right support from the professionals, family and friends etc.

"You just feel like you're alone. You feel like it's only you, You're in your bubble. I found that with depression, one of the most important things you could realise is that you are not alone. You're not the first to go through it, you're not going to be the last to go through it. I wish I had someone at the time who could

just pull me aside and say, hey it's going to be OK, it will be OK. Have faith that on the other side of your pain is something good" The Rock

"It doesn't have to take over your life, it doesn't have to define you as a person, it's just important that you ask for help. It's not a sign of weakness" Demi Lovato

"We can no longer afford to be silenced by stigma that portray mental health conditions as a matter of weakness or moral failing" Lady Gaga

"To all of those like me who overschedule, overthink, overwork, over-worry, and over-everything, please know you are not alone" Ryan Reynolds

"Mental health is a sensitive subject amongst a lot of people, but it doesn't need to be. We need to talk about it more, get rid of the stigma" Prince Harry

"It is okay to have depression, it is okay to have anxiety, and it is okay to have an adjustment disorder. We need to improve the conversation. We all have mental health in the same way we all have physical health" Prince Harry

    I think the last quote from Prince Harry sums it up quite well. We all have our physical health and mental health. At times we struggle with our physical health, and at times most people will struggle with their mental health at varying degrees. I have been there with depression myself, and it is debilitating. I have worked with many people with different types and mental health problems, and it can happen to anyone at any time, and it is important for people to open up and talk about what is going on in their lives and get the support they need. I think men especially bottled up their emotions and problems, and that is why suicide is higher in men.

The statistics regarding mental health are quite worrying, and it is important that we start to see that mental health is very real, very much out of someone's control in many cases, just as physical health, and get rid of any stigma regarding mental health, and support your family, friends and loved ones who may just be going through hard times in their lives and may be suffering with the mental health.

Here are some worrying statistics about mental health: -

- 1 in 4 people will have a common mental disorder at some point in their lives (NHS 2014)
- 75% of those with a diagnosable mental health disorder receive no treatment at all (Davies, 2014)
- 57% of people would not feel able to disclose a mental health condition they were suffering from to anyone else (Capita, 2015)
- Every year 300,000 people with a long-term mental health condition lose their jobs (Labour Force Survey 2016-17)
- Somewhere in the world, a suicide takes place every 40 seconds (NHS, 2014)
- For every 1 suicide, there are 25 attempts (International Association for Suicide Prevention, 2017)
- Men are three times more likely as women to commit suicide (NHS, 2014)

Supporting a loved one who is facing mental health issues can be a challenging and emotionally taxing experience. Mental health conditions such as depression, anxiety, bipolar disorder, schizophrenia, and others, can have a significant impact on an individual, as well as on their relationships with family and friends.

In this chapter, we will explore various aspects of supporting loved ones with mental health issues, including understanding mental health, offering emotional support, providing practical assistance, promoting self-care, seeking professional help, and fostering open communication.

Supporting a loved one with mental health issues requires compassion, patience, understanding, and a willingness to provide both emotional and practical support. By educating yourself about mental health, offering emotional support and providing practical assistance, prompting self-care, encouraging professional help, and fostering open communication, you can be a source of strength and comfort for your loved one in their journey towards healing and recovery. Remember that supporting someone with mental health challenges is a marathon and not a sprint.

Emotional support is a fundamental aspect of helping a loved one cope with mental health challenges. Listening attentively, showing empathy, and validating their feelings are essential components of providing emotional support. Let your loved one know that you are there for them, that you care about their well-being, and that they are not alone in their struggles.

Avoid judgement, criticism, or dismissive attitudes towards their feelings and experiences. Instead, offer encouragement, reassurance, and a non-judgemental space for them to express themselves freely. Your presence, understanding, and compassion can make a significant difference in their journey towards recovery and healing.

In addition to emotional support, practical assistance can also be valuable in supporting a loved one with mental health issues. This may include helping them with daily tasks, such as cooking, cleaning, running errands or managing appointments at times when they are struggling with the mental health. Offering practical support can alleviate some of the stress and burden they may be experiencing due to their mental health condition.

Encourage your loved one to engage in self-care activities, such as exercise, hobbies, relaxation techniques, or social outings. Help them establish routines and structure in their daily lives, as consistency, and predictability can be beneficial for managing symptoms of mental illness. By providing practical assistance, you can empower your loved one to focus on their recovery and well-being.

Self-care is essential for maintaining mental and emotional well-being especially for individuals dealing with mental health issues. Encouraging your loved one to prioritize self-care practices that promote relaxation, stress management and overall health is so important. This may include getting enough sleep, eating nutritious meals, exercising regularly, and engaging in activities that bring joy and fulfilment.

Help your loved one identify coping strategies that work for them, whether it be mindfulness, meditation, journalling, creative expression, or spending time in nature. Encourage them to seek professional help when needed and to adhere to their treatment plan, whether it involves therapy, medication, hypnotherapy or other interventions. By promoting self-care, you can support your loved one in building resilience, managing symptoms and improving their quality of life.

Whilst your support and encouragement are valuable, it is essential to recognise that professional help may be necessary for your loved one's mental health treatment. Encourage them to seek help from mental health professionals, such as therapists, counsellors, hypnotherapists, psychiatrists or support groups.

Professional intervention can provide specialised care, evidence-based treatments, and personalized strategies for managing mental health conditions.

Support your loved one in finding the right mental health provider and in attending appointments regularly. Offer to accompany them to therapy sessions or doctor visits if they feel anxious or overwhelmed. Remember that mental health professionals are trained to assess, diagnose, and treat mental health disorders effectively, and their expertise can complement the support you provide to a loved one.

Understanding mental health resources and services

The Mental Health Act is a legal framework that governs the assessment, treatment and rights of individuals with mental health disorders. It provides a mechanism for the compulsory detention and treatment of individuals who are deemed to be at risk to themselves or others due to their mental health condition.

There are several key sections of the Mental Health Act that outline the circumstances under which an individual can be detained for assessment and treatment. These sections include: -
- Section 2: - this section allows for the detention of individuals for assessment in a hospital for up to 28 days. It is used when there is a belief that an individual is suffering from a mental disorder that requires assessment and treatment, and they may be at risk to themselves or to others.
- Section 3: - This section allows individuals to be detained for treatment in a hospital for up to 6 months. It is used when there is a need for ongoing treatment of a mental health disorder and the individual is a risk to themselves or others if they are not detained.
- Section 4: - This section allows for the emergency detention of individuals for up to 72 hours for assessment. It is used in situations where there is an urgent need for assessment and treatment of a mental health disorder, and the individual is unwilling to consent to voluntary treatment.
- Section 5 (2): - This allows for the detention of individuals who are already in hospital for treatment under Section 3. It permits the extension of detention for up to 6 months following the initial detention period.
- Section 5 (4): - This section allows for the transfer of individuals from one hospital to another for treatment under the Mental Health Act. It is used when it is deemed necessary to move an individual to a different hospital for their care and treatment.
- Section 135: - This section allows for the detention of individuals in their own homes for assessment by a doctor. It is used when there is a need to assess an individual's mental health state, but they are unwilling to go to a hospital for assessment.
- Section 136: - This section allows for the detention of individuals in a public place for assessment. It is used when the police have concerns about an individual's mental health and believe that they may be at risk to themselves or others.

These are just a few of the key sections of the Mental Health Act that outline the circumstances under which an individual can be detained for assessment and treatment. The Act is designed to balance the rights of the individuals with mental health disorders, and protect others from harm.

Chapter 5

Substance Abuse and Mental Health

Substances abuse can be described as overindulgence and excessive use of an addictive substance. i.e. alcohol and other drugs. Mental health refers to a person's mood, thoughts and ability to function and relate to others. Mental illness is the condition that disrupts this mental wellbeing.

Neuroplasticity
3 important principles of brain learning, healing and adaptation
1. Repetition: - (e.g. child learning to tie their shoelaces)
2. Focused attention: - releases a learning / memory neurotransmitter (acetylcholine)
3. Pleasure from learning (seeing reward and benefits) releases a pleasure neurotransmitter (dopamine)
Unfortunately, this works for us or against us in addictions
3 important principles of our brain, thoughts, words and actions
1. Thoughts: - change our brain genetics (epigenetics) electromagnetic signals and chemicals
2. Words: - express thoughts and reflect our attitude, which give life or death to our body and soul
3. Deeds (actions): - we have free will to influence our emotions, thoughts and all of the processes above. This creates a positive or negative feedback loop.
Unfortunately, this works for us or against us in addictions

Drugs are chemicals, chemicals can be poisons.

Routes of administration: - there are 4 ways a drug can be administered into the body.
1. Oral dose
2. Inhalation
3. Injection
4. Rectal dose

The closer the drug is administered to the blood stream, the greater the impact but the shorter the effect.

Drug effects on the brain
Stimulants – depressants – hallucinogens

4 phases of addiction
- Expérimental
- Social / recreational
- Harmful dependency / daily pre-occupation
- Using to feel normal

Phase 1:- experimental – learns that experimenting with the substance makes one feel good. Does not generally recognise any serious negative consequences. Learns to trust the drug. Learns how much to use (substance) to feel good.

Phase 2:- social – more regular use or practice. Makes this a part of social life. Uses or practices at appropriate times and place. Makes 'safe' rules for self-regarding use. Turns into problem without warning.

Phase 3:- daily pre-occupation – harmful dependency. Becomes a harmful dependency. Begins to lose control over use/practice. Cannot block out the emotional pain. Unresolved problems produce more stress and pain. Life-style centres on compulsive behaviour. Self-imposed rules broken regularly. Deteriorating health, emotions, relationships, spirituality.

Phase 4:- using to feel normal – full blown addiction - Problems have snowball effect. Loss of control and dignity. Broken family relationships. Paranoid thinking – delusion. No desire to live. Geographic escapes. Spiritual bankruptcy.

Phases of addiction – intervention
1. Experimentation – drug information, education, harm minimisation.
2. Social – drug information, education, harm minimisation, counselling
3. Harmful dependency – medical, support group, counselling, detox, rehab.
4. Addiction – medical, support group, counselling, detox, rehab

<u>Stages of change</u>
this helps us identify the stage a person is in and what their next step forward is.
Stage 1: - pre contemplative – have not considered they have a drug problem, therefore not thinking about changing their drug use patterns
Stage 2: - contemplative – have identified that they have a drug problem, thinking about making changes. However, no change occurs.
Stage 3: - decision – know they have a drug problem, planning to do something about it.
Stage 4: - action – treatment starts. Drug use declines and or stops
Stage 5: - maintenance – ongoing treatment, strategies developed to prevent relapse. Monitoring of progress.

<u>Stage 1: - Pre-contemplative</u>: - no problem identified; no change sought. Interception: - regular contact, they need to have their level of awareness raised. Harm minimisation strategies. Do not enable their drug use. Allow them to experience the consequences of their drug use.

<u>Stage 2: - Contemplative: -</u> problem is identified. No change occurs. Interception: - same strategies as pre-contemplation. Do a costs v benefits exercise with them to motivate change towards decision (stage 3)

<u>Stage 3: - Decision:-</u> know they have a problem. Plan to change.

Interception: - need to give 'very clear' options of pathways at this point. Refer to phases of addiction model, track their phase of drug use and refer to intervention suggested. Be specific e.g., detox, counselling etc.

<u>Stage 4: - action: -</u> gets treatment. Drug use declines and or stops.

Interception: - assist and encourage them in their treatment. Regular contact to monitor their progress.

<u>Stage 5: - maintenance: -</u> treatment continued. Strategies to prevent relapse.

Interception: - work with relapse prevention plan. Do not assume they are ok because they are in treatment (90% of people relapse). Follow-up plan.

Alcohol

Alcohol is a drug. It enters the blood stream and into the brain rapidly from the stomach. Alcohol is an addictive drug (like other drugs that target the brain chemicals we naturally make.

Alcohol depresses the brain activity. Alcohol slows down messages going to and from the brain.

Standard drink: - what's that?

1 standard drink is any drink that contains 10 grams of alcohol.

- 10 grams of alcohol, in one glass of wine 100ml
- 10 grams of alcohol, in 1 mid strength beer 375ml
- 10 grams of alcohol, in 1 nip of spirits 30ml

Why are females affected by alcohol more than males? Alcohol is broken down by the liver. Females have smaller livers than males. Females have proportionately more body fat and less water than males (alcohol is not taken up by fatty tissues). Females produce less dehydrogenase, an enzyme that breaks alcohol down.

Alcohol: - mothers and their babies

Alcohol passes straight to the baby via the placenta. If the mother is drunk – so is the baby. Alcohol has a toxic effect on the developing cells and organs it kills brain cells.

Alcohol effects: - children and adolescents

Children and adolescents absorb alcohol faster than adults (their livers metabolise alcohol less efficiently). Self-reporting shows that many adolescents and teenagers do not drink socially – they drink to get drunk, smashed, wasted etc.

Adolescents are at serious risk from alcohol because of their physically smaller size. Low tolerance to alcohol, lack of drinking experience and their intent of drinking to get 'plastered'

Binge drinking: - 'alcohol poisoning'
- Binge drinking can lead a person to suffer alcohol poisoning
- Alcohol poisoning = blood alcohol levels rising to dangerous point and shut down critical organs.
- Causing loss of consciousness, slowing the breathing and heartbeat. Vomiting can occlude the airway. Used with other drugs can have a lethal effect.
- People do die from too much alcohol.

How do you know someone has 'alcohol poisoning?'

You can't wake them by pinching, prodding or shouting. Their skin is cold, pale, bluish or purplish (they are not getting enough oxygen). Breathing very slowly, (10 seconds between each breath)

Vomiting without waking up. Conscious and vomiting heaps. Someone can die 'sleeping' it off in the corner.

Poly Drug use: - Poly – many

Alcohol is often involved in poly drug use. Poly drug use causes exacerbated effects.

Cannabis

Cannabis the drug contains over 420 chemicals. When combusted form over 2000 chemicals. No other illicit drug is found to have all these chemical properties.

- Cannabis acts on specific areas in the human brain. The areas are called cannabinoid receptors. These receptors normally receive our own cannabis type chemical (anandamide – human brain cannabinoid)
- THC a cannabinoid, targets cannabinoid receptors and it interferes with normal brain functioning.
- Anandamide – is the brains own THC just like endorphins are the brains own morphine. Anandamide plays an important role in regulating mood, memory, appetite, the same areas the cannabis affects.
- Cannabis uses is associated with greater psychotic symptoms and increased potential risk of aggression. Users experience significantly more delusional ideas and other psychotic symptoms compared to non-users.

Stimulants

They stimulate brain activity. Speed up messages going to and from the brain.
- Amphetamines (speed, go-Ey, whiz, uppers, base, ice)
- Methylamphetamine (ICE)
- Crystalline methylamphetamine

Adverse effects from amphetamines can be fatal.

Amphetamines can be smoked, injected, snorted, pills drinks.
- Effects on the body usually last about 4-6 hours however can be up to 36 hours depending on the quality and amount taken.
- Amphetamines / ecstasy cause large amounts of potent chemicals to be released in the brain. Adrenaline – noradrenaline – serotonin – dopamine. These chemicals regulate emotions (depression / anxiety) mood (happy / aggression) BP, HR, temperature, sweating, airways, pain perception.

Amphetamine use – physical patterns you can look for
- Amphetamines cause hyperactivity of the CNS (Brain)
- Large pupils, nausea / vomiting, racing pulse, C/O chest pain, rapid breathing, fainting, increased BP, headaches, sweating – hot (high temperature.

Amphetamine use – behavioural patterns to look for
- Users become hyper-alert
- Overconfidence
- Easily startled, anxiety
- Confusion, increasing agitation
- Aggressive violent outbursts, extra strength
- Amphetamine induced psychosis
- Paranoia (delusions, generally excessive use)
- Out of touch with reality. Increased risk of suicide,
- Impulsive violence, potential for homicide.

A person affected by amphetamines (brain stimulant) very awake, opposite to collapse, serotonin depleted and prone to homicidal or suicidal behaviour)

Psychosis – intense paranoia, confusion, anxiety, visual and auditory hallucinations, out of control rages, delusions.

<u>Health risks associated with ICE (Methylamphetamine)</u>
<u>Speed (Amphetamine)</u>
- Ingredients: - acetone, lithium, toluene (brake fluid) hydrochloric acid, pseudoephedrine, red phosphorus, sodium hydroxide, sulfuric acid, anhydrous ammonia.

<u>Ecstasy – methylenedioxymethamphetamine</u>
<u>(Ecstasy, E, Ecky, XTC, the hug drug, love drug, dance drug, X, MDMA</u>
- ONE PILL COULD KILL
- Effects – lasts about 3-4 hours (peaks in about 2 hours)
- Physical patterns – large pupils, C/O Headache, increased BP nausea / vomiting, teeth grinding, tongue and cheek chewing, jaw clenching, dry mouth, sweating – extreme rise in temperature

- Behavioural patterns – feeling of well-being (euphoria), feeling of increased closeness to others, lack of inhibitions, increased confidence, inability to sleep, anxiety, paranoia, psychotic (out of touch with reality)
- Serotonin levels are seriously affected in ecstasy users and are at risk of death from serotonin toxicity. Hot skin rising temperature (over 40 degrees) can be fatal, proteins begin to break down.
- Jerky body movements.

Inhalants

Inhalants are chemicals that give of fumes, these fumes have mind-altering qualities that can result in intoxication. Inhalants have similar effects to alcohol and cannabis. (depressant effects on the brain)

- Glues, paints, petrol lighter fuel refills, hair sprays, nail polish, removers, air fresheners, white out, deodorants etc
- Inhalant abuse – volatile substance mis-use (VSM)
- Acute effects for most solvents occur 3-5 minutes after inhalation. (10-20 breaths are sufficient) euphoric effects can last between 3-6 hours
- Effects include: - exhilaration and euphoria. Similar effects to alcohol (depressant) risk taking behaviour, drowsiness, slurred speech, confusion, disorientation, irritability, agitation, sneezing, coughing, runny nose, glazed eyes, blood shot eyes, large pupils, chest pain, nose bleeds, sores around mouth and nose.
- Signs of use: - paint staining on skin, hands, mouth, strong smell of chemicals on breath and clothes.

Brain development
- Neuroscience suggests brain structure and function are not fully mature until mid-20s (the adolescent brain is at risk)
- Finding suggest chronic inhalant abuse can result in substantial structural brain abnormalities as well as marked cognitive deficits.

VSM Special note
- It is thought that some volatile substances sensitise the heart to adrenaline. This sensitivity in combination with a sudden fright, anxiety, stress or physical exertion can lead to potentially fatal heart rhythms in matter of minutes. Do not try to restrain them or chase them but rather contain the situation.
- High doses can result in convulsions and unconsciousness, breathing depression and heart failure.
- Sudden death from VSM: - sudden sniffing death syndrome – lethal heart rhythms, bronchospasm (asthma)

Neuroplasticity
- A single dose of many addictive drugs will produce a protein called DFosB (delta Fos B). each time the drug is used more DFosB accumulates until it throws a genetic switch affecting which genes are turned on or off.
- Flipping this switch causes changes that persist long after the drug is stopped. Leading to irreversible damage to the brain's dopamine system and rendering the person more prone to addiction.
- Nondrug addictions such as running and sucrose drinking, also lead to accumulation of AFosB and the same permanent changes in the dopamine system.
- An addict experiences cravings because his plastic brain has become sensitised to the drug or experience. Sensitisation is different from tolerance. As tolerance develops, the addict needs more and more of a substance or porn to get a pleasant effect.
- As sensitisation develops, he needs less and less of the substance to crave it intensely. So sensitisation leads to increased wanting, though not necessarily liking. It is the accumulation of DFosB, caused by exposure to an addictive substance or activity that leads to sensitisation.

Common medications
Antipsychotics (distortion of perception and reality)
1st generation antipsychotics
- Haloperidol (serenace)
- Chlorpromazine (Thorazine)

2nd generation antipsychotics
- Olanzapine (Zyprexa) can be weight gaining, effects various neurotransmitters particularly dopamine antagonist. Wide acting anti-psychotic (also anti-depressant)
- Clozapine (Clozaril)
- Risperidone (Risperdal)
- Quetiapine (Seroquel)
- Amisulpride (solian)

3rd generation antipsychotics
- Aripiprazole (abilify)

Anti-depressants (depression / anxiety / OCD)
MAIO (not good with other medications as they can clash a lot)
- Monoamine oxidase inhibitors – reduce enzymes that break down neurotransmitters at synapse

Tri-cyclic / tetra cyclic (antidepressants that help with insomnia
- Amitriptyline (endep) – long standing effectiveness plus mild pain relief
- Trimipramine (submental) long standing effectiveness, slightly less side effects
- Imipramine (Tofranil) long standing effectiveness

SSRI (selective serotonin (5HT) re-uptake inhibitor
- Fluoxetine (Prozac) can hype people up, for those with no energy
- Sertraline (Zoloft) first preference in the middle. 50mg tablets

- Paroxetine (aropax) slightly sedating, 20mg tablet
- Fluvoxamine (Luvox) more sedating, for those with insomnia,
- Nefazodone (serzone) not as much positive feedback
- Citalopram (cipramil)

SNRI serotonin and noradrenaline Re-uptake inhibitor)
- Venlafaxine (Effexor) for panic attacks / depression

Mood stabilisers (bi-polar)
- Carbamazepine (Tegretol) for epilepsy – anticonvulsant. For erratic, manic, racy thoughts. Acts as a buffer, slows down electrical activity in the brain, flattening side effect.
- Sodium valproate (Epilim) similar to Tegretol
- Lithium (lithcarb) generally used for bi-polar

Benzodiazepines (anti anxiety)
- Diazepam (Valium) more even sedation, long acting for ongoing anxiety, 35 hr
- Oxazepam (serapax) occasional panic attacks, 4–6-hour peaks and wears off
- Alprazolam (Xanax) as for serapax
- Flunitrazepam (Rohypnol)
- Temazepam (normison) for insomnia
- Nitrazepam (Mogadon) more severe insomnia
- Clonazepam (rivotril or pizza) longer acting than diazepam

Orthomolecular science)
Recent progress in brain science has identified the molecular biology of many mental diseases. And this research provides a roadmap for developing effective drug-free therapies, aimed at true normalisation of the brain.

"The world will eventually learn the wisdom of Pfeiffer's law, for every drug that benefits a patient, there are natural substances that can achieve the same effect.

The primary raw materials for the synthesis of many neurotransmitters are nutrients – amino acids, vitamins, minerals, and other natural biochemicals, that we obtain from food.
- Serotonin is produced from the amino acid tryptophan, a constituent of protein, and the final reaction step requires Vitamin B-6 as a cofactor.
- Dopamine can originate from either of 2 amino acids. Decarboxylase and PLP (Vitamin b-6) With iron and folate also involved in the process.
- Norepinephrine is produced from dopamine, with copper (Cu) having a decisive role.

In another example, zinc (Zn) and B-6 are required for the synthesis and regulation of GABA. There are numerous other examples of the decisive role of nutrients in neurotransmitter synthesis.

Good mental health requires proper neurotransmitter activity at synapses. The dominant factor is reuptake. In which the neurotransmitter molecules are whisked away from the synapse and returned to the original brain cell like a vacuum cleaner inhaling dust particle.

The population of transporters generally has a more dominant effect on synaptic activity than the number of neurotransmitters present. Transporters are continuously produced in the brain by genetic expression, the process by which information in a gene is used to produce protein.

The rate of production of transporters is enhanced by certain nutrients and inhibited by others.

Undermethylated: - reduced serotonin – depression

Over methylated: - excessive dopamine activity. Anxiety and Paranoid schizophrenia.

Biochemical treatment of schizophrenia

Therapy using vitamins, amino acids, and other chemicals that are natural to the body,

The primary repeat offenders of mental illness are the following.
- Copper (overload)

- Vitamin B-6 deficiency
- Zinc deficiency
- Methyl / folate (vitamin B-9) imbalances
- Oxidative stress (overload)
- Amino acid imbalances

Nutrient deficiencies that impair brain function are
- Zinc, methionine, folic acid, vitamins B-6 and B12, niacin, niacinamide, DHA, EPA, AA (essential fatty acids), antioxidants (se, GSH, Vitamins C & E etc, magnesium

Nutrient overloads that impair brain function
- Copper, folic acid, iron, methionine, SAMe, toxics such as lead, mercury, cadmium, etc

The 3 musketeers of antioxidant protection in the brain
- Glutathione – first line of defence
- Metallothionein – natures back up system
- Selenium – speeds up the process

Chapter 6

Stress

We all go through stress at different times in our lives. Stress can be good for us in certain situations, but when out of control and negative, it can cause serious problems in our lives and is very much a big factor in our bodies breaking down and the start of dis-ease in our bodies.

So, what is Stress?

As I said above, Stress isn't all bad, in fact, we couldn't't survive without it, as it helps us to adapt to our environment, and when we face challenges, it can help us meet these challenges and overcome them.

When the body experiences acute stress, there are a range of physiological responses that occur to prepare us for what we call the 'fight or flight 'response. Our respiration increases, our heart rate increases, nutrients are mobilized the immune system is activated, and our awareness heightens. At the same time as all of this is happening, our body also starts to divert resources which are being used for different processes in our body such as digestion and reproduction etc.,

and these are diverted to this fight or flight response and immediate survival. This perfectly regulated response to stress provided our ancestors with the energy they needed to survive in dangerous environments.

When stress is beneficial to us, it is named 'eustress 'or positive stress, and this kind of stress can motivate us., it can give us more focus, and more energy, can improve functions, and enhances our ability to thrive in the environment we are in.

But what happens when stress exceeds your capacity and ability to cope? It becomes 'distress', negative stress. This makes the person feel unpleasant, often decreases performance, and can lead to mental, emotional, and physical problems. Prolonged distress can lead to the breakdown of the body and dis-ease, and there are links to long-term stress with cancer. We will go into this in much more detail in a chapter further down the line in the book.

Stress in many ways is like turning on a superpower, it is getting your body ready to take on a challenge such as surviving, exceeding, or conquering whatever problem comes your way.

Stress is an automatic reaction which can help you perform at your best. When stress is being used in a good way it is like pressing a button for ultimate power.

So what happens during the stress response?

When the body perceives a stressor, the Hypothalamus-Pituitary-Adrenal (HPA) axis is activated. The axis consists of the Hypothalamus and Pituitary Gland which are located in the brain, and the adrenal glands, which are located on the top of the kidneys.

When this axis is activated, it causes the release of several different hormones such as cortisol and epinephrine (aka adrenaline). These orchestrate and govern the stress response.

The first stage of the stress response is called the alarm reaction. Cortisol is the hormone responsible for many of these physiological changes. The problem with this is that when cortisol production is too high for too long, numerous problems follow, such as health problems, anxiety, and depression.

The human body is constantly working to keep balance or homeostasis. Your body can recover very quickly from positive stress, but with distress (negative stress) your body cannot maintain homeostasis because the intensity and the frequency of the stressor exceed its capacity to cope.

Long-term distress can come in all sorts of ways including divorce, death of loved ones, financial problems, chronic injury or illness, and over long periods of time this is destructive. This is one of the main things that you need to get under control in your life, and in the later chapter about cancer, we will show why it is one of the main contributory factors in the formation of cancer in your body.

So, how does intense emotion cause the brain to form intense memories? It is well known that emotions can trigger a rise in stress hormones, and these hormones trigger activity in the amygdala. The amygdala increases memory-forming activity which engages the frontal lobes and what is called the basal ganglia to 'tag' these memories as important.

The problem with this can be that the memories are stored with more emotional and sensory details which can trigger rapid unintended recall of these memories.

So, what does the amygdala do?

Well, it has a great deal to do with the fight or flight response as we have discovered, and it controls the release of adrenaline which is good for running away from tigers, but I am not sure you will be encountering many of them. What it does do, is it suppresses logical processing in the frontal lobe, it creates the 'fear 'sensation, it hijacks your logical thinking in favor of emotional response, and therefore it isn't so good for making decisions or communication.

So how do you know when you are stressed?

You will hear many people around you say they are stressed. But what does being stressed actually mean? What you really do need to know is how to control Stress.

Stress is like having a superpower, but if you can't control it, then you will crash, burn, and explode. But if you learn to control stress, you also learn how to use your power.

How do you know when you are stressed? Some of the symptoms of stress could be: -
- Your stomach goes round, and you feel sick
- You want to cry
- You feel exhausted
- You can't sleep and are wide awake half the night
- You can't think straight
- Sweaty hands
- A feeling something bad is going to happen

What you need to start doing to control your stress is to Recognize and Realize when you are stressed.

Other signs of Stress can be rambling and ranting, bloodshot eyes, frazzled looks, and unkempt hair.

The next time you feel stressed about something, a good technique is to write down what you feel. Just write down and notice what comes from being stressed. You can only control your stress, when you start to recognize when you are getting stressed.

Stages of Stress
1. Recognise your challenger, this could be a text with bad news, or someone wanting to punch or hurt you. There are many challenges in life, and it is so important to recognise who and what your challenger is.
2. Stage two is about assessing the challenger. This is a lightning-fast reaction in your body, where you must decide about how serious the challenge is to you. If it is someone a lot bigger than you about to punch you, then this is a very serious challenge, but if it's something small, then it is no challenge.
3. The next thing that happens is that your body mobilises your forces. When your brain assesses that this is indeed a serious challenge for you, it does all it can to prepare you to take the challenge on. This is when your brain activates your stress circuit, this is what is called the Hypothalamic-Pituitary-Adrenal (HPA) Axis. It floods your body with energy, sugar, and glucose which provides immediate fuel to your muscles, to deal with the stress at hand. There are a number of other things that happen with your body during this time when your body is preparing you to deal with a very stressful incident: Your heart beats faster and you start to breathe faster. Your blood is taken away from your digestive system and rushes into muscles and brain. Your body releases painkillers, and this is all done to protect you from injury. It also dilates the pupils in your eyes so you can see better and sharpens your senses so you can act faster and be stronger.
4. This is where we face the challenger, as we have the heightened perception, stamina, and energy to deal with the problem.

5. This is where we go into recovery, and where the brain starts to calm the body down. Your heartbeat starts to slow down, your breathing goes back to normal and releases hormones such as oxytocin which make you more sociable so you might be able to talk about what happened.

Stress can be a positive, and can be a lifesaver if you are about to do something difficult such as performing, exams, sports etc.

The problem is we get stressed due to everyday life, work, when minor things come up, when we don't have a challenger, and this is where stress becomes a problem.

When we get stressed like this, our body does all the above, and we are filled with this energy and there is no outlet.

Many times, we get stressed over the smallest things, and things which are way down the line such as an exam, or work that needs to be done, so you can't use the energy from the stress response to deal with anything, you just sit burning and eventually blow up.

We need to learn how to turn on and turn OFF the stress button.

Stress is designed to help you perform and act now. For example, if you have an exam in a few weeks, could you use your stress to help you revise now? You need to redefine it to something you can take on NOW and not worry about what is down the line.

A fantastic way to deal with stress is something called the STOP technique. It is a tool which can be used when something has just happened that you feel you need to react to, and you are feeling very strong emotions. The idea of this technique is to give yourself a few seconds or minutes to STOP and PAUSE and take that time to decide how you want to respond, rather than react.

1. STOP: make the decision to not react, but instead, pause

2. TAKE YOUR TIME: breathe… just breathe and bring all your attention to just breathing for a moment. Count each breathe until you reach five, and take this time to focus on your breathing and then

3. OBSERVE: observe what is going on for you right now, what are you feeling in your body? No judgement, just observe.

4. PROCEED: decide how you want to proceed in the next minute. Don't make any decisions about the big picture, or what you want to do in the coming days and weeks, but what you want to do in the next few minutes now that you have had time to take a step back. Maybe doing nothing, not taking any action or even walking away, or consciously responding to the problem. Make a conscious decision about how you want to respond, rather than automatically reacting to the situation.

<u>How does stress affect the body?</u>
Stress can affect the body in so many ways, so it is very important you start to learn how to control your stress and don't let things get to you. Later in the book we discuss mindfulness, and being in the present moment, and this is so important.

Some of the affect's stress can have on your body are:
- Skin: - acne, psoriasis, eczema, dermatitis, and skin rashes.
- Stomach: - peptic ulcers, inflammatory bowel disease, stomach cramps, acid reflux, nausea, and weight fluctuations.
- Pancreas: - elevated secretions of insulin, diabetes, damaged arteries, and obesity.
- Immune system: - immune suppression, increased inflammation, chronic health conditions including cancer.
- Head: - mood swings, depression, anger, irritability, lack of energy, concentration problems, anxiety, panic attacks.
- Heart: - increased blood pressure, increased heart rate, higher cholesterol, and increased risk of heart attack and stroke.
- Intestines: - decreased nutrient absorption, reduced metabolism, inflammatory bowel disease.
- Reproductive system: - reduced fertility, erectile dysfunction, low libido
- Joints: - aches and pains, inflammation, tension, lowered bone density, tightness in muscles and joints.

Your body can recover quickly from positive stress, but with negative stress (distress), your body cannot maintain homeostasis if the intensity or frequency of the stressor exceeds its capacity to cope.

If the neurotransmitters such as dopamine, norepinephrine, and serotonin have been depleted, the brain will search for ways to get back to balance through actions or inactions that flood the body with feel-good chemicals to meet those needs.

- Low Dopamine: - no motivation, no interest, impatient, inattentive, boredom, addictions, impulsive, and forgetful.
- Low Serotonin: - overwhelmed, worried, anxious, regretful, sorrowful, resentful, needy, moody, over-giving, and rigid.

Grumpy old lady

A young lady sat on a bus, at the next stop a loud and grumpy old lady came and sat by her ... she squeezed into the seat and bumped her with her numerous bags.

The person sitting on the other side of the young lady got upset and asked her why she didn't speak up or say anything.

The young lady responded with a smile," It is not necessary to be rude or argue over something so insignificant, the journey is so short, I get off at the next stop."

This response deserves to be written in GOLDEN letters. - "It is not necessary to argue over something so insignificant, our journey together is so short."

If each of us realized that our time is so short, and to darken it with quarrels, futile arguments, not forgiving others, discontentment, and a fault-finding attitude would be a waste of time and energy.

Did someone break your heart? Be calm, the journey is short. Did someone betray, bully cheat or humiliate you? Be calm, and forgive, the journey is so short.

Whatever troubles anyone brings us, let us remember that our journey together is short, no one knows the duration of this journey, and no one knows when their stop will come. Our journey is so short, let us cherish friends and family, let us be respectful, kind and forgiving to each other, and let us be filled with gratitude and gladness.

Life really is short. If people can start to live their own lives, and don't let others impact on their life so much and get the most out of their own lives. You really don't know what is going on in someone else's life for them to act the way they do, so focus on yourselves, and being the best you can be, whilst trying to be kind to others.

Chapter 7

Cancer

Over the next chapter, I hope to show you why Cancer is not actually disease, but it is your body's last ditch attempts to wake YOU up to the abuse your body has been put through.

- We all know that smoking is bad for your body, and your health, yet there are many who continue to smoke, not knowing what changes are happening inside their body as their body tries to fight to keep the person's body in homeostasis.
- We all know that alcohol is bad for your body, and your health. (Yes, it is a drug and poisonous to your body. Doh.), Yet many people keep drinking not realising how hard their body is working to balance their body.
- We all know that meat is bad for us, especially red meat, as the body takes such a long time to digest meat, which is sometimes left putrefying in our colon and gut for years.
- We all know that processed foods are full of chemicals, and preservatives just to keep them from going off. There have been tests on certain fast-food delights that when left out, did not start to go off or get mouldy for many months, yet many people stuff their body with processed foods, and think that their body will continue to be fine even though we abuse it so much.

FACT

Cancer and other debilitating disorders are not actual diseases, but instead they are desperate attempts by the body to stay alive for as long as circumstances permit!

It would perhaps astound you to learn that a person who is affected with the main causes of cancer (which constitute the real illness), would most likely die quickly unless he grew cancer cells.

Cancer will only occur after the body's main defence or healing mechanisms have already failed.

In extreme circumstances, exposure to large amounts of carcinogens can bring about a collapse of the body's defence's within several weeks or months and allow for rapid and aggressive growth of a cancer tumor, but generally it takes many years, and even decades for the so called 'malignant tumours' to form and become noticeable diagnostically.

Here is a novel thought.... what if... cancer is on our side and not against us.

Unless we change our perception of what cancer really is, it will most likely resist treatment.

So, what if cancer is indeed part of the body's complex survival responses, and not actually a disease.

Cancer can be the greatest opportunity to help restore balance to all aspects of your life, but it can also be the harbinger of severe trauma and suffering. You are always in control of your body!

The human body must have a certain amount of life sustaining energy. You may either use this inherent energy in a nourishing and self-sustaining way, or in a destructive way.

If you choose negligence or self-abuse over loving attention and self-respect, your body will very likely end up having to fight for its own life.

So, in a nutshell, the main issue is not whether you have cancer...but how you perceive it.

Cancer is one of the many ways that your body tries to change the way you see and treat yourself.

FACT: - damaged or faulty genes do NOT kill anyone

Cancer does NOT kill a person afflicted with it.

Would you like to know what really kills a cancer patient? What kills a cancer patient is NOT the tumor, but the numerous reasons behind cell mutation and tumour growth. These root causes should be the focus of every cancer treatment.

Have any of you suffered from trauma, guilt, shame, resentment and Stress? Constant conflicts, resentment, guilt, shame, stress, can easily paralyze the body's most basic functions, and easily lead to the cancerous growth.

Many cancer patients are burdened by some sort of poor self-image, past emotional conflict, trauma, unresolved conflict or issue, worry, that still lingers in their Subconscious mind and cellular memories. Yes, cellular memories, we will get that later in the book.

FACT: - The physical disease cannot occur, unless there is a strong undercurrent of emotional uneasiness and deep-seated frustration.

Many cancer patients may suffer from a lack of self-respect or worthiness and often have unfinished business in their life. Cancer can help them come to terms with such conflict and even heal together. The way that you deal with weeds, is that you pull out the weeds, along with their ROOTS.

FACT: - It is a medical fact that every person has cancer cells in their body, at ALL times in their life. Let me say that to you again.

EVERY person always has CANCER cells in their body in their life. The thing is though, these cancer cells remain undetected through standard tests until they have multiplied to several billion. Yes several billion! We have around 36 trillion cells in our body.

Curing cancer has nothing to do with getting rid of a group of detectable cancer cells.

Here is another fact for you: -

Treatments like chemotherapy and radiotherapy are capable of poisoning or burning many cancer cells, but they also destroy healthy cells in the bone marrow, gastro-intestinal tract, liver, kidneys, heart, lungs, which leads to permanent irreparable damage of entire organs and systems of the body.

Let me ask you a question. What do you think causes the falling out of hair, and sickness, and not being able to be touched as it's too painful? The cancer? No, the cancer isn't there to kill you. Why would an intelligent cell want to kill you, when in the end it kills itself? We will go through this more in detail later, but quite frankly your hair falls out, and it is too painful to be touched, because your body is inflamed due to the chemotherapy, and your immune system is so depleted because of these treatments.

The poisons of Chemotherapy drugs alone cause so much severe inflammation in every cell of the body, that even the hair follicles can no longer hold onto the strands of hair.

FACT: - Cancer can have no power or control over you unless you allow it to grow in response to the beliefs, perceptions, attitudes, thoughts and feelings you have, as well as the life choices that you make.

Another question. Would you be as afraid of cancer if you knew what caused it, or at least understood what its purpose was? I don't think you would!

When you hold on to anger, resentment, fear, expose yourself to the sun, don't get enough sleep, eat junk food, the chemical additives, artificial sweeteners, can you start to see why your body eventually needs a way to make you see what you are doing to it, and that it is under pressure, and basically crying out for you to change, for a chance to heal itself.

Cancer is merely an indication that something is missing in our body, and in our life. Cancer shows that our physical, mental, and spiritual life as a whole is standing on shaky ground and is fragile to say the least.

There is NO cancer that has not been survived by someone else, regardless of how advanced the cancer is. The problem is that when the cancer is diagnosed, most cancers are NOT given a chance to disappear on their own. They are immediately targeted with a deadly arsenal of weapons such as Chemotherapy, radiation and the surgical knife.

And unfortunately, this is when sleeping tumors that wouldn't' have caused much harm to the body, may now be aroused into powerful defence reactions and become aggressive. It makes absolutely no sense, that when you need to strengthen the body's most important healing system – the immune system – you would then subject yourself to radical treatments that weaken and destroy the immune system.

FACT: - Did you know that chemotherapy is so poisonous, that leaking a few drops of the drug onto your hand, can severely burn it, and if it drops on a concrete floor, they can burn holes in it, and the spilling of any chemotherapeutic drug in the hospital or anywhere En-route is classified as a major biohazard.

Just imagine the holes chemotherapy creates inside your blood vessels, lymphatic ducts, and organ tissues when you undergo infusion after infusion.

Yes, the drug kills cancer cells, but along with them, many of your healthy cells too. Your ENTIRE body becomes inflamed.
"

Chemotherapy and radiation can increase the risk of developing a second cancer by up to 100 times
Doctor Samuel S Epstein

"My studies have proven conclusively that cancer patients who refuse chemotherapy and radiation, actually live up to 4 times longer than treated cases'
Doctor Jones, Professor, University of California

Suffering from a disease, means that there is something wrong with the human engine. Medical practitioners however are not trained to deal with root causes of chronic illness. Their training is dedicated to alleviating or shutting down the symptoms, that indicate the body is trying to deal with an underlying imbalanced situation. When you remove the symptoms, you suppress the mind and body's attempt to deal with the actual real underlying problem.

Temporary cancer shrinkage through Chemotherapy and radiation, has never been shown to cure cancer or extend life. In other words, you can live with an untreated tumor for just as long as you would with one that has been shrunken or eliminated by chemotherapy and radiotherapy.

The bottom line is that tumors almost never kill anyone unless they obstruct the bile duct or any other vital passages. And in primary cancers, the tumor is never health endangering or life threatening.

The fact is that chemotherapy has never been shown to have curative effects for cancer. In contrast, the body can still cure itself, which it does do in the first place by developing cancer. Cancer is really more of a healing response than it is a disease. The disease is the body's attempt to cure ITSELF from an existing imbalance.

FACT: - Chemotherapy can give the patient life threatening mouth sores, and it attacks the immune system by destroying literally billions of immune cells (white blood cells). It inflames every part of the body!

If you have cancer, you may well think that when you feel tired, it is unfortunately just part of the disease. This is rarely the case, and the feeling of being tired is more likely to be anemia, which is a common side effect of chemotherapy drugs.

Did you know that Chemotherapy drugs can decrease your red blood cell levels? and this reduces the oxygen availability to the 30 trillion cells in your body.

By permanently damaging the body's immune system, chemotherapy has become a leading cause of treatment caused diseases, such as heart disease, liver disease, intestinal diseases, pain disorders and rapid ageing.

Let me say this again... cancer cells are not part of a malicious disease process. When the Doctor says the cancer has spread (metastasized) throughout the body, it is NOT the cancer cell's purpose or goal to disrupt the body's vital functions, infect healthy cells, and kill you.

Self-destruction is not the theme of any cell unless it is old, worn out, and ready to be turned over. The simple fact is that cancer cells are like all other cells, and know that if the body dies, they will also die as well.

A cancerous tumor is neither the cause of progressive destruction, nor does it lead to the death of the body. The cancer cell does not have the ability to kill anything.

Do you know what leads to the demise of an organ or the entire body? The wasting away of healthy cell tissues, which results from deprivation of nutrients and life force.

The reduction of nutrient supplies to the cells of an organ is not caused by cancerous tissue, but the reduction of nutrition to the cells causes the cancer cells.

A cancer cell is a normal healthy cell, that has undergone genetic mutation to the point that it can live in anaerobic surroundings (an environment where oxygen is NOT available).

If you deprive cells of oxygen, which is their primary source of energy, some of the cells will die, but others will manage to alter their genetic software program and mutate in a most ingenious way. The cells will be able to live without oxygen and will adapt to derive some of their energy needs from such things as cellular metabolic waste products.

Here is another fact for you... the more infections that are suppressed through medical interventions and prevented, the less efficient the immune system becomes, as well as the liver, kidneys, lymphatic and digestive systems in keeping the body's cell tissues free from harmful deposits.

So, let me say this again... cancer is NOT a disease, it is the body's most desperate and final defence mechanism at its disposal.

It only takes control of the body when all other measures of self-preservation have failed.

The body is always trying to tell us if something is wrong, but it is only when it has tried repeatedly to warn us that we are causing irreparable damage, that it tries to tell us in more drastic ways, in a final attempt to try and get us to stop abusing our bodies.

If we are ever to truly heal cancer in a person's life, we must understand that the body while allowing some of its cells to grow abnormally is actually acting in its best interest.

FACT... Cancer is NOT an indication that the body is about to destroy itself.

You, as consciousness, soul and spirit, are the ONLY true source of energy and information that run your body. Your presence in the body, and what you do, eat, drink, feel and think, determine how well your genes can control and sustain your physical existence.

If you, the conscious presence, are no longer present in your body, the energy and information are withdrawn from every cell. We know this to be physical death, you are no longer present, and your eyes are empty.

Cancer only strikes when there are parts of us that are not alive anymore, be it physically, emotionally and spiritually, and that unfortunately happens to many people long before they do actually die the physical death.

Cancer can resurrect these congested, suppressed areas whether they are physical or non-physical in nature.

How do we start this resurrection? We can start to realize how deeply we have harbored intense negative emotions towards others, and ourselves, such as trauma, hurt, hate, anger etc, and at the same time notice that we have allowed certain foods, beverages, drugs such as painkillers, steroids and antibiotics to contaminate and congest our beautiful body.

Here is the wake-up call!! Cancer is the wake-up call...

How does it do this? It prompts us to take our life back when it is no longer meaningful.

Cancer only occurs when channels or ducts of circulation and elimination have been consistently blocked for a long time.

So, what is a cancer cell?

"It is a cell that has lost its ability to fulfil its pre-programmed responsibilities of ensuring balance or homeostasis in the body. Instead of fulfilling its natural duty, such a cell has turned itself over to a new line of occupation that you could describe as a 'sewer worker"

During every single day in your adult life, the body turns over about 330 billion cells. Out of these an estimated 1% become damaged in the process and turn cancerous. Thats 3.3 billion cells every single day that are damaged and turn cancerous.

Your immune system is programmed to detect these cells and destroy them through a highly sophisticated arsenal of weapons including T killer Cells.

The bodies clean up force is so efficient and perfectly timed that the cancer cells stand no chance of surviving. It is essential for the body's own survival that these kind of cancer cells are created every day, as they make certain that the immune system remains stimulated to keep its self-purification and defence system up to date.

In reality, cancer is an extended immune system response, to help clear up an existing condition of congestion that suffocates a group of cells.

So, why would the immune system try to hinder the body's efforts to prevent waste products entering the bloodstream and killing the body?

The cancer cells are far too precious, and too useful for the body to eliminate them. Cancer cells do NOT randomly spread throughout the body, they lodge themselves in other places that are also congested, in other places that are oxygen deprived also.

So why would the immune system want to collaborate with cancer cells to make more larger tumors?

Because cancer is a survival mechanism NOT a disease.

"The body uses the cancer to keep deadly carcinogenic substances and metabolic waste matter away from the lymph and blood, and therefore from the heart, brain and other organs. Killing off cancer cells would in fact jeopardize its survival"

The body only attacks a cancerous tumor after the congestion that has led to the tumor growth in the first place has been broken up.

FACT... Normal cells turn cancerous when they do NOT get enough oxygen to do their metabolic work. Without cell metabolism, the body would turn cold and lifeless within minutes.

Without the use of oxygen, and to keep some sort of metabolism going, the cells have to mutate into anaerobic cells that are capable of utilising accumulated metabolic waste products and delivering at least some of the required energy and heat in the body.

What happens when you eat meat?

Did you know that the most blood thickening agent is food protein, particularly if it is derived from an animal source. "When compared to a carnivorous animal like a lion or wolf, your stomach can only produce only $1/20^{th}$ of the hydrochloric acid needed to digest such a concentrated meal"

The concentration of the hydrochloric acid in cats and wolves is at least 5 times higher than in human beings.

Most of the animal protein will therefore pass undigested into the small intestine where it will either putrefy (80%) or enter the bloodstream (20%).

With regular consumption of animal protein, including meat, fish, eggs, poultry, cheese, milk etc., more and more intrahepatic stones are formed in the bile ducts of the liver, and this reduces the liver's ability to breakdown these proteins.

Protein foods are the most acid forming and blood thickening foods, so when this protein ends up in the blood, circulating, it thickens the blood. To avoid a stroke or heart attack, the body will dump the proteins into the tissue fluid or connective tissue surrounding the cells. This process thins the blood (for now), and staves off the imminent threat of cardiovascular complications (for now).

The problem is this dumped protein begins to turn the intercellular fluid into a gel-like substance, and nutrients that are trying to make their way to the cells get caught up in this thick soup, which increases the risk of cell death due to starvation.

To avoid cell death, the body then tries to remove the protein from the intercellular fluid, the body rebuilds the protein and converts it into 100% protein collagen fibre.

Over a certain amount of time, the build-up of waste in the cells deprives them of oxygen and nutrients and they start to suffocate in their own waste, and this dramatic damage of the cell environment leaves them with no choice but to mutate into abnormal cells.

Cell mutation does NOT occur because the genes of the cell decided to have a bad day and decided to play malignant.

Genes do NOT switch themselves on or off without a reason.

FACT... genetic blueprints have NO control or power to do anything.

Genetic blueprints are merely there the help the cell reproduce itself. The problem is that the genetic blueprint becomes altered when the environment of the cell undergoes major changes.

With the reduction of cell oxygen concentration in the environment, the genes then generate a new blueprint, that enables them to survive without oxygen and use metabolic waste for energy.

ALL OF THESE ADAPTATIONS MAKE CANCER A SURVIVAL MECHANISM TO KEEP THE PERSON ALIVE, FOR AS LONG AS CIRCUMSTANCES PERMIT.

Certain fats such as trans fatty acids or trans fats also attach themselves to cell membranes, making it difficult for the cells to receive oxygen, glucose and water, and oxygen deprived, dehydrated cells become damaged and turn cancerous.

Do you know what kind of polyunsaturated fats lead to a high risk of skin cancer and other cancers? Vegetable oil, mayonnaise, salad dressings, and most brands of margarine.

Did you know that margarine is just one molecule away from being plastic?

"Cancer has only one prime cause. It is the replacement of normal oxygen respiration of the body's cells by an anaerobic cell respiration" Dr Warburg, winner of the Nobel Prize in Medicine 1931

"lack of oxygen clearly plays a major role in causing cells to become cancerous" Dr Harry Goldblatt, Journal of experimental medicine 1953

"oxygen plays a pivotal role in the proper functioning of the immune system, i.e., resistance to disease, bacteria and viruses. Dr Parris Kidd

"Cancer is a condition within the body, where the oxidation has become so depleted that the body cells have degenerated beyond physiological control" Dr Wendell Hendricks, Hendricks Research Foundation

"Starved of oxygen the body will become ill, and if this persists, it will die" Dr John Muntz, Nutritional Scientist

Protein-cancer connection

The protein-cancer connection came to light after large scale scientific studies including 'The China Study' which demonstrated a virtual absence of cancer among people who don't eat animal proteins.

Research has also shown that meat contains several carcinogenic compounds, including some that are formed during cooking or processing of meat including heterocyclic amines and nitrosamines. They also found that meat contains other potential carcinogens heme iron, nitrates, nitrites, hormones and salts.

All these substances have been found to affect hormone metabolism, increase cell proliferation, damage DNA, and promote damage of cells, all of which can lead to cancer.

It has been estimated approximately 35% of cancer can be attributed to diet. According to the China study, and other cancer research over the past 60 years, cancer could become a rare illness if animal proteins were avoided altogether, along with cutting sugar, and processed food out of our diets, and also dealing with the psychological issues such as stress and trauma.

For a normal person, the immune system tackles and kills the cancer cells easily and quickly. So, a cure is an end to a disease.

In cancer statistics, The American cancer society listed some of 'their' cancer cure rates as high as 45% to 55%, yet we read from other sources that the cure rate for conventional cancer treatment is less than 3%. So, who is telling the truth? The answer is, the reason why ACS and other cancer society's claim such high rates is since they use a '5-year survival' rate, i.e. ability to live for 5 years.

This basically means that if the cancer originates in the liver, and after 5 years you have no liver cancer, but you have lung cancer, you are still considered cured, and your figure is added to the cure rate. Or you have cancer, and you survived for 5 years, but you died from the cancer treatment after 5 years and 1 day, you are still considered cured, according to their cure rate statistics.

Or you have been 'cured 'of cancer by conventional treatment, and due to the destruction of your immune system caused by the toxic treatment, you fall sick by catching a simple cold or pneumonia, and you died, you are still considered 'cured ' of cancer, and your name is added to the cure rate.

Of course, the motive behind this is the profiteering of billions of dollars, that the medical and pharmaceutical companies get from existing and potential cancer patients.

The cancer statistics from alternative treatments, natural treatments, and holistic treatment protocols, shows that the cure rate is 90%. Natural cancer treatments have a 30 times higher cure rate than orthodox cancer treatments of radiotherapy, chemotherapy and surgery.

"The American people and most of the rest of the world's population have been brainwashed by television and every other media source to 'go to the doctor' at the least sign of any medical problem. But doctors don't know how to be well themselves, or how to get you well. If they did know, they wouldn't be dying of cancer, or other horrible diseases at the same – or greater – rate than the general population.

Dr Lorraine Day, MD

"My studies have concluded conclusively that untreated cancer victims usually live up to 4 times longer than treated individuals" Dr Hardin Jones, professor of medical physics and physiology, University of California, Berkeley.

If everything is left to medicine, the cancer will kill you, if not, the treatment will finish you off.

Cancer must not be treated like it is a bacterial invasion, and the patient will be healed when the bacteria has gone and the invasion has stopped. Cancer is a process of evolution, where the patient's own cells mutate and metastasize all over the body.

Cancer is a nutritional, toxic, environmental condition in the human body, and in most cases can be reversed successfully through the application of a sound nutritional approach, and common-sense lifestyle changes.

"The cause of cancer is no longer a mystery, we know it occurs whenever a cell is denied 60% of its oxygen requirements. Cancer above all other diseases has countless secondary causes. But even for cancer there is one prime cause. The prime cause of cancer is the replacement of the respiration of oxygen in normal body cells by a fermentation of sugar. All normal body cells meet their energy needs by respiration of oxygen, whereas cancer cells meet their energy needs in great part by fermentation. All normal body cells are thus obligate aerobes, and all cancer cells are partial anaerobes" Dr Otto Warburg, in the Prime causes and prevention of cancer.

"the basic cause of disease is no longer a mystery, the basic cause is the habits of improper diet, inadequate exercise, negative mental attitudes, and the lack of spiritual attunement, which combine to produce toxic conditions and malfunction of our bodies.

The elimination of the habits that cause illness is done through the positive approach of developing proper habits that cause health, combined with corrective techniques that remove the ill effects of our former incorrect ways" Stanley Burroughs

"Alternative medicine explores the stressors (environmental, chemical, biological, psychological and emotional) in a patient's life, that cause a weakening of a particular energy field, which in turn allows the manifestation of a disease condition in a weakened area. To maintain a state of health, all energy systems within the body need to exist in a state of balance or equilibrium. Imbalance leads to conditions of discomfort (dis-ease), which eventually spirals into ill health if not corrected. The Chinese and Indians (Ayurvedic Medicine) had worked all of this out thousands of years ago"

"Orthodox or allopathic medicine utilizes poisonous substances (drugs) in non-lethal dosages in order to suppress symptoms in an affected area. This approach neither addresses the cause of the disease condition, nor is it responsible for healing the patient. Rather the use of drugs often will temporarily mask the outer manifestations of the malady, while at the same time drive the disease deeper into the body, only to reappear later, as a more serious and chronic health threat.

One of the many flaws of the orthodox approach is that it focuses on the disease condition itself, rather than the patient. The term Wholistic (or holistic) sprang up to distinguish those physicians whose gestalt considers all the physical, emotional and spiritual energies interacting with the patient". Ken Adachi, in forbidden cures, Suppressed alternative therapies.

"17 out of 20 cancer victims shouldn't't have cancer, they have been murdered by the callous indifference of the people with power" Dr Vernon Coleman, F.R.S.M, Sunday Independent, November 1987

"And we have made ourselves living cesspools, and driven doctors to invent names for our diseases" Plato

"If I contracted cancer, I would never go to a standard cancer treatment centre, cancer victims who live far from such centre have a chance" Professor Georges Mathe, French Cancer Specialist

"chemotherapy and radiation can increase the risk of developing a second cancer by up to 100 times"
Dr Samuel Epstein, Congressional Record, Sept 9, 1987

« *Chemotherapy and radiation do not make the body well. They destroy, they do not heal. The hope of the doctor is that the cancer will be destroyed without destroying the entire patient. These therapies do kill cancer cells, but they kill a lot of good cells too, including the cells of the immune system, the very cell that one needs to get well. If a cancer patient survives the treatment with enough immune system left intact, the patient may appear to get well at least temporarily, but they will have sustained major damage to their body and their immune system. How much better is it to nourish the immune system directly using natural therapies to assist it in getting you well instead of destroying it by the use of the conventional therapies. Then the immune system itself can kill the cancer cells without any side effects and heal your body at the same time"* Lorraine Day MD, Woman who cured herself of breast cancer naturally

Mangosteen Fruit

The mangosteen fruit contains Xanthones – biologically active plant compounds, which have many properties including antioxidants, and potent COX2 inhibition to reduce inflammation and pain.

Xanthones in mangosteen have the ability to eradicate and destroy cancer cells.

Not only does it induce apoptosis (programmed cell death) of the cancer, but it effectively destroys cancer cells resistant to modern chemotherapy treatments.

One In Vitro study showed Garcinone E, a xanthone, to be more effective than 5 commonly used chemotherapy agents. As a COX2 inhibitor, mangosteen blocks production of Prostaglandin E2 impeding promotion and progression of cancer when DNA damage occurs, and it also attacks tumour cells directly.

Guyabano / Soursop

This is the natural cancer killer. It fights cancer cells, lowers blood pressure and increases the immune system. The Guyabano tree, its fruit, leaves and bark, is a natural cancer cell killer. A scientific research study in 1976 shows that one chemical is 10,000 times more potent than the chemotherapy drug Adriamycin.

Extracts from the tree were shown to effectively target and kill malignant cells in 12 types of cancer, including colon, breast, prostate, lung and pancreatic cancer.

What's more, unlike chemotherapy, laboratory tests show that the compound extracted from the Guyabano tree selectively hunts down and kills only cancer cells. It does not harm healthy cells.

A study at Purdue University found that leaves from the Guyabano tree killed cancer cells among 6 human cell lines, and were especially effective against prostate, pancreatic and lung cancers.

The Guyabano tree consists of many chemicals, but what makes the Guyabano tree special is that the tree contains a natural compound named 'acetogenins'. Research has found that this compound can slow the growth of tumor cells, and it is toxic to tumour cells without harming healthy cells. The tree produces the acetogenins in the leaves, stem and bark, and you can drink the extracts of the tree and this will help you fight against cancer.

Oberlies et al (1995) researched the capability of acetogenins to block, or inhibit the cell growth of tumour cells, and they tested this on several cell types.

Results showed that the more acetogenins were added with the cancerous cells, the more the cell growth was blocked, and in addition to this, the non-cancerous healthy cells were not affected by the acetogenins and the cell growth was not blocked.

Sodium Bicarbonate

An oncologist in Rome called Dr Tullio Simoncini discovered that Bicarbonate Soda destroys cancer cells.

Sodium Bicarbonate is safe, inexpensive and unstoppably effective when it comes to cancer tissues. It is an irresistible chemical, and it is a cyanide to cancer cells, as it hits the cancer cells with a shock wave of alkalinity, which allows more oxygen into the cancer cells that they can't tolerate. Cancer cells cannot survive in the presence of high levels of oxygen.

Sodium Bicarbonate is an instant killer of tumors.

The Bicarbonate maple syrup (molasses as an alternative to maple syrup) cancer treatment focuses on delivering natural chemotherapy in a way that it effectively kills cancer cells but significantly reduces the brutal side effects experienced with most standard chemotherapy treatments.

The bicarbonate maple syrup treatment is a very significant treatment which every cancer patient should be aware of, and it can be combined with other natural treatments.

This treatment works like a trojan horse. Cancer cells gobble up sugar so when you encourage the intake of sugar (maple syrup) it is like the trojan horse.

The treatment is a combination of pure 100% maple syrup and bicarb soda. When mixed and heated together, the maple syrup and bicarbonate soda bind together. The maple syrup targets the cancer cells (which consume 15 times more glucose than normal cells), and the baking soda which is dragged into the cancer cell by the maple syrup, being very alkaline forces a rapid shift in ph killing the cell. The actual formula is to mix 1 part baking soda, with 3 parts (pure 100%) maple syrup in a small saucepan. Heat for 5 minutes, take 1 tsp several times a day.

The apple cider vinegar ¼ teaspoon and ¼ teaspoon bicarb soda, taken 2 or more times a day is another treatment, as is lemon and bicarb soda. Honey may be able to be substituted for the maple syrup if you are unable to get the maple syrup.

Breuss cancer treatment

Rudolf Breuss a healing practitioner from Austria said cancer can only live on the protein of solid food, therefore, if you drink nothing but vegetable juice and teas for 42 days the cancerous tumour dies off while the body continues to do well. Do not drink more than half a litre per day. The cocktail is made up of beets, carrots, celery roots, black radishes and potato.

The recipe is 300 grams red beets – 100 grams carrots – 100 grams celery root – 30 grams black radish – and potato. Mix all the vegetables in a juicer and strain to get rid of any sediment.

The actual Breuss instructions are:-
1. First thing in the morning – ½ cup of cold kidney tea
2. 30-60 minutes later, 2 cups of warm herb tea made from st john's wort, peppermint and lemon balm
3. After 30-60 minutes take some vegetable juice and salivate well before swallowing
4. 15-30 minutes later, another sip of vegetable juice. You should take some juice throughout the day.
5. In between drink warm or cold sage tea without sugar, as much as you like, and at noon and in the evening, half a cup of kidney tea.

No other food should be consumed during the treatment.

Anti-cancer fruit and vegetables

1. Garlic: - garlic can help stop cancer-causing substances from forming in your body, speed DNA repair, and kill cancer cells.

2. Broccoli: - it contains a compound called sulforaphane, and this helps boost the protective enzymes in the body and flush out cancer causing chemicals. It also targets cancer stem cells. Eat it raw or steamed

3. Tomatoes: - tomatoes owe their red colour to a phytochemical which is called lycopene. This is an antioxidant, and it has been shown to stop the growth of certain cancer cells, such as breast, lung and endometrial. Watermelon, pink grapefruit and red bell peppers also have lycopene.

4. Berries are among the best source of antioxidants. They also contain ellagic acid which has cancer preventing properties which can destroy cancer causing substances and slow the growth of tumours

5. Carrots contain carotenoids, beta-carotene and alpha carotene. Beta carotene is believed to slow cancer cell growth, and protect cells from damage caused by toxins

6. Apples contain Polyphenols, which can prevent inflammation, cardiovascular disease and infections. Some research also shows polyphenols may modulate certain processes that lead to cancer development, and furthermore, another study in 2018 shows that apple phloretin inhibits growth of breast cancer cells without affecting healthy cells. The polyphenol inhibits a protein called glucose transporter 2, which plays role in advanced cancer cell growth.

7. Walnuts contain a substance called pedunculagin, which the body metabolises into urolithins, and these bind to estrogen receptors and may play a role in preventing and fighting breast cancer

8. Dark chocolate contains polyphenols, flavonoids and antioxidants and may have preventative effect on cancer. Research in 2022 also showed that people who ate more chocolate had a 12% lower risk of death from cancer.

9. Grapes contain resveratrol which has shown promise as a tool for fighting cancer.

Miracle Mineral Supplement (MMS)

The 3 things that all cancers have in common are
1. The body is overwhelmed with toxins and waster matter
2. The immune system is weak and depleted
3. There is a large presence of pathogens inside and around the cancer cells, which may include bacteria, viruses, parasites, fungi and yeast.

There is one substance, sodium chlorite which may have the most immediate and balanced effects on all the diseases causing factors listed above.

The product MMS (miracle mineral supplement) is a stabilized oxygen solution of 28% sodium chlorite in distilled water.

The magic happens when you add a small amount of lemon or lime juice, or citric acid to the MMS as chlorine dioxide is formed. Once the chlorine dioxide is ingested, it oxidizes harmful substances such as parasites, viruses, bacteria, yeast, fungi etc within a matter of hours, and at the same time it boosts the immune system 10-fold.

MMS doe'not cure anything, it allows the body to heal itself.

There are many other natural remedies, and therapies for cancer treatment which include IV Vitamin C, water fasting, The Budwig Diet, The Keto Diet, intermittent fasting, Raw Vegan diet, green juice diet, Epigenetic Diet, Coley's toxins, Bob Beck Protocol, Black Cumin Seed oil, Alkaline water, Pao Pereira, Oxalic acid, Fenbendazole – turmeric, CBD oil, Bee venom, and may other treatments. I don't cover them in this book, but I do go a little more into them in the 3 day 'Awakening 'Workshop, and in private and group sessions.

The other really important factor in healing from cancer is the emotional and psychological part. It has been proven that trauma, stress, anger, and all other negative emotions cause cancer and your body to break down with dis-ease.

It is so important to rid yourself of deep-rooted trauma and stress, and even if you don't think you have any trauma, or negative emotions in your body, you most likely do, and clearing these emotions is the most important thing for you to do for you to heal from cancer.

The best way to ger rid of negative emotions and release trauma, is through hypnosis.

I have the greatest respect for the nurses, health care assistants, and other support staff, surgeons in hospitals around the world, and many doctors also, who do an incredible job caring for people, but I think medical professionals need to start looking at how they are treating their patients, and is it to benefit the pharmaceutical companies, or do they truly want to help their patients.

When my father was diagnosed with pancreatic cancer, I went to see the oncologist, the 'medical professional', who, when I said I was an alternative medicine therapist, called me a 'witch doctor', to which we then had an interesting conversation as to how toxic the chemotherapy drug was, and what would happen if we put this on her hand, let alone inside her body.

Eastern medicine, alternative medicine, 'voodoo medicine' as this oncologist saw it, has been around for many thousands of years, and I think it has done well to help people over that time.

Western medicine, conventional 'orthodox' medicine, has been around a couple of hundred years, and it not about dealing with the cause, but with the symptoms, and 'popping pills. Yet cancer was virtually unheard of for thousands of years, as was diabetes and many other diseases, but in the time of modern medicine, cancer is on the increase, diabetes is at its highest level ever at the moment, and many other diseases are increasing including asthma, and this is because they are treating the symptoms, and not actually what is really behind the body being in 'dis – ease'.

I have two people come up to me recently saying they were palliative and nothing they could do, and it astounds me that a medical professional would give this negative information to someone. There are two words which many doctors should look up in a dictionary. 'Placebo', which is when something positive is said to someone, and 'nocebo', which is where a doctor says, 'sorry, you are going to die'. This is crazy!

Because that person, looks at this 'trained' professional, and listens to those words, and believes them because, hey he is a doctor. So, what happens? That person then starts to deteriorate, because the doctor said they are going to die, so they are going to die… What utter rubbish!

I remember working as a support worker in the community and being called out to this lady who had kidney disease, and she refused to have dialysis and the doctors then very wisely, advised her that if she didn't have dialysis, she had around 6 months (with their crystal ball of course).

I went to talk to this lady, and basically told her to forget what the doctors, nurses etc said, and asked this lady what she loved to do. She said, 'I love going on cruises', to which I said, 'go and enjoy yourself, go on cruises, enjoy, and have fun'. Do you know how long this lady lived? It was about 18 months later; I heard she had passed away.

The nocebo effect, especially coming from a doctor, will have that exact affect and that person will do exactly as that person said they would and die. The placebo affect has the opposite effect on the brain and the psyche and gives that person hope.

Another gripe of mine with regards to oncologists and cancer wards, is that, as you have seen in this chapter, meat is a carcinogenic and feeds the cancer. Sugar, cakes, sweets, and any other things containing sugar etc., feed the cancer, it is like giving the cancer cells a wonderful meal. The cancer cells love glucose remember, and as you will see in the next chapter, with someone who has cancer, we need to get the body into an alkaline state, and not in an acidic state. It is beyond belief that medical professionals are still saying to people with cancer to eat meat and sugar and feeding the cancer.

Later in the book, we are going to be looking at epigenetics, neuroplasticity and quantum embodiment, and how YOU can turn your lives round.

The thing is the doctor doesn't cure you! The therapist doesn't cure you! They can be a catalyst to help you get better, but you cure yourself, you heal yourself. Even with hypnosis, the hypnotherapist is a catalyst, the give you suggestions, but it is YOU who heals yourself, and it is YOU who cures yourself. And as epigenetics, and neuroplasticity will show you later in the book, it is NEVER too late to change your life and heal yourself.

www.thevikingbuddha.com

Chapter 8

Trauma

For this chapter I want to run quickly through an area of life where many people go through traumatic events, whether it be one off events, or years of trauma, to different types of trauma / PTSD. Many of us have had either bad childhoods, abusive relationships, or other traumatic events which have affected us.

What is trauma?
Many situations can be traumatic, and most of the time traumatic situations are unpredictable, and out of the person's control.

When somebody goes through a traumatic experience, they often undergo changes in their brain, and their bodies. This will most of the time, end up with the victim experiencing overwhelming feelings of anxiety and helplessness.

Trauma is an encounter resulting in severe psychological and physical stress. It can result from a single occurrence, or a series of events. No matter how long the trauma lasts, it can still cause harm, and effect a person psychologically, emotionally, physically and spiritually.

So, a traumatic event is a singular incident such as a earthquake, fire, flood, burglary which causes emotional, spiritual, physical and psychological harm. After the traumatic event, the person may feel physically threatened, emotionally upset, and unsure how to respond.

They may also be in denial and might behave as though the event didn't affect them.

Some common incidents which can cause trauma are: -
- Child abuse and neglect.
- Car crashes.
- Job loss.
- Fires.
- Sexual assault, rape or sex trafficking.
- Physical assault, murder or torture.
- Intimate partner violence.
- Suicide and poverty.
- Life threatening medical conditions.
- Earthquakes, floods, and other natural disasters
- Witnessing homicide or suicide.

Trauma can cause so much stress and can be devastating for the person suffering with it. After a traumatic incident, there are numerous techniques that can be used to help the victim regain emotional equilibrium.

If symptoms of trauma persist, and affect a person's personal life, work life, school, sleep, etc., then it is time for that person to get help to deal with the trauma.

In children, trauma manifests in different ways, such as intense emotions, violent behaviour, difficulty sleeping, obsessive thinking about the experience. These are signs that a child may need help.

There are different types of trauma and below we will go through them: -

1. Community violence: - this is where it is predatory violence such as robbery, rape, stabbings, beatings, shootings, homicides, which people may experience as victims or witnesses.

2. Complex trauma: - This trauma is where the person is exposed to multiple or prolonged traumatic events over a period of time, such as child abuse, domestic abuse, psychological maltreatment, neglect, physical and sexual abuse. Exposure to this kind of violence can affect a person deeply, resulting in emotional dysregulation, loss of safety and direction, deep anxiety, and the lack of ability to detect or respond to danger cues, which leads to subsequent or repeated trauma exposure.

3. Domestic violence: - this includes actual or threatened physical or sexual violence and also emotional abuse between adults.

4. Early childhood trauma: - this type of trauma generally refers to children aged 0-6, who have been subject to traumatic experiences such as childhood abuse, sexual abuse, witnessing domestic violence, natural disasters, sudden loss of parents, painful medical procedures.

5. Natural disasters: - this type of trauma generally comes from one off event such as tornadoes, hurricanes, earthquakes, fires, floods, explosions, but can also be caused by something like COVID19

6. Refugee and war zone trauma: - this kind of trauma includes exposure to war, political violence, torture, and refugee trauma can be a result of living where there is bombing, looting, shooting, as well as being forced to leave their homes due to the above.

7. School violence: -This includes teacher victimisation, bullying, cyber bullying, fights at school, and can cause problems many years after especially with things like bullying and cyber bullying.

PTSD

PTSD can have a significant effect on a person's life who is suffering with it, and their day to day lives and functioning.

The symptoms for PTSD normally develop in the first month after the traumatic event, but occasionally there might be a delay of sometimes months and even years before symptoms start appearing.

PTSD sufferers may go for long periods where their symptoms are not as noticeable, which can then be followed by periods where they are worse. For others their symptoms are always there and can be made worse by triggers.

Symptoms of PTSD can vary from person to person, but on the next page are some of the symptoms which can be found in people who have PTSD

1. Re-experiencing: - flashbacks, nightmares, distressing and repetitive sensations and images, physical sensations such as pain, Sweating, nausea and trembling. Others may have constant negative thoughts about the experience, which leads them to constantly question it, and prevent them from coming to terms with it.

2. Emotional numbing and avoidance: - A person with PTSD may try in any way they can to avoid being reminded of the traumatic event, and this may mean avoiding certain places, people, that remind them of the trauma and may avoid talking to anyone about their experience. Many people try to push the traumatic memories out of their mind, by distracting themselves by doing hobbies or focusing on work. Emotional numbing is where the person tries not to feel anything at all, but this can lead to the person feeling withdrawn and isolated.

3. Hyperarousal: - Some people with PTSD may find it hard to relax, feel very anxious, and may be constantly looking for threats and may be easily startled. This unfortunately often leads to angry outbursts, insomnia, irritability, and difficulty concentrating.

Other problems with people who have PTSD may include: - depression, mental health problems, phobias, suicidal ideation, self-harming, substance abuse, destructive behaviour, headaches, chest pains, stomach problems, dizziness etc.

PTSD in children

Children with PTSD can have similar symptoms as adults, such as nightmares and insomnia. They can also have loss of interest in activities, headaches, stomach problems, difficult behaviour, avoiding things related to the traumatic event, and even re-enacting the event over and over in play.

Complex PTSD

Complex PTSD is when the person has repeatedly experienced traumatic events such as abuse, neglect or violence. This kind of PTSD is thought to be more severe if: -

- The parent or carer caused the trauma.

- The trauma was experienced over a long period of time
- the person was alone during the trauma
- there is still contact with the person who caused the trauma
- the events happened early in life

If this happened in childhood, it could affect the child's development, self-confidence and also create behavioural problems and other issues as they get older.

The symptoms of PTSD include
- difficulty in controlling emotions
- loss of attention and concentration
- feelings of shame and guilt
- headaches, dizziness, chest pains, stomach problems.
- Cutting themselves off from friends and family
- Relationship difficulties
- Self-harm, drug and alcohol abuse
- Suicidal thoughts

This is again just a short introduction to trauma and is part of the bigger picture in this book about finding yourself, healing yourself, and finding your life purpose and the law of attraction and living your best life.

With regards to dealing with trauma and PTSD, talk therapies such as counselling, CBT, DBT, psychotherapy can help with coping skills etc., but if you really want to deal with the trauma and release it, then you need to be going right to the root of where the problem is stored, and that is your subconscious mind. The best way to deal with trauma and PTSD is hypnosis, EMDR, IEMT, etc., by using techniques such as trauma release, timeline therapy, narrative exposure therapy, and dealing with the problem so that it loses its hold on you.

You can release all the trauma which has been holding you back, and you can let it go. As a master hypnotist, speaking quite frankly and honestly about this, unfortunately the NHS and other authorities refer you for CBT/DBT/ Counselling, which is quite frankly just like putting a plaster over your trauma, much like it deals with symptoms of disease and illness.

The plaster, which is your coping skills through CBT, or talk therapies, does just that, it gives you coping skills at best, and you still have that trauma or multiple traumas like a bag of rocks holding you back, and weighing you down,

The reason for this is that your traumatic events, phobias, fears are not held in your conscious mind, so no amount of talk therapy will rid you of your phobia, at best they put the plaster on and help you cope with the trauma. Trauma is stored in your subconscious mind, and the only way to banish your trauma for good and release it, is to access your subconscious mind. There are a few ways you can do this through EMDR / IEMT/ Brain spotting, NLP etc., but quite frankly the best way to rid you of all your trauma, fears, phobias, is hypnosis. It works, it is very effective of dealing with all your trauma, and you throwing away all the rocks in that bag holding you back.

You can release it, so you can go forward in your life. Hypnosis is the way to do this.

Chapter 9

Gut Brain Axis

Your gut has a mind of its own. It is referred to as our 2nd brain and connects via the gut brain axis. The gut brain axis is a term for the communication network that links your brain with your gastrointestinal tract. But it's not just a one-way street. Communication goes both ways. Your gut informs your brain, and your brain also sends messages to your gut.

How does this happen? Well, they are connected physically through millions of nerves, most significantly the vagus nerve, one of the biggest nerves linking the gut and brain. They also communicate through biochemical signalling involving hormones, neurotransmitters and immune system proteins.

There are trillions of bacteria living in your gut. They are not just passing inhabitants. They interact with both the brain and the gut, influencing things like your immunity, mood and even behaviour. Did you know that 90% of serotonin, the feel-good hormone, is produced in your gut? These tiny microbes play a huge role in that. That's why when your gut is unhappy, you might feel low or anxious. Also, if you have ever felt your stomach churn when you are nervous or stressed, that is the gut brain axis in action. This is because your brain and gut are constantly talking to each other in real time, reacting to different situations. The gut brain axis concept is a revolution in how we think about our bodies and health.

We are not just individual organs functioning separately, but a complex, interconnected system where every part as an impact overall. Understanding this can open doors to managing our health in ways we never imagined before.

The enteric nervous system

Embedded in the lining of your gastrointestinal system that stretches from your oesophagus to your anus, is a complex network of 100 million neurons. This entire system functions independently and is often referred to as the body's second brain. This network is the ENS, and it plays a vital role in some critical processes in your body. One amazing thing about the ENS is that it is self-sufficient. It can carry on its functions without any input from the brain or the spinal cord. In fact, if you somehow manage to disconnect it from the central nervous system, it will continue to work just fine on its own, coordinating all your digestive processes like a pro.

The Vagus nerve is like the hotline between the brain and the gut relaying signals back and forth, however it is interesting to note that around 90% of these signals are going from the gut to the brain, not the other way around. The Enteric Nervous System (ENS) doesn't just handle digestion, it also interacts with the local immune system, regulates blood flow and even affects your emotions. Your gut can also influence your feelings and mental state. Have you ever had a gut feeling about something? That is your ENS at work, or felt nauseous before a big presentation or performance? That is your ENS responding to stress and anxiety.

About 90% of your body's serotonin, the feel-good hormone, is produced in your gut under the influence of the ENS and the gut microbiota.

GI system – from ingestion to absorption

The GI system comprises of various things. Imagine a ling winding tube that starts at your mouth all the way down to your anus. This tube along with a few helper organs like the liver, pancreas, and gallbladder, forms your GI system. It is around 30ft long.

Our journey starts at the mouth, the moment you take a bite, your teeth and salivary enzymes start breaking down the food, both mechanically and chemically. The food then makes a quick slide down the oesophagus and lands in your stomach. The mixing pot.

Your stomach with its muscular walls and potent gastric juices, churns and breaks down the food further into a semi liquid mess called chyme. Your stomach lining has got you covered literally by producing a layer of mucus to protect itself from the acid.

The next stop is the small intestine, this is about 20 ft long and is the superstar of digestion and absorption. Here your food meets bile from the lover and stored in the gallbladder, that helps digest fats and pancreatic enzymes that break down proteins and carbohydrates. The small intestines inner lining, the mucosa, is covered in millions of tiny fingers like projections called villi and microvilli. They look a bit like a shaggy carpet under a microscope. This design massively increases the surface area for absorption. If you could flatten out the small intestine, it would have the surface area of a tennis court. At this point most nutrients from your food have been absorbed and sent into the bloodstream, ready to fuel your body. What remains is mostly water and indigestible fibres, which move into the large intestine or colon.

The colon's main job is to absorb remaining water and electrolytes, transforming the watery waste from the small intestine into more solid stuff. Also residing in the colon are trillions of gut bacteria happily feasting on the fibres, producing essentials vitamins and gases. Finally, the leftover waste now formed into a solid, semi solid, or liquid depending on how much you trust that street food cart. Then it is stored in the rectum until it's time for great exit.

The nervous system

The nervous system is your body's electrical wiring. It is a complex network of nerves and cells called neurons, that carry messages between the brain and the rest of the body. It is divided into 3 parts, the CNS, central nervous system, the PNS, peripheral nervous system, and the ENS, the enteric nervous system. The CNS is the big boss, consisting of the brain and the spinal cord. This is where all the critical decision making happens. The brain is like the command centre, processing information and sending out instructions. The spinal cord on the other hand, is the main highway for these messages, carrying them to and from the brain. But the CNS can't do all this on its own.

The PNS is the loyal sidekick, it connects the CNS to the rest of the body. So, if the CNS is the central government, the PNS is like local administration, bringing the CNS decisions to every corner of your body. The PNS is split into the somatic and autonomic systems. The somatic system controls voluntary actions like reaching for that piece of chocolate cake, while the autonomic system handles the stuff you don't have to think about like making your heartbeat faster when you see said chocolate cake.

The autonomic system is further divided into the sympathetic, the fight, flight freeze system, and the parasympathetic system, which is the rest and digest system. These guys ensure your body responds appropriately in different situations, whether you are running from a bear or lounging on the couch.

The ENS, this maverick runs the entire show down in your gut, independent of the brain and the spinal cord. This network of around 100 million neurons, lines your GI Tract and manages every aspect of digestion, from the oesophagus to the anus, and it doesn't stop there, as it also communicates with the CNS influencing your emotions and mental state.

The Vagus Nerve

The vagus nerve, also known as the 10th cranial nerve, is one of the longest and most complex nerves in the human body. The name vagus actually comes from the Latin word for wandering, and boy does it wander. Starting in the brainstem, just behind your ears, it meanders down your neck, branches out into your chest and heart, and then goes all the way down to your abdomen, touching pretty much every major organ on the way. It is like the route 66 of your body. The vagus nerve is like a superhighway for signals between your gut and your brain.

The vagus nerve plays a crucial role in the rest and digest part of your nervous system - The parasympathetic system. It regulates heart rate, stimulates the digestive organs, and helps control respiratory rate. All this makes it essential for maintaining homeostasis, keeping your body's internal environment balanced and stable. But where it gets really interesting for us is how the vagus nerve acts as a two-way communication link between your brain and your gut. It carries signals from the brain to the gut, about 10% of the traffic, and from the gut to the brain, a whopping 90%. That means most of the time, it is your gut talking to your brain, not the other way around.

On the gut to brain pathway, the vagus nerve helps inform the brain about what is happening in the gut. For instance, if you have eaten something that your body is having a hard time digesting, the gut will send a distress signal to the brain via the vagus nerve, which might result in feelings of discomfort or nausea. On the flip side, the brain to gut pathway, allows the brain to control gut function. Ever felt butterflies in your stomach when you are nervous or anxious? That is your brain sending signals to your gut via the vagus nerve.

The vagus nerve is also a key player in our moods and emotions. It is involved in the production and regulation of certain neurotransmitters like serotonin, our beloved feel-good hormone. In fact, stimulating the vagus nerve has been explored as a treatment for depression and anxiety.

What are the microbiota and microbiome?

The microbiota refers to the 10 to 100 trillion symbiotic microbial cells harboured by each person. Primarily bacteria in the gut. The human microbiome consists of the genes these cells harbour. Simply put microbiota is the name for the whole ecological community of microbes that live in a particular location, in our case the human body. These microbes include bacteria, but also viruses, fungi, and other microscopic organisms.

The microbiome on the other hand, refers to the collection of all the genetic material of these microbes. Imagine the microbiota as a bustling city full of diverse citizens. Then the microbiome would be like the combined knowledge, skills and characteristics of all these citizens. Where do these microbial buddies hang out? Well, they have set up shop all over your body, your skin, mouth, nose, and especially your gut. In fact, your gut is like the New York city of your microbiota, home to the largest, densest population of microbes.

Here is a mind-blowing fact. There are as many microbial cells in your body as there are human cells. You are just as much a microbe as you are human. These microbes are not just peaceful co-inhabitants, they are essential for our health and well-being. Your gut microbiota helps with digestion, especially foods that your stomach and small intestine have trouble breaking down. They play a significant role in the immune system, keeping harmful bacteria in check and even help regulate your metabolism.

Emerging research suggests that the gut microbiota can even influence our mood and mental health. The composition of your microbiota is influenced by your diet, lifestyle, birth method, c-section, or natural birth. Whether you were breastfed, your environment, and even your age. It is like a microbial fingerprint unique to you.

What makes your gut microbiome unique.

The microbiome is like your personal microbial ecosystem, with a population as diverse as the inhabitants of a bustling city. But what shapes this metropolis of microbes inside us?

Genetics: - your DNA doesn't just determine your eye colour or whether you can curl your tongue, it also influences your microbiome. Studies have shown that identical twins, who share 100% of their genes, have more similar microbiomes, than fraternal twins who share about 50% of their genes.

birth: - how you came into this world has a significant impact on your initial microbiome. Babies born vaginally acquire different microbes than those born through a c-section. The former are exposed to their mothers vaginal and faecal microbes, where the latter are first exposed to the skin microbiota and the general environment

Breastfeeding: - breast milk is not just nutrition; it is also a way for mothers to pass beneficial bacteria to their babies. This kick starts the development of the baby's microbiome and immune system.

Diet: - the impact of diet can't be overstated. Just like how different populations of people eat different cuisines, different types of gut bacteria prefer different kinds of food. Some love fibre, others protein, and others sugar. So, the composition of your diet heavily influences the composition of your gut microbiome. The more diverse your diet, the more diverse your microbiome.

Lifestyle: - This also plays a key role, are you a night owl, or a morning person, do you run marathons or binge watch tv shows? All of these choices influence your microbiome. Regular physical activity has been linked to more diverse microbiome.

Age: - your microbiome changes as you grow. Newborns have a vastly different microbiome from toddlers, who have a different microbiome from teenagers, and so on. As we age, the diversity of our microbiome tends to decrease

Environment and geography: - the microbes in your home, your city, and your part of the world all influence your personal microbiome

The composition of your gut microbiome is linked to everything from digestion to immunity to mental health, and even to conditions like obesity, allergies, and autoimmune diseases.

The impact of diet on the gut microbiome

Our diet is one of the most significant factors shaping the composition of our gut microbiota. Our microbial friends need to eat too. Just like any city different residents have different preferences.

Some love the bustling marketplaces, filled with fibre rich foods like fruits, vegetables and whole grains, while others prefer the quieter corners where protein hangs out, and of course there are those who go for the sugary fast-food joints.

Each food you eat can nourish different type of bacteria. I diet rich in diverse foods can support a diverse microbiome, which is generally healthier and more resilient. A diet lacking in diversity, say one dominated by processed high sugar or fat foods can lead to a less diverse microbiome.

Fibre is good for your microbiome, and this is found in fruits, vegetables, whole grains and legumes. They ferment this to produce short chain fatty acids, which have numerous health benefits including nourishing the gut lining, reducing inflammation, and even protecting against cancer.

Polyphenols: - these are plant compounds with antioxidant properties found in foods like berries, tea, and dark chocolate. Our gut bacteria help break down polyphenols into a form our bodies can use, aiding in everything from heart health to brain function

Probiotics / prebiotics

Probiotics are good bacteria found in fermented foods like yoghurt, sauerkraut, and kimchi.

Prebiotics are the foods that bacteria love to eat.

What you need to do is limit processed foods, high sugar foods and unhealthy fats, these can lead to an imbalance in your gut bacteria, often favouring harmful bacteria and leading to a less diverse microbiome.

Food as medicine

Food is more than just calories. Every bite you take is a complex package of nutrients, fibre, and phytochemicals that can significantly influence your health and the health of your gut microbiome. Your body and particularly your gut, is a bit like a highly sophisticated chemistry lab. The foods you eat interact with your body's natural chemistry to either promote health or contribute to disease.

So, what does a balanced medicinal diet look like?

1. Fruits and vegetables: - these are superheroes of the diet. They are packed with fibre, which your gut microbes absolutely adore. And they are a rich source of vitamins, minerals, and antioxidants which protect against cell damage.

2. Whole grains: - such as oats, brown rice, whole grain bread, pasta, are an excellent source of fibre and can help promote a healthy diverse gut microbiome.

3. Lean protein: - this includes plant-based proteins like beans, lentils, tofu as well as lean meats, poultry, fish and eggs, and it is essential for cell growth and repair.

4. Healthy fats: - foods rich in monounsaturated and polyunsaturated fats like avocados, nuts, seeds, olives, and fatty fish such as salmon or mackerel are important for brain health, heart health and keeping inflammation at bay.

5. Fermented foods: - these are the probiotics of the food world. Foods like yoghurt, kimchi, sauerkraut, and kefir, are filled with beneficial bacteria that can help maintain a healthy gut microbiome.

6. Spices and herbs: - many spices and herbs have antioxidant and anti-inflammatory properties.

7. Certain types of fibre, called prebiotic fibre, act as food for our beneficial gut bacteria. When they ferment this fibre, they produce compounds called short chain fatty acids, which nourish our gut cells, help maintain a healthy gut lining and even have anti-inflammatory effects. Promoting regularity, where fibre adds bulk to the stool, helping prevent constipation and promoting regular bowel movements. A healthy gut is a cornerstone of a strong immune system and fibre, by promoting a healthy microbiome, plays a crucial role in maintaining our immune health.

8. Fruits, vegetables, whole grains, nuts, seeds are all excellent sources of dietary fibre, each offering a unique blend of different types of fibre, so aim for a variety of these foods to reap the most benefits. Beans and lentils are fibre powerhouses offering both soluble and insoluble fibre whole grains like oats and brown rice. Fruit and vegetables, especially when eaten with the skin provide a good mix of soluble and insoluble fibre.

Stress

When your body is stressed, remember one of the key hormones released is cortisol, which helps your body respond to stress, but cortisol also influences your gut in various ways. It can alter your gut motility, how quickly food moves through your gut, increase gut sensitivity, and even change the composition of your gut microbiota. What's more, your gut and brain are in constant communication. When you are stressed, your brain sends signals to your gut, which can lead to gastrointestinal symptoms.

Stress triggers the release of hormones like cortisol which can alter gut function. Stress affects the speed at which food moves through your digestive system. It can also alter the balance of bacteria in your gut, often leading to a decrease in beneficial bacteria, and an increase in potentially harmful ones. This dysbiosis imbalance can negatively impact our health in many ways, including impairing our immune system and potentially contributing to mood disorders. Stress can make your gut more sensitive, meaning you might feel discomfort or pain more readily. This is particularly relevant for people with IBS where stress can exacerbate symptoms.

Microbiota gut brain axis

This is a bi-directional communication between your gut and your brain, and your gut microbiota is a key player here. Research has shown that the types and balance in your gut can influence your brain's response to stress.

Did you know that your gut bacteria are responsible for producing many of the neurotransmitters that influence your mood and stress response. The majority of your body's serotonin, a neurotransmitter that helps regulate mood is produced in your gut.

Your gut microbiota also plays a critical role in regulating inflammation in your body, and chronic inflammation has been linked to increased stress and anxiety. The vagus nerve acts as the communication highway between your gut and brain,

Role of gut health and the immune system

When we think of the immune system, we often picture white blood cells and lymph nodes. What we don't immediately imagine is the bustling metropolis of microbes living in our gut. 70% of our immune cells reside in the gut. Our gut is a key player in our immune health. Our gut also acts as a physical barrier to harmful substances. The intestinal lining prevents pathogens, toxins, and allergens from entering the bloodstream, acting as a front-line defence. A healthy intact gut lining is critical to this protective role. A significant proportion of our immune cells live in the gut. They are on constant high alert, ready to jump into action at the first sign of an invader.

Our gut microbiota plays a crucial role in educating and regulating the immune system. Certain bacteria stimulate the immune system while others can suppress it, creating a balanced immune response. Dysbiosis, or an imbalance in gut bacteria can disrupt this harmony, leading to immune related issues.

Microbes in our gut also produce substances that have anti-microbial properties. These substances can directly inhibit the growth of pathogenic bacteria, keeping us protected from infections.

Eating a balanced varied diet is key, consuming plenty of fibre, as well as fermented foods rich in probiotics can help support a healthy diverse gut microbiota. Also, certain nutrients are crucial for maintaining the health of your gut lining, including zinc, Vitamin A, and omega 3 fatty acids and drinking plenty of water supports digestion and helps maintain the health of your gut lining

Gut microbiota and the immune response

They significantly impact our immune response. From birth our gut microbiota plays a vital role in training our immune system. The first 1000 days of life are crucial in shaping a child's microbiome, and in turn, the development of their immune system. During this period, exposure to a diverse array of microbes teaches the immune system to discern between harmful pathogens and friendly residents, setting the stage for robust immune health in later life.

- Balancing immune responses: - the gut microbiota is all about balance, particularly when it comes to immune responses. Consider this, our gut houses around 70% of the body's immune cells. By stimulating certain immune responses and suppressing others, our gut microbiota ensures our immune system functions optimally
- regulating inflammation: - certain microbes are inflammation tamers. For instance, some bacteria strains produce short chain fatty acids, like butyrate, which is known for its anti-inflammatory properties. Studies have shown that butyrate producers can represent up to 20% of the total gut microbiota in healthy individuals, underlining their importance in maintaining gut health.
- Protecting against pathogens: - our gut microbiota plays a crucial role in what is known as colonization resistance, effectively acting as a shield against invading pathogens. By taking up available space and nutrients in the gut, our resident gut microbes create an environment that is less than welcoming for potential invaders. However, maintaining a balanced, diverse gut microbiota is key to preserving this immune supporting synergy.

When this balance is disrupted in a state known as dysbiosis, things can start going south. Dysbiosis can lead to impaired immune response, making us more susceptible to infections. It is also linked to chronic inflammatory and autoimmune conditions.

For instance, studies have shown that people with inflammatory bowel disease, IBD, often have a less diverse gut microbiota, with increased levels of certain harmful bacteria, and decreased levels of beneficial ones, that's why nurturing a healthy gut microbiota is crucial, and not just for digestion. This includes eating a diverse, fibre rich diet, a staggering 70-80g per day is what our hunter gatherer ancestors consumed, avoiding unnecessary antibiotics, managing stress, and leading to a gut friendly lifestyle.

The major gut hormones and their functions

The gut hormones are the chemical communicators in our body that play a crucial role in several processes, from digestion to mood regulation. Hormones are chemical messengers produced by our body that travel in our bloodstream to tissues or organs. They regulate many bodily functions, from simple needs like hunger and thirst, to complex systems like reproduction and even emotions and mood.

- Ghrelin: - often referred to as the hunger hormone, Ghrelin, is produced in the stomach and pancreas. When your stomach is empty, ghrelin is released and travels to your brain, signalling that it is time to seek out food and eat. Interestingly, levels of Ghrelin are also known to increase when we are stressed, which might explain why some of us are prone to stress.
- Cholecystokinin (CCK): - is produced in the small intestine in response eating, especially when the meal is high in fat or protein. CKK has multiple roles. It stimulates the release of digestive enzymes from the pancreas and bile from the gallbladder to help break down food. It also acts on the brain to promote feelings of satiety, essentially telling us that we have eaten enough.

Reset your gut

Your gut is your 2nd brain. Your brain and your gut have a very intimate relationship. Bloating, brain fog, inflammation, trouble sleeping, fatigue, acne, hair loss, auto immune disease and food intolerances are all signs of an unhealthy gut. Your intestines have about 39 trillion organisms in it, we like to call this collection of micro-organisms – the Microbiome.

The Microbiome uses the Vagus nerve, which is an extremely important cranial nerve that travels through your body and controls your heart rate. The microbiome uses this nerve to send messages to your brain. If your gut is not happy, your brain is not happy.

Our bodies are very complexed, in factors such as sleep, food intolerances, hormones, genetics, exercise, all play key factors in what we like to call a healthy body.

- 95% of your serotonin (the happy hormone) is manufactured in your digestive system.
- 80% of your immune system is manufactured in your digestive system.

<u>How to eat properly</u>
1. Eat until satisfied, not full, not until your belly is aching. Overeating is causing the production of free radicals in the body, which ultimately effects ageing and overlading our digestive system. Use smaller plates and smaller bowls.
2. Cut your food into smaller pieces, eat mindfully. Eat slowly, take your time, and chew your food until it is basically mush. This is going to help with your digestion, because your enzymes in your mouth can now use that food, chew it up and help your body to fully digest it.
3. Do not drink while eating. What happens when we are drinking directly before eating or while we are eating is that we are creating a blockage, our body can no longer allow the enzymes that are in our mouth to mix with our food, so that it can be properly digested. Do not drink while eating or before eating.
4. Make time for eating mindfully: - sitting down in a calm environment, not talking on the phone, no distractions,
5. No snacking: - after a meal your body needs time to break down what you have eaten. When we are snacking, especially straight after a meal, you are basically overloading your digestive system, which leads to not only bloating, over time

will cause weight gain. Give your body at least 3 hours in between every single meal or use intermittent fasting.

6. Use salt-free additives like herbs.: - you should not be consuming more than 2300mg of sodium per day.

Grocery list

First thing in the morning drink a warm cup of water with lemon. Then a glass of water with a capful of apple cider vinegar and cinnamon.

- Fats: - Extra virgin olive oil, avocados, raw nuts-peanuts, almonds, walnuts
- Dairy: - Kefir, Greek yoghurt,
- Protein: - Organic chicken breasts, beans, lentils, salmon, tuna, herring, lamb turkey, eggs
- Carbohydrates: - Gluten free oats, buckwheat, white or brown rice, sweet potatoes
- Vegetables and fruit: - Squash, turnips, Brussel sprouts, cabbage, arugula, kale, beetroot, Swiss chard, spinach, mushrooms, kiwi, pineapple, orange, lemons, limes, coconuts, passion fruit, zucchini, carrots, green peas, broccoli, sauerkraut, lettuce, watercress, white onion, blueberries, raspberries, celery, garlic cloves.

Add ons

- Organic mustard, Himalayan salt, collagen powder, extra virgin coconut oil, turmeric, cinnamon, raw honey, black pepper, ginger root, bone broth, pickles, Kefir, all herbs and spices, chia seeds, flax seeds, sunflower seeds

Beverages

- bone broth, kombucha, coconut oil, purified water, nut milk, celery juice, ashwagandha tea, green tea

prebiotics (increase healthy gut bacteria)

- lentils, oats, bananas, artichokes, asparagus, garlic, leeks, nuts, onions, kefir, sauerkraut, tempeh, kimchi

Hormonal belly

If you are eating right and not losing weight despite a healthy lifestyle. You are craving sweets, sugar and salt uncontrollably. Your mood swings are off the charts, you are restless but can't sleep and have irregular periods. This could well be a hormonal belly. This type: _

- Lays low on the abdomen, protruding below the navel, the hormones are imbalanced. High estrogen, low estrogen, low testosterone, low DHE, high cortisol, high insulin.

Lower belly fat with a hormonal belly doesn't respond to exercise, no matter what you do it doesn't go away,

1. Daily nutrient imbalance: - not eating enough of the foods that your body needs to get all the nutrients. You are not eating enough and when you do eat it is not very balanced. Your body needs specific nutrients for it to heal itself.

2. high insulin levels: - This is caused by consuming excess refined and processed starches. What happens next is your body is unable to break this down, and utilize these types of foods for energy, for fuel, so now we have a problem, the pancreas will send insulin to take that glucose out of your blood and send it to your cells, and when that happens your body is flooded with a spike of insulin to do this. The solution is to have a diet that is lower in carbs, a higher in fats and protein. Because if your body is using fats and protein for energy, your body is not going to struggle with insulin management to the level where it can cause you to gain weight.

3. Insulin resistant: - when this happens you will not be able to shuffle the carbs out of the blood into the cells, so then your body is going to be starving at a cellular level.

4. High cortisol levels: - this is cause by anxiety, depression, lack of sleep, PTSD, all of these things can cause your body to surge in cortisol levels. When your body is creating cortisol, it is taking away from your progesterone and your testosterone, so high levels of stress will drop your testosterone, and drop your progesterone, and it will put you in a state of estrogen dominance. We fix this by having correct meal timing, adequate sleep,

5. High levels of estrogen:- women have lower belly fat that hangs over waist line. Men have extra fat tissue on breast area. We can fix this by eating vociferous vegetables, kale, broccoli, sprouts, etc. these foods naturally detox excess estrogen through the liver, so that it can be released in the body as a fibre supplement. If you are estrogen dominant, you are storing excess fat because of it. Lower consumption of red meat, pork, processed food, refined carbs, and exercise more.

6. Low growth hormone levels: - with this you will have a challenging time growing your muscles. This is relatively related to how you sleep and how you sleep at night, it is important to sleep in pitch black, so that our bodies can release more melatonin. This will improve your sleep and help lower your body temperature while you are sleeping.

<u>How to fix a hormonal body</u>

1. Adaptogens: - ashwagandha, this can balance your mood and give you a feeling of 'I'm doing ok'. It can reduce your cortisol levels, as well as your blood sugar levels.

2. Adding B1 into your diet (thiamine): - this is also known to turn your food into energy. This is another nutrient we become deficient in when we are highly stressed. B1 is a stress reliever.

3. Potassium: - when our cortisol levels are high for a long period of time we start to lose nutrients in our body. Potassium is one of them. Eat your bananas.

4. Deep breathing: - for stress reduction. Controlled breathing helps to stimulate the PNS, known as the rest and digest system.

5. Laugh more: - this helps keep your cortisol levels down.

6. Resolving guilt: - change habits, forgive others, learn to forgive yourself.

7. Exercising regularly: - this can help promote good health, which may help lower your cortisol levels.

8. Create a sleep routine: - avoid caffeine 6 hours before bedtime.

9. Cope with your triggers: - traffic, co-workers, neighbours,

Foods that cure hormonal belly
1. Probiotics: - support healthy gut microbiome, which will improve your mood, lower your stress, promote regularity, aid in digestion, will help your body absorb all nutrients in your food. Probiotics create a happy environment in your gut.
2. Prebiotics: - prebiotics are what the probiotics use to feed off, leeks, onions, chicory root, asparagus, bananas. Prebiotics will help sustain the balance in your gut, along with the probiotics which create the environment for a healthy gut
3. Anti-inflammatory herbs and spices: - ginger root, turmeric,
4. Protein: - salmon, chicken, eggs, keep protein sources
5. Fats: - play crucial role in getting rid of a hormonal belly. Nuts, seeds, avocados, nut butters, olive oil, it will help balance out hormones
6. Apple cider vinegar: - this is great for revving up your bowel flow.
7. Magnesium: - nuts, seeds, wheat germ, dry beans. Improves your insulin sensitivity, naturally lowers blood glucose levels,

Exercise for hormonal belly
- We need to be increasing our NEAT. Non-Exercise Activity Thermogenesis. Choose steps instead of elevator. Walking, shopping,
- Training style: - metabolic resistance training. Drop set: - 15lb dumbbells to do shoulder press. Supersets: - hip thrusts, squats.

Weight gain belly
- If you have rolls that is weight gain.
1. Portion control: - ger rid of frozen dinners, processed foods, packaged foods. Take time reading labels when grocery shopping.

2. Don't drink your calories: - avoid sugary fruit juices, sodas, alcohol, avoid sugar and cream into your coffee.
3. Drink water that is infused with lemon, lime, drink lots of water, apple cider vinegar. Your weight gain belly is because you are craving things, wanting more and more of those types of cravings.
4. Move your body for at least 30 minutes. A sedentary lifestyle is the biggest culprit of your weight gain belly.
5. Quit sugar: - cut out sugar, sodas, sweets, chocolate.

Bloated belly
- This bloat typically happens above the naval, more like pregnant belly appearance,
- 1: - consume no more than 2300mg sodium per day. Eliminate processed foods. No fast-food life.
- No carbonated drinks, alcoholic drinks. Watch your lactose
- Eat slower, stop overloading. Chew food, make mush.
- More water. Journal food. Food intolerances.

Too many carbs in diet
- Your gut may be extremely irritated and bloated because you may be holding onto water. Culprit could be eating way too many carbs.
- Symptoms and signs you are eating way to may carbs are
1. You are bloated: - 1 gram of carbs will bind into 3 grams of water. The more carbs you eat, the more water you are going to proportionally hold onto.
2. You are experiencing brain fog: - lethargic, strong urge to lay down, long break, excess carbs cause rise in blood sugar, which ultimately lead you toa crash. Also, your serotonin and melatonin levels in your brain increase and that gives you a feeling of drowsiness.
3. Insulin resistance: - signs of this are frequent urination, very thirsty all the time, this is because the excess carbs you are consuming you could possibly become hyperglycaemic. Excess amount of glucose in your bloodstream.

4. Eat sweet potatoes and brown rice.

Digestion remedies that work
- Ginger water: - sliced ginger root, weight loss benefits, empties stomach out and lowers blood sugar levels.
- Water, lemon, turmeric, cinnamon
- Blueberries contain polyphenols which are antioxidants
- Water and apple cider vinegar.

Intermittent fasting
- 16;8: - fast for 16 hours and eat in 8-hour window.
- 20:4 warrior fast: - you fast for 20 hours and eat for 4 hours. Start at 2pm and stop at 6pm
- OMAD: - one meal a day: - just eat one meal in a day
- Fed state is when body is digestion stage and digesting food. It is hard for your body to burn fat, because your insulin levels are high. After that your body goes into post absorbative state, which is where your is processing a meal. This state last 8-12 hours after your last meal. It is easier for your body to burn fat currently because your insulin levels are low.
- Because we don't enter the fasting state until 12 hours after our last meal, it is rare that our bodies are ever in this fat burning state. This is one of the reasons why many people start intermittent fasting and will lose so much fat without changing what they eat. Fasting outs your body in a fat burning state which you rarely make it during your normal eating schedule.

Nighttime routine to optimise your weight loss
1. Brush your teeth
2. Skincare routine
3. create my peaceful environment
4. Avoid these foods for 3-4 hours before bed: - MSG, caffeine, saturated fat, spicy foods. Alcohol

Leaky gut syndrome
- Increased intestinal permeability occurs when tight junctions of your intestinal walls loosen, this may allow harmful substances such as bacteria, toxins, and undigested particles to pass into your blood stream. The cause of this is a mystery, but leaky gut may contribute to several conditions such as IBS, Crohn's disease, celiac disease, chronic liver disease, food allergies, diabetes, PCOS,

The colon's main job is to absorb remaining water and electrolytes transforming the watery waste from the small intestine into more solid stuff. - the poop…

Also residing in the colon are trillions of gut bacteria happily feasting on the fibres, producing essential vitamins and gases. Finally, the leftover waste now formed into a solid or semi solid or liquid depending on how much you trust that takeaway. Is store in the rectum.

The nervous system, central, peripheral and enteric

The nervous system is basically your body's electrical wiring. It is a complex network of nerves and cells called neurons that carry messages between the brain and the rest of the body. This is divided into 3 parts. The CNS, PNS, and ENS. The CNS is the big boss consisting of the brain and the spinal cord

This is where all the critical decision making happens, the brain is the command centre. The spinal cord is the main highway for these messages carrying them to and from the brain. But the CNS can't do all this on its own, so enter the PNS. This connects it to the rest of the body. So, it is like central government and local administration. Bringing the CNS decisions to every corner of your body. The PNS is split into the somatic and autonomic systems.

The somatic system controls voluntary actions like reaching for cake, while autonomic system handles the stuff you don't have to think about, like making heartbeat faster.

The autonomic system is further divided into the sympathetic nervous system (fight flight freeze) and parasympathetic (the rest and digest system). These systems ensure your body responds appropriately in different situations.

The ENS runs the entire showdown in your gut, independent of the brain and spinal cord. This network of around 100 million neurons, lines your GI tract and manages every aspect of digestion from the oesophagus to the anus, and it doesn't stop there, it also communicates with the CNS influencing your emotions and mental state.

How does the ENS affect our mood an mental health? Can we use this knowledge to treat mental health disorders.

The Vagus Nerve

The vagal nerve, also known as the 10th cranial nerve, is one of the longest and most complex nerves in the human body. The name vagus comes from the Latin for wandering.

Starting in the brain stem just behind the ears, it meanders down your neck, branches out into your chest and heart, then goes all the way down to the abdomen, touching pretty much every organ on the way, it is like the route 66 of your body.

The vagus nerve is like a superhighway for signal between your gut and your brain. The vagus nerve plays a crucial role in the rest and digest part of your nervous system, The parasympathetic system, it regulates heart rate, stimulate the digestive organs, and helps control respiratory rate. All this makes it essential for maintaining homeostasis, keeping your body's internal environment balanced and stable.

The vagus nerve caries signals from your brain into your gut, about 10% of the traffic, and from the gut to the brain 90%. That means most of the time, it is your gut talking to your brain. Not the other way round. On the gut to brain pathway, the vagus nerve helps inform the brain about what is happening in the gut. For instance, if you have eaten something your body is having a hard time digesting, the gut will send a distress signal to the brain via the vagus nerve, which might result in feelings of discomfort or nausea.

On the flip side, the brain to gut pathway allows the brain to control gut function. The vagus nerve is also a key player in our moods and emotions. It is involved in it is involved in the production and regulation of certain neurotransmitters, like serotonin, our beloved feel-good hormone.

What are microbiota and microbiome

Microbiota refers to the 10 to 100 trillion symbiotic microbial cells harboured by each person. the human microbiome consists of the genes these cells harbour. Simply put, microbiota is the name for the ecological community of microbes that live in a particular location. These microbes contain bacteria, but also viruses, fungi, and other microscopic organisms. The microbiome however refers to the collection of all the genetic material of these microbes

Imagine the microbiota as the bustling city, full of diverse citizens. Then the microbiome would be the combined skill, knowledge, and characteristics of all these citizens. These all hang out all over your body, skin, mouth, gut. There are as may microbial cells in your body as there are human cells.

Your gut microbiota helps with digestion, especially food that your stomach and small intestine have trouble breaking down. They play a significant role in the immune system. Keeping harmful bacteria in check and even help regulate your metabolism. The gut microbiota can influence our mood and mental health.

Factors affecting the composition of the microbiome

The microbiome is like your own personal microbial eco system, with a population as diverse as the inhabitants of a bustling city.

Your DNA doesn't just determine your eye colour, or whether you can curl your tongue, it also influences your microbiome. Studies have shown that identical twins who share 100% of their genes, have more similar microbiomes than paternal twins. How you came into this earth has a significant impact on your initial microbiome. Babies born vaginally acquire different microbes than those born through a c section. The former are exposed to their mothers vaginal and faecal microbes, whereas the latter are first exposed to the skin microbiota and general environment.

Breastfeeding is another factor. Breastmilk is not just nutrition it is also a way for mothers to pass beneficial bacteria to their babies. This kick starts the development of the baby's microbiome and immune system.

The impact of diet can't be overstated. Different types of gut bacteria prefer different kinds of food. Some love fibre, others love protein and others love sugar. So, the composition of your diet heavily influences the composition of your gut microbiome. The more diverse your diet, the more diverse your microbiome. Lifestyle also plays a key role. Are you a night owl? Or morning person. Do you run marathons or binge watch tv shows? All these choices influence your microbiome. Regular physical activity for example has been linked to a more diverse microbiome.

Your microbiome changes as you grow. Newborns have a vastly different microbiome from toddlers, who have a different microbiome to teenagers, and so on. As we age, the diversity of our microbiome tends to decrease,

Environment and geography are also important, the microbes in your home, city, and part of the world, all influence your personal microbiome. The composition of your gut microbiome is linked to everything, from digestion, immunity, to mental health an even to conditions like obesity, allergies, and autoimmune diseases.

<u>The impact of diet on the gut microbiome</u>
- Fibre is found in fruits, vegetables, whole grains, legumes, many gut bacteria love fibre. They ferment it to use shortchange fatty acids which have numerous health benefits including nourishing the gut lining, reducing inflammation, and even protecting against cancer.
- Polyphenols, these are plant compounds with antioxidant properties found in foods like berries, tea, and dark chocolate. Our gut bacteria help break down polyphenols into a form our bodies can use, aiding in everything from heart health to brain function
- Probiotics are found in fermented foods like yoghurt, sourcrout, and kimchi.
- Prebiotics are the foods that bacteria love to eat,

Food as medicine: - the importance of a balance diet

Food is more than calories, every bite you take is a package of nutrients, fibre, phytochemicals, that can significantly influence your health and the health of your gut microbiome. The foods you eat interact with your body's natural chemistry to either promote health or contribute to disease.

- Fruits and vegetables: - high fibre, rich source of vitamins, minerals and antioxidants. Which protect against cell damage.
- Whole grains: - oats, brown rice, whole grain bread, pasta, excellent source fibre.
- Lean protein: - beans, lentils, tofu, lean meats, poultry, fish and eggs. Protein is essential for cell growth and repair.
- Healthy fats: - avocados, nuts, seeds, olives, fatty fish, salmon or mackerel, are important for brain health, heart health and keeping inflammation at bay.
- Fermented foods. They are the probiotics of the food world. Yoghurt, kimchi, sauerkraut, kefir are filled with beneficial bacteria, that can help maintain a healthy gut microbiome.
- Spices and herbs: - antioxidant and anti-inflammatory.

Prebiotics, probiotics, symbiotics

Probiotics are live beneficial bacteria that when consumed in adequate amounts have health benefits. Picture them as friendly new neighbours moving into bustling city. Lactobacillus and bifidobacterium. These friendly bacteria can help balance your gut microbiome, support immune system, and even promote mental health. Find these foods in fermented foods like yoghurt, sauerkraut, kimchi, kefir and kombucha. They need to contain live cultures.

Prebiotics are types of dietary fibre that act as food for these friendly bacteria. These are found in many fruits and vegetables. Garlic, onion, asparagus, bananas, apples.

Symbiotics are a combination of the two, these are foods that contain both probiotic and prebiotics. Yoghurt and banana combined.

Understanding role of dietary fibre in gut health

Dietary fibre has big role to lay gut health. As it passes through our digestive system it performs various tasks that help keep gut healthy. Prebiotic fibre act as food for our gut bacteria. When they ferment this fibre, they produce compounds called short chain fatty acids (SCFA) which nourish our gut cells, help maintain gut lining, and also anti-inflammatory effects. Fibre adds bulk to the stool, preventing constipation. Foods high in fibre tend to be more filling. Beans and lentils, brown rice, fruits and vegetables. Nuts and seeds.

Fibre types: - soluble and insoluble
- Soluble: - dissolves in water, when it does it forms a gel like substance in our stomach. Lower cholesterol, regulate blood sugar levels, promote weight management. Oats, peas, beans, citrus fruits, carrots, apples,
- Insoluble: - does not dissolve: - promote bowel regularity, prevents constipation, supports gut health. Whole wheat flour, nuts, beans, vegetables such as cauliflower, green beans, potatoes. Skin of fruits.

Understanding stress response
- The first reaction to stress is alarm stage, and where your adrenal gland produces adrenaline. Also known as epinephrine. Which causes heart rate to increase, more blood to muscles.
- Resistance stage: - if stress continues. Adrenal glands release another hormone cortisol. Regulates body.
- Exhaustion stage: - during stage might feel drained and burnt out.
- When your body is stressed, one of key hormones that is released is cortisol, which helps body respond to stress, but cortisol influences gut in various ways, it can alter your guts motility, increased gut sensitivity, and change composition of gut

microbiota. Your gut and brain are in constant communication, when you are stressed your brain sends signals to your gut which lead to gastro-intestinal symptoms.

How stress affects the gut and vice versa

Stress affects the gut by releasing cortisol. It can cause dysbiosis and impairing immune system, and mood disorders. Stress can make gut more sensitive. Such as IBS etc. The gut microbiota plays a significant response, it can influence brains response to stress.

The role of gut health in the immune system

About 70% of our immune cells reside in the gut. Our gut is a key player in our immune health. Our gut acts as a physical barrier to harmful substances, the intestinal lining prevents pathogens, allergens, toxins from entering the blood stream, acting as a front-line defence. A healthy intact gut lining is critical to this protective role.

Immune cell home, a significant proportion of our immune cells live in the gut, they are on constant high alert, ready to jump into action at the first sign of an invader.

Our gut microbiome plays a crucial role in educating and regulating the immune system, certain bacteria stimulate the immune system, while others can suppress it, creating a balanced immune response.

Dysbiosis, or an imbalance in gut bacteria can disrupt this harmony, leading to immune related issues,

Production of anti-microbial substances. Our gut microbes also produce substances that have anti-microbial properties, these substances can directly inhibit the growth of pathogenic bacteria keeping us protected from infection.

Eating a balanced varied diet is key. Eating fibre and fermented foods can help support a healthy diverse gut microbiota. Hydration drinking plenty of water helps with hydration and helps support healthy gut balance.

Gut microbiota and immune response

From birth our gut microbiota plays a vital role in training our immune system. The first 1000 days of life are crucial in shaping a child's microbiome. And in turn the development of their immune system. During this period, exposure to a diverse array of microbes teaches the immune system to discern between harmful pathogens and friendly residents. Setting the stage for robust immune health in later life

The gut microbiota is all about balance. Particularly when it comes to immune responses. Our gut houses around 70% of our immune cells. By stimulating certain immune responses and suppressing others, our gut microbiota ensures that our immune system functions optimally. Regulating inflammation. Certain gut microbes are inflammation tamers, for instance some bacteria strains produce short chain fatty acids which is known for its anti-inflammatory properties.

Our gut microbiota plays a crucial role in what is known as colonisation resistance, effectively acting as a shield against invading pathogens. By taking up available space and nutrients in the gut our resident gut microbes create an environment that is less than welcoming for potential invader. However, maintaining a balanced diverse gut microbiota is key to preserving this immune supporting synergy. When this balance is disrupted in a state known as dysbiosis, things can start going south. Dysbiosis can lead to impaired immune response, making us more susceptible to infections. It is also linked to chronic inflammatory and auto immune conditions.

The major gut hormones and their functions

- Ghrelin: - the hunger hormone. Ghrelin is produced in the stomach and pancreas. When your stomach is empty, ghrelin is released and travels to your brain, signalling that its time to seek out food and eat. Levels of ghrelin are also known to increase when we are stressed.

- Cholecystokinin CCK, is produced in the small intestine in response to eating, especially when the meal is high in fat or protein. CCK has multiple roles, it stimulates the release of digestive enzymes from the pancreas and bile from the gallbladder. It also acts on the brain to give feelings of satiety.
- Glucagon-like-peptide-1 (GLP-1): - this hormone is secreted in response to food intake, plays a key role in maintaining glucose balance. It promotes insulin release, reduces glucagon production a hormone that raises blood sugar levels and slows gastric emptying, which all contribute to regulating blood glucose levels
- Peptide YY: - this hormone is released in the lower gut after eating and is responsible for creating a feeling of fullness. It also slows down the rate in which food is moved from the stomach to the small intestine thereby contributing to satiety and helping with overall weight regulation.
- Serotonin: - this neurotransmitter plays a role in various bodily functions including mood regulation, bowel movements, and nausea.

Enzymes in the digestive system

Enzymes are proteins that speed up the rate of chemical reactions. In the digestive system these reactions involve breaking down the food we eat into most basic components. Proteins into amino acids. Carbohydrates into simple sugars. Fats into fatty acids and glycerol. These tiny particles can then be absorbed by our bodies and used as fuel for various cellular functions,
- Amylase: - produced in the salivary glands and the pancreas, this starts working the moment you take your first bite of food. Amylase breaks down complex carbohydrates like starches into simpler sugars.
- Pepsin: - this is the main gastric enzyme secreted by the lining stomach. It begins the process of protein digestion by breaking them down into smaller fragments called peptides.

- Trypsin: - secreted by the pancreas, trypsin carries on where pepsin left off, it breaks down the peptides into even smaller units, preparing them for the final stage of protein digestion
- Peptidases: - these enzymes are located in the walls of the small intestine, and perform the final act in protein digestion, breaking own the peptides into individual amino acids, which can then be absorbed into the bloodstream.
- Lipase: - produced by the pancreas and small intestine, lipase is responsible for breaking down fats into fatty acids and glycerol.
- Lactase, sucrase, and maltase: - these enzymes found in the lining of the small intestine are tasked with the breakdown of specific sugars. Lactase breaks down lactose the sugar found in dairy products

Factors disturbing gut health
- Stress: - chronic stress can wreak havoc on your gut, when we are stressed our bodies release stress hormones like cortisol, which can alter gut motility, and create environment more hospitable to harmful bacteria. This can result in a host of gut issues from IBS, indigestion, acid reflux.
- Poor diet: - diets high in processed foods, sugars and unhealthy fats but low in fibre can disrupt the balance of our gut and microbiome. These eating habits can promote the growth of harmful bacteria, at the expense of beneficial ones, leading to a condition known as dysbiosis. This can pave the way for various health issues from obesity and type 2 diabetes to heart disease and certain types of cancer
- Sleep: - lack of sleep can alter the composition and diversity of our gut bacteria. Which can impact everything from our metabolism to our mental health.

How environmental factors impact gut health
Our environment plays a critical role In shaping the diversity and functioning of our gut microbiota. It begins the moment we are born as we acquire our first microbes during birth and

continue to accumulate more as we grow. From there our environment continues to shape our microbiome throughout our lives

Air pollution is one factor that can affect our gut health. Tiny particles of particulates from air pollution can be inhaled and eventually make their way into our guts. Studies have shown that these particles can alter our gut microbiota composition and increase permeability leading to a condition often referred to as a leaky gut.

This allows bacteria and other potentially harmful substances to leak into the bloodstream leading to inflammation and other health problems.

Water quality. Our drinking water can be a source of variety of microbes, some beneficial and some potentially harmful. The quality of our water whether its tap water or bottled can influence the composition of our gut microbiota. Water treated with chlorine commonly used to disinfect drinking water can kill off beneficial gut bacteria. On the other hand, contaminated water can introduce harmful microbes into our system causing a range of gut problems.

Pesticides and antibiotics

Pesticides can harm our microbiota directly or indirectly by reducing the biodiversity of our diets. Antibiotics on the other hand can wipe out significant portions of our gut bacteria including the beneficial ones, leading to a decrease in microbiome diversity.

Our modern ultra clean environment might be partly to blame for the rise in allergies and autoimmune diseases. As our immune systems aren't being trained by enough diverse microbes.

Understanding genetic factors affecting gut health

Our genes can also influence the bustling community of microbes in our gut. Genetics can play a part in shaping our gut microbiota in several ways. Our genes can affect the physical environment of our gut such as its PH level, immune response, and the type of mucous lining it has. This environment in turn can influence which type of bacteria can thrive there.

Superfood: - beverages: - Kombucha

Kombucha is a fermented beverage much like cultured yoghurt, cheese, kefir, kimchi, and sauerkraut, and made by fermenting tea, generally black tea or sometimes green and oolong tea and sugar with a symbiotic culture of bacteria and yeast. Also known as SCOBY, generally for 10 days, it is then bottled for 1 to 2 weeks to contain released CO_2 and encourage carbonation. From there, bottled kombucha is placed in a refrigerated environment to slow down the carbonation and fermentation processes. The scoby comprises various acetic acid bacteria and yeast.

After fermentation kombucha is a cocktail of chemical components, including sugars, tea polyphenols, organic food, acid fibre, ethanol, amino acids, including lysine, and essential nutrients such as copper, manganese, zinc, water soluble Vitamin C, and many B vitamins, and enzymes. It is rich in probiotics, and probiotic bacteria are like the friendly bacteria present in the gut and they help with diarrhoea and IBS. They can also strengthen immune system.

Superfood: - sauerkraut

Sauerkraut is a traditional European dish. It is made from fermented cabbage. It is made by mixing shredded cabbage and salt and pressing it down on the mixture. The beneficial bacteria present on the surface of the cabbage and from the air in the environment start to break down the natural sugars in the cabbage into lactic acid. The fermentation could take 3-5 days to complete. It is loaded with nutrients and is low in calories. It is an excellent source of vitamins and minerals, including iron, calcium, selenium, manganese, and folate. it also has high fibre. studies show that fermented cabbage has antioxidant and anti-inflammatory properties because of phytochemicals, Vitamin C and iron contributing to a more robust immune system.

Superfood: - Kimchi

Kimchi is a traditional Korean recipe made with salted fermented vegetables, which involve Korean cabbage, and seasonings like sugar, salt, onions, garlic, ginger, red chilli powder and seafood. It may include other vegetables including radish, celery, carrot, cucumber, spinach, scallions, beets and bamboo shoots. Several bacteria are involved in kimchi fermentation, but probiotic lactic acid bacteria are the dominant species in the fermentation process. It contains vitamins such as Vit A, C, B complex, sodium, calcium, potassium, iron, and phosphorus, also gingerol, isocyanide and chlorophyl

Supplementation and gut health
The food we eat is losing its nutritional value. How it is grown, transported, and how we store and cook it. Unless you buy your produce from a local farmer's market, and take every precaution to store it effectively, there is almost a loss of 50% or more nutrients in your food.

Factory foods are highly processed and offer very little or no nutritional value. The companies that manufacture these processed and fast foods rely on taste, convenience and obviously on how much profit they will earn by the end of the day.

A woman needs at least 25g of fibre every day and a man needs more than 40g per day. A dietary supplement such as Psyllium can help.

Organic whole husk psyllium. Psyllium is a heavily sprayed crop which many sources are contaminated with pesticides, herbicides and fertilisers. You should only use organic psyllium husk, non-GMO and ensure it is 100% pure with no added compounds.

Glutamine: - proteins are made up amino acids, which are like the building blocks of the human body. When you eat proteins, your body breaks them down into their constituent parts, amino acids. Now 20 different amino acids join together in various combinations to make all types of proteins. Our bodies can't make some of these amino acids, hence they are known as essential amino acids. These 9 essential amino acids we need to get from our diets. Whereas 11 amino acids can be manufactured by the body and are termed as non-essential amino acids and there is no need to get them from your diet.

Glutamine is one of the most abundant amino acids found in the human body, one remarkable fact about glutamine us that it is conditional amino acid. Studies have shown that in exceptional circumstances, like when there are muscle wounds or a patient has AIDS, which is a muscle wasting disease, glutamine can be very helpful. Glutamine is abundantly found in animal foods like beef, eggs, poultry, fish and even green leafy vegetables like spinach and cabbage. Glutamine is an essential nutrient for our gut, it has an anti-inflammatory effect on the gut.

You don't need probiotic supplements. One quart of fermented vegetables can give you approximately a trillion beneficial microbes. A high-quality yoghurt from raw cow's milk has nearly a few hundred billion CFUs. Include various probiotic rich foods in your diet.

Sleep

Sleep deprivation is not only linked with grumpiness and grogginess, but also with increased risk of chronic diseases. In a study, lack of sleep on a regular basis less than 6 hours or more than 9 hours, can increase the risk of death by 10%. The common symptoms of sleep deprivation are feeling fatigued throughout the day, lack of creativity, unwanted weight gain as lack of sleep increases appetite and cravings for junk food and fried foods.

You may even start to look old as your skin will start to appear bad because of excessive cortisol which is the stress hormone which is released during sleep deprivation which breaks down collagen. This causes skin wrinkling, and premature aging. There will also be no energy for workouts, your reaction time will drastically reduce rendering at higher risk when driving, and lastly your immune system will suffer which can make you more vulnerable to cold and flu. Quality of sleep is more important than quantity, however a minimum period of sleep is important as well. So how much sleep also depends on your age, how stressed you are and other variables.

A newborn needs the most sleep around 14-t7 hours. Toddlers and preschool need around 11-14 hours. School age 9-11 hours. Teens 8-10 hours and going into adulthood and beyond 7-9 hours' sleep.

Sleep cycles

It is still not clear why we sleep. Your bran is fully functional when you sleep, and sleeps with main function to repair and rejuvenate, and rebuild. A good night's sleep gets you ready to face the world with a lot of energy and vigour.

A sleep cycle consists of all four stages plus the REM sleep. Each cycle lasts up to 90 minutes. With each stage lasting from 15-20 minutes, followed by the REM sleep which can last up to an hour. Seven to nine hours of sleep consist of 3-5 sleep cycles, including 3-5 REM sleep cycles.

Note non-REM sleep happens during the early part of the sleep usually between the hours of 10pm and 1pm. This is the time where there is maximum repair and rejuvenation.

- Stage 1: - is when your body starts to doze off and within 3-5 minutes sometimes even within seconds when you are super tired or when napping. Your brain starts to produce alpha and theta brainwaves. Your body temperature starts to drop, eye movements slow down, it is easy to be awakened from when in this stage. This stage can last up to 10-15 minutes or so, when you enter stage 2.
- Stage 2 is where your brain waves are in the form of sleep spindles, eye movements completely stop, hence the name non-REM sleep, heart ate slows down, and body temperature drops. This is also a stage where one's nap should usually end.
- Stage 3 and 4 is where you start to enter the deep sleep and your brainwaves convert into delta waves, there is zero eye movement, and no muscle activity. Stage 3 and 4 is when your body rejuvenates to restore and rebuild. This is where your immune system gets a boost, this is where large amounts of growth hormone is released. This is super beneficial for you and your body is completely nonresponsive to the outside stimuli and that is why it is very tough for you to wake up from these stages especially stage 4.

- Stages 1,2,3,4 are the NON-REM stages and are also the dreamless phases of sleep with virtually little or no eye movement.

Steps to heal your gut

1. Eliminate food triggers: - identify foods that may be causing inflammation or irritation in your gut and eliminate them from your diet. Start with the most common foods that cause allergic reactions like gluten, conventional dairy and all related products like cheese and butter. Then you can eliminate eggs, peanut, shellfish, soya.

2. Avoid junk food and fast food: - it is best to remove anything that comes in a wrapper or a box. The idea is to avoid processed foods that have an ingredient list. Processed foods can contain ingredients that can be harmful to the gut, such as preservatives, artificial sweeteners and additives. Abstain from alcohol, tea, coffee etc.

3. Avoid conventional dairy and farmed meats: - stop conventional dairy while healing your gut. It is one of the most common foods that can cause food allergies, it is also loaded with antibiotics, hormones and other unwanted compounds that play havoc with your gut health. CAFO meats, which are grain fed meats from Confirmed Animal Feeding Operations, these contain tons of antibiotics, which can affect your gut health, farmed seafood: - fish and seafood are a major source of human exposure to contaminants like methyl mercury, and PCBs. Limiting your consumption of farmed raised fish is vital because their contaminant levels are generally higher than wild water species.

4. Eat a plant-based diet: - vegans and vegetarians have a more diverse and stable microbial population than omnivores.

5. Include foods high in prebiotic content: - eat at least 5 to 8 servings of fresh and seasonal fruits and vegetables daily. Legumes, lentils, beans, steel cut oats.

6. Include foods high in probiotic content: - yoghurt, kefir, kimchi, kombucha. Buttermilk and raw milk. Fermented vegetables. Pickles, miso.

7. Stay hydrated.: - water is essential.
8. Reduce stress
9. Get enough sleep
10. Exercise regularly
11. Build a meditation and mindfulness practice.

Chapter 10

Hormone rollercoaster

Stress and hormones are intimately connected. Stress is at the very root of all disease. It starts into play a cascade of inflammatory events within the body and the release of hormones and neurochemicals, which can then manifest their way into disease states. How you respond to these stressors has a definite effect on your physiology. Thoughts create a physiological response. Your stress perception can either have a positive or negative effect. Much of this is based on your perception on a given stressor. There is an emotional component to every mental, physical and spiritual aspect of your life.

Sleep

Sleep provides time for our conscious minds to rest and our subconscious minds time to process. We need approximately 8 hours of sleep per night. Losing as little as 1 hour of sleep leads to hormonal imbalances that eventually leads to a whole host of other health problems. It contributes to cognitive decline, decreased immune function, and obesity, and increases our risks of heart disease, stroke, and diabetes.

Did you know that stress sabotages your sleep. Same with a glass of wine. If you are waking up between 1,2 3 or 4 in the morning, that glass of wine may be responsible for that. Physical and mental illness is also a factor that can be sabotaging your sleep. Taking various medications can also have an impact on your quality of sleep and how deep you sleep. Eating late and trying to digest those foods particularly if they aren't healthy foods is also going to affect your sleep because it is going to raise your body temperature. If you are a shift worker, this can have a significant effect on your hormone imbalance, and whether you get good quality sleep.

Exercise and hormones

Did you know that 65% of Americans are overweight, and 30% of these people presume that they are at a normal weight. 70% of obese individuals perceive they are just a little overweight. If you are overweight carrying around that extra weight, it is holding onto fat, estrogen, and increasing your health risks. Excess weigh contributes to diseases such as cancer, heart disease, diabetes, autoimmune diseases.

Environmental impact

We are consuming a very high processed and sugar laden diet, and this is severely impacting your hormones. Foods are grown in fields with pesticides and fields that have been stripped of vital nutrients and minerals. Our water supply is polluted. The air we breathe today is not the same our parents were breathing. There are a lot more pollutants such as cadmium, and other heavy metals that we are breathing in from the air. Cell phones and electronic devices are having an impact on our own electromagnetic field. We are all energy. If you are using cosmetics and creams and lotions made from chemically derive substances, you are being exposed to xenoestrogens.

Diet

This is a major factor on hormone balance. A poor diet creates inflammation, and inflammation leads to the manifestation of a whole host of diseases.

Genetically modified organisms or GMO, the pesticides, herbicides. There is enough research on this to show that this is contributing to obesity, hormone imbalances, depression, autoimmune disorders, autism, etc.

Adrenal fatigue

The adrenals are vital to hormone imbalance particularly cortisol. There are many symptoms from hormonal imbalances which affect the adrenals including fatigue, sugar cravings, salt cravings, sleep difficulties, mood changes, hair loss, pain, weakened immune system, brain fog, food insensitivities and allergies, weight gain, digestive issues, insulin resistance, altered thyroid and sex hormones, mineral depletion, healing impairment, headaches and pre-menstrual syndrome.

Some of the symptoms are associated with low progesterone. Symptoms of low estrogen are hot flushes, night sweats, forgetfulness, vaginal dryness, headaches, urinary incontinence, fatigue, low libido, menstrual irregularities. Insomnia, dry skin,

Symptoms of low testosterone are low libido, thinning pubic hair, mood changes, fatigue,

Hormone regulation

Each endocrine gland has a function and produces hormones. Hormones are interdependent and must be able to communicate with each other. Communication breakdown is affected by genetics, age, gender, stress, emotions, diet, environment, food sensitivities, and gut health.

HPA Axis (Hypothalamus-Pituitary-Adrenal)

There are many branches of communication within the HPA axis. One hormone breaks down to another hormone and each has an important function. There are many branches of communication within the HPA axis. When this communication system is stressed for one reason or another, there is a breakdown in that communication. One hormone communicates with the next.

Most of our hormones start out as cholesterol. And from cholesterol become what is known as pregnenolone, or the mother hormone. This starts breaking down into your progesterone, which breaks down into cortisol. Pregnenolone also becomes DHEA which breaks down into testosterone, estradiol, and estrone, estrol.

Now, if your body is under a lot of stress, these hormones are going to start to be stressed as well, because the most important thing is to keep our cortisol level up. As your body is trying to keep that cortisol level up, it is going to start pulling away from your DHEA, which will then affect your testosterone, and your estrogen, it's going to start pulling away from your progesterone, so that is going to be affected, and the next thing you know you have complete hormonal imbalance.

So simply replacing estrogen and progesterone without dealing with things that are stressing your cortisol balance, or any upstream or downstream effect from this, will only have a very limited response.

STRESS is the root of all health problems. The stressors can be from your diet, your environment, and just general chronic day to day stress. And when that stress occurs, everything is going to try to keep your cortisol level up, and in the process, start shunting away from other areas.

Thyroid symptoms occur when excess cortisol blocks the production of your thyroid stimulating hormone which happens in the brain, or prevents the conversion of your T4 to T3, this happens at the level of the thyroid gland itself

Then symptoms can occur, and these can include fatigue, cold intolerance, weight gain, memory problems, poor concentration, depression, hair loss, dry skin, infertility. These are also symptoms you can see with a progesterone issue.

When your cells get the amount of T3, which is the most active most potent form of thyroid hormone, your body is going to feel healthy, and it is going to work the way it should. When that conversion is not happening, for various reasons, then it is a lot harder for that thyroid to operate as it should.

Factors that affect thyroid function

Factors that contribute to proper production of thyroid hormones: - nutrients, iron, iodine, tyrosine, zinc, selenium, Vits E, B2, B3, B6, C, D. Factors that increase conversion of T3 to RT3: - stress, trauma, low calorie diet, inflammation – cytokines etc, toxins, infections, liver/kidney dysfunction, certain medications. Factors that inhibit proper production of thyroid hormones: - stress, infection, trauma, radiation, medications, fluoride (antagonist to iodine), toxins including pesticides, mercury, cadmium, lead, autoimmune disease. Factors that increase conversion of T4 to T3: - selenium, zinc. Factors that improve cellular sensitivity to thyroid hormones: - Vitamin A, exercise, Zinc,

Testing for hormonal imbalances
- Blood v saliva testing
- Urine testing
- Food sensitivity testing
- Heavy metals
- Nutrient testing

What tests should you get?
- Cholesterol, 25 (OH)D, cortisol's, DHEA, 17-OH progesterone, secretary IgA, FSH, LH, Gliadin Antibody, progesterone, Estrone, Estradiol, Estriol, TSH, Free T4, Free T3, Thyroid antibody, reverse T3 and Thyroglobulin Antibody.

Get off the hormonal roller coaster
- Get Water filters, check on radiation,
- Diet: - it is about nourishing the body. NON-GMO foods, grass fed meat and dairy. Hormone free. Mediterranean diet, paleo diet. Nuts, seeds, fresh fruit, vegetables, fish

Chapter 11

Obesity and insulin resistance

<u>What is the obesity epidemic?</u>
Since the 1960's we have been lied to, we have been told to be low-fat based, on faulty research. There are two schools of thought: - calorie number -v- calorie type. Calories in/calories out is NOT a good human model. The body is not a simple furnace, and calories don't really matter nearly as much as we are led to believe.

<u>What happens if we ignore this?</u>
Insulin Resistance leads to obesity, diabetes and probably more. This current epidemic is growing unchecked. In the past 30 years, the number of people diagnosed with diabetes has quadrupled. The problem is treating Type 2 diabetes patients with insulin makes them fatter. Insulin resistance is also linked to several diseases, such as poorly controlled seizures in kids, dementia, type 2 diabetes, heart disease, high cholesterol, high blood pressure, non-alcoholic fatty liver disease and stroke.

<u>Why does what we have always been told: - FAIL?</u>
The eat low fat, high carb, exercise more diet, DOES NOT WORK. When we process food it enters the stomach, it is then mixed with stomach acid, released into the small then large intestines, and the remains are excreted as stool.

Hunger is controlled by numerous overlapping hormonal systems, and we consciously decide to start/stop eating in response to hormonal signals. These hormones also regulate fat growth, so obesity is a hormonal disorder and NOT a caloric disorder. The calories in − calories out = body fat seems logical, but it is wrong. Measuring caloric intake is simple, but measuring calories expenditure is complicated. Our bodies don't deal in calories, but in hormones, enzymes and metabolic processes with complex feedback loops. Your total calories out is not just basal metabolic rate and exercise. Your total energy expenditure (calories out) is made up of Basal Metabolic Rate, thermogenic effect of food eaten, non-exercise activity, thermogenesis, excess post exercise oxygen consumption and exercise.

The real problem to obesity and weight gain is carbohydrates. Our bodies don't need a lot of carbohydrates, and these should not be refined carbohydrates.

Carbohydrate metabolism and hunger

When we eat carbohydrates and sugar, our blood sugar rises, the pancreas responds by secreting insulin, the insulin brings the blood sugar back down. Refined carbohydrates trigger the pancreas to overshoot so blood sugar drops too low, and we get hungry again. The low blood sugar makes us irritable and anxious, we feel bad, and it triggers us to eat again,

Carbohydrates equal sugar. Starches break down into carbohydrates, carbohydrates break down into sugar. Sugar has ZERO nutritional value. Table Sugar = sucrose which is glucose + fructose. Fructose cannot be used by any cell in the body, it has to be metabolised in the liver first, and excess fructose is changed directly into fat in the liver. High levels of fructose will cause fatty liver, this is crucial to developing insulin resistance in the liver and to insulin resistance overall.

Carbohydrates and the intestines

Carbohydrates can lead to leaky gut. There are trillions of bacteria that live in our gut all the time. We need them to digest things we couldn't otherwise use. We also need the bacteria to make some neurotransmitters like serotonin. Processed foods, medications and stress all kill these bacteria.

With carbohydrates, the blood glucose moves into the liver, the liver can only store so much glucose, so it makes glycogen. The liver can only store so much glycogen, so it makes triglycerides (fat). Another thing which causes obesity are the toxins in processed foods which are called obesogens. They include monosodium glutamate and soy protein isolates. They block hormone receptor sites on cells so hormones can't do their jobs.

We have been duped for the past 30 years, where cholesterol has been portrayed as the clog in our arteries. Cholesterol is NOT the enemy. Heart disease is not about fat. Yes, cholesterol is deposited in the arteries of the heart, but this is as a response and not the cause of heart disease. Heart disease is about inflammation and oxidative stress.

The low-fat high carb diets contribute to dental disease. periodontal disease is a direct result of sugar in the diet. Low-fat high carb diets lead to periodontal disease, the body is trying to defend against chronic inflammation.

What is insulin?

In most cases of Type 2 diabetes, your body still produces insulin. And the real problem is Insulin resistance. Insulin is a hormone that allows glucose to enter our cells. Without insulin, this blood sugar has nowhere to go and accumulates in the blood stream. Insulin controls this process in order to maintain steady blood levels of glucose.

In type 1 diabetics, the immune system is attacking the beta cells in the pancreas than make insulin. So they can't make any, or at least not enough. For them insulin is a medication, and most necessity for survival. Although Type 1 is an autoimmune disease as the immune system is attacking own body. And we discuss the autoimmune system later in this book.

In type 2 diabetes, the vast majority of type 2 diabetics, about 95%, still make insulin, but their cells become resistant. The remaining 5% of type 2 diabetics, also develop an immune response to their own beta cells, but this happens over time rather than suddenly. The other 95% of type 2 diabetics, have a problem of too much insulin, so why the hell are they being given more insulin, instead of actually dealing with the issue, which is the glucose not being delivered to the cells, and insulin resistance.

With high glucose and high insulin in the body this can cause a whole host of problems and health issues. High glucose can cause erectile dysfunction. High insulin lowers testosterone in men, and it also raises testosterone in women, and can cause acne, oily skin, more facial hair, and it also affects the menstrual cycle, and can also cause poly cystic ovarian syndrome. This is caused by chronically increased levels of insulin.

High levels of insulin cause men's bodies to convert some of their testosterone to estrogen, leading to estrogen effects in their bodies, these include development of breast tissue or man boobs.

Did you know that over 75 million Americans have metabolic syndrome? Metabolic syndrome is a name for a group of medical disorders occurring simultaneously in an individual. These include central obesity, obesity around the abdomen, high triglycerides, low HDL, high fasting glucose, and high blood pressure. It is also known as insulin resistance or syndrome X.

What happens when we are resistant to insulin?
This is where we have too much glucose and too much insulin. Our cells only have room for so much glucose, and then they take glucose and make glucagon. Glucagon is the storage form of glucose in the cells. Once that limit is also reached, glucagon is made into triglycerides (fat). You also need to realise that when you get stressed and your body releases cortisol, cortisol is a stress hormone, and this also can make us fat by raising glucose levels.

Glucagon- the anti-insulin
Where insulin tries to save energy in the body. Glucagon wants to spend it. Glucagon wants to body to release its stored energy, by triggering fat cells to release fat, and triggering liver cells to release glucose. It also activates ketogenesis, or the making of ketones. It also activates autophagy, which is the clean up of cellular debris.

Because insulin and glucagon work against each other, to activate and inhibit metabolic processes, the balance of these hormones dictates which process actually occurs.

Just before awakening, the body secretes higher levels of adrenaline, growth hormone, glucagon, and cortisol, but NOT insulin, to prepare for the coming day, this explains why the blood glucose is slightly higher first thing in the morning.

Dietary protein raises insulin levels, but not blood glucose, and it does this by simultaneously raising other hormones such as incretins and glucagon.

A deeper dive into insulin resistance

Hormones are molecules that deliver messages to a cell. To do this, these molecules bind to a receptor on the cell surface, very much like a key fitting into a lock. This can either open, or close a channel in that cell surface, which either allows entry of another molecule or prevents it from entering.

In the case of insulin, which we know now is a hormone, it acts on its receptors to bring glucose into a cell. The door opens, and the glucose enters. Insulin is a key regulator of energy metabolism. It is one of the fundamental hormones that promote fat accumulation and storage. Without insulin, glucose builds up in the blood stream and quickly becomes toxic. This is what happens in type 1 diabetics.

Type 1 diabetes is an auto-immune disease, that causes the destruction of insulin producing cells in the pancreas, resulting in dangerously low levels of insulin. For those of us with a functioning pancreas, the essential step that creates insulin resistance is still a rise in blood sugar. Any rise above fasting levels, will overtime, promote insulin resistance. The higher the blood sugar, and the more frequently it occurs, the ore insulin resistance is provoked.

Fructose is another thing that worsens this, as it causes several things such as inflammation, growth of visceral or deep abdominal fat, increased blood triglycerides, and a fatty liver. They are all powerful blockers of insulin, and they worsen insulin resistance.

Elevated insulin is a main culprit of weigh struggles. The constant release of insulin triggered by our diet or sugary and starchy foods bathes our cells in insulin,

Every one of our cells has a certain number of receptor channel sites that act like gates. The insulin molecules fit into these receptors like a key into a lock. This opens the channel and allows the glucose from sugar and starch to enter the cell. The ore insulin that is around, the more congested these gates become, and the cells then become resistant to the insulin, and the keys don't open the gates anymore, leading to high levels of glucose in the blood, despite high levels of insulin. Which here again raises the question, why conventional medicine feels the need to give more and more insulin to Type 2 diabetics. Crazy right\? Anyways let's carry on...

So, what happens at mealtimes when you eat carbohydrates, there is more glucose available than the body needs, so insulin moves glucose into the cells, especially the liver, and triggers insulin release from the pancreas.

What happens to glucose normally inside the cells?
Glucose inside the cells is made into glycogen in order to save space. Glycogen is stored mainly in the liver, with a small percentage in the muscle cells. We can covert glucose to glycogen and back again easily. The liver has only a limited storage space for glycogen, once it is full, excess carbohydrates are turned into fat. Several hours after a meal, the blood sugars and insulin levels start to drop, less glucose is available for use in muscles, brain and other organs. This is when the liver starts to break down glycogen into glucose, where it is released in general circulation for energy.

During fasting, in a short term fast the body has enough energy from glycogen to function, but during a prolonged fast, the body can make new glucose from its fat stores, a process called gluconeogenesis.

Why do we get fat?
because our body's set weight thermostat is set too high, and this is because our insulin levels are too high. Reducing carbohydrates should reduce weight. But the main missing piece of this problem is insulin resistance.

When insulin no longer fits into the receptor, the cell is called insulin resistant. Less glucose gets through the partially open door of the receptor, the cell notices the lower glucose level, and asks the body for more insulin, which it does. The cell then makes more insulin receptors that get incorporated into the cells walls, but the fit is still poor, but more receptors are available, allowing potentially a normal amount of glucose to enter, but as we develop more insulin resistance, our bodies increase our insulin levels to get the same result of glucose into the cell. Unfortunately, constantly elevated insulin levels cause obesity.

High blood glucose levels, trigger the pancreas to make ore insulin, and when there is a lot of both glucose and insulin around, the cell can only hold so much glucose before it is full. Too much glucose in the cell is toxic, so the cell down regulates the receptor to slow its entry, the resistance creates a vicious circle, there is too much glucose outside the cell pushing its way in, so the insulin receptors are down regulated even more, high persistent levels of insulin cause insulin resistance. But there is good news, as reversing the high insulin levels, reverses insulin resistance.

Prolonged insulin resistance actually alters brain cells, and normal brain function becomes impaired. It compromises our short-term learning and may damage our long-term memory. Did you know that insulin resistance accounts for about 80% of dementia cases. It is referred to as type 3 diabetes. Alzheimer's was thought to be due to sedentary lifestyle, however, recently early-stage Alzheimer's patients have shown that insulin resistance is a key factor. The brain accumulates plaques, called amyloid beta peptides, and these are protein bits that the body produces normally, and when they build up in plaques, they may disrupt brain function including memory, mood. Motor function and learning.

The debilitating effect of insulin resistance and how it can affect your body and potentially cause so many health issues in your body including: - migraines, MS, peripheral neuropathy, mood disorders, PCOS, menstrual problems, skin problems, thyroid issues, autoimmune problems, osteoarthritis, kidney problems, fibromyalgia, cancer, and much more.

what should you eat

you should eat more healthy food as a general rule of thumb, but to turn around insulin resistance, you should keep carbohydrates down to a minimum. Remove all added sugars from your diet and watch for fake sugars. No fructose except for fruit. Avoid all processed foods, refined carbs such as white sugar, white flour, bread, cakes, sweets, chocolate.

If you are insulin resistant, your diet should contain just vegetables, fruits, prebiotics, probiotics, lean grass-fed meat and cold water fish etc. do not eat processed meats such as hot dogs, burgers, sausages, salami etc.

Intermittent fasting

Fasting helps with every aspect of metabolic health, from weight loss, high blood pressure, insulin resistance, inflammation, lowering cholesterol. It also helps repair gut microbiome, improves neurogenerative disease like dementia and Alzheimer's, and reboots struggling immune system.

3 meals a day without snacks is a 12 hour fast. For insulin resistance longer is better. A 3-day fasting period can kill cancerous cells, reboot your entire immune system. Cancer cells must have glucose to grow. Take it away and they stop growing.

The shorter the time of actual eating is, the faster the insulin returns to low levels. What foods are best kept out of diet after fasting. No processed foods, chemicals and sugars. During fasting you can have black coffee, black tea, water still or sparkling and salt.

Science behind fasting

- Your Body has over 30 trillion cells. Cells need nutrients to function properly. When they don't get enough nutrients, they stop being able to do their job. Our bodies are designed to self-heal. We come pre-programmed with an array of healing responses like autophagy, that our bodies tap into when we fast. Combining fasting and food choices with our hormones, will lead to a greatly improved level of health.

Our hunter gatherer ancestors fasted involuntarily. Once they found food they feasted, typically followed by days of fasting. Eating all day goes against our genetic code. If we don't have type 1 diabetes, we don't have to worry about our sugar dropping too low. When sugar isn't available, we burn fat for energy, and blood sugar levels will remain in the normal range, even during prolonged fasting, due to the livers ability to make glucose out of fat.

Our bodies get energy from 2 sources, sugars and fat. When we stop eating, our blood sugar drops, triggering our bodies to use fat for fuel. This happens about 8 hours after the last meal. And this is when the fasting benefits begin. Intermittent fasting has anti-ageing affects. It also helps with pre and post injury healing.

The cellular level healing benefits include increased ketones, increased mitochondrial stress resistance, increased antioxidant defences, increased autophagy, increased DNA repair, decreased glycogen stores, an decreased insulin levels.

The more often we enter the fasting state the more repair can happen in our bodies, it's like sleep, the body heals at a deeper level when we are asleep. Fasting allows the brain and body to recover from the stresses of the modern world. Our bodies stop using glucose and start using ketones from fat for fuel. Change when eat and you will undo the years of damage poor living has done to your health

Fasting and autophagy

Autophagy is the repair process triggered by fasting. Cells do this to become more resilient by detoxification, repair, removal of diseased / damaged cells. Necessary healing state for the human body

Over time our cells accumulate a variety of damaged organelles, proteins, oxidized particles, and harmful substances. This cellular junk causes our cells to become dysfunctional. Autophagy allows our cells to detox these malfunctioning parts out of the cell, rejuvenating an rebooting it. Viruses are a great example, they don't have an energy system, so they must work of ours. If our cells are in a sugar burner state, viruses will enter our cells, will fuel themselves on sugar, and gain energy to multiply quickly. If our cells are in a stage of autophagy, where there isn't sugar to consume, viruses will lose energy, and the ability to replicate.

Fasting can help restore autophagy's ability to shut down viral replication. Cells also have many internal organelles, think, parts in a factory. When those get worn down, autophagy removes these older parts that accelerate the ageing process, suppress our immune system, and sap our energy.

Autophagy is an amazing process. Cells can't detox synthetic man-made chemicals or heavy metals, like lead or mercury. All these substances will thus build up in our cells and interfere with how the cells works. When cells are in a state of autophagy, and sense that they are malfunctioning, they will initiate cellular death called apoptosis. This is important because cells containing toxin loads, can turn into cancer cells. Removing damaged cells is key to our long-term health by preventing disease.

Repairing mitochondria, the parts of the cell that make energy, also happen during fasting. Cells in autophagy remove damaged or dysfunctional mitochondria, counter acting degeneration or inflammation that can lead to cognitive disabilities, muscle weakness, chronic fatigue, an impairment in hearing and vision. This process also helps with liver and gastrointestinal function.

Liver cells stuffed full of glycogen are less efficient, leading to diabetes, fatty liver disease and high cholesterol. Fasting triggers liver cells to release glycogen and stored insulin. Fasting also gives cells a reason to use the sugar stored in the fat cells

Your liver is one of the hardest working organs in your body. The goal is to get rid of excess glycogen and fat in the liver. All our blood flows through the liver, as that happens, the liver cleanses the blood of toxins as well as sugar. Once the liver cell is full of sugar, and can't pull out anymore from the blood, all that sugar, glycogen fat takes up space and interferes with the cells functions of burning fat, breaking down hormones, and making good cholesterol for the body and brain to use.

Fasting creates a space in the blood for this extra sugar, so it starts moving out of the liver cells. Now the liver can get back to what it is best at doing for us. The same goes for fat cells. The body is asking for glucose, sugar, to come out of the cells, thus the process of glucose to glycogen to triglycerides to fat reverses in order to keep the blood level of glucose constant. The extra insulin is stored in the liver and fat. Thus, fasting also releases this excess insulin as well. Which means that the pancreas doesn't have to make it. Fasting increases growth hormone production by 5 times which means better muscle mass and brain function.

Dopamine is a pleasure hormone. Eating a food that tastes good triggers dopamine release. People who eat all the time get dopamine hits constantly. These people become dopamine resistant. They have to eat more to get to their base dopamine level, and of course their weight continues to climb.

Fasting stops age related decline in the dopamine receptor numbers in our cells, it also can make our dopamine receptors more sensitive. Fasting for 72 hours, repairs the immune system. Chemotherapy patients did a 3-day water only fast, on the 3rd day, the bone marrow released what are called stem cells, which become new undamaged white blood cells, allowing the body to function at its best.

The how of fasting

- We finish dinner, and don't eat or drink after that apart from water.
- After about 8 hours, our bodies will start making ketones from fat for energy
- At around 12 – 15 hours, these ketones flood our blood streams and go to our brains, turning off hunger, and giving a boost to our physical and mental energy
- Cells then move into autophagy, repairing, detoxing, and regenerating themselves. The liver continues to break down fat, releasing glycogen, glucose, and insulin. Gut bacteria will start to regrow good bacteria to help lower blood pressure, and more mood enhancing neurotransmitters. And help with blood glucose balance.
- Weight loss happens with fasting 15 hours a day as this is enough to flip the metabolic switch to fat burning.

- Autophagy fasting anything over 17 hours. Gut reset fast 24 hours. Fat burner fast 36 hours. Dopamine fast 48 hours. Immune reset fast, more than 72 hours. Skip breakfast, it is NOT essential.
- Every morning just before we wake up, a natural circadian rhythm burst out levels of growth hormones, cortisol, epinephrine, norepinephrine, this triggers to liver to make new glucose. This jolt of hormones and glucose wakes us up, and gets us going in the morning.

Fitness and Exercise

- Exercise is a poor method of weight loss. The human body quickly adjusts to exertion, and weight loss does not result. If we do exercise and don't have enough fat or protein in the diet, the body will eat away at muscle stores when we exercise.
- The less muscles content we have, the slower the metabolism will be.
- Exercise is a good thing, as it helps keep us young. Daily physical activity is important.
- The benefits of exercise are bone health, thinking more clearly, increase strength. Exercise is effective for removing heavy metals through sweating.
- Running raises cortisol levels due to what the muscles perceive as chronic stress. High cortisol as we know will raise our blood sugar, so if our goal is to keep our blood sugar lower, this works against that goal. Cortisol also triggers the body into holding onto fat, an also decreases growth hormone production.

Intermittent fasting is not a diet, it is a way of eating. It is basically cycling fasts and mini eating. Why try intermittent fasting in the first place? To lose weight, to build muscle, to improve digestion, improve inflammation, increase energy levels.

Human beings can only be in 2 states. Fast state or fed state. Today we live a world where food is available in over abundance. More than 60% of calories in the USA comes from processed foods. Genetically we are designed to be in fed and fasted state almost equally, and that is what intermittent fasting pattern of eating focuses on

Intermittent fasting myths

1. one should eat 5-7 smaller meals a day to keep the metabolism ticking... this has no effect on metabolism compared with eating 2 or even 1 meal per day. The major players that affect metabolism are your BMR an activity level.

2. One should not eat more than 30g of protein in a single meal as the human body cannot digest it...... this statement is false.... If we give more protein, our bodies simply take a longer time to digest the proteins. on average whey will digest at 10g / hour and whole food proteins are digested at 4-6g/hour.

3. Breakfast is the most important meal of the day.... breakfast simply means break + fast... break the fast. It's a myth... it's all about greed... commercial .. corn sugar, artificial cereals. Huge profit margins....

4. Fasting decreases your metabolism.... Just like eating fewer meals won't have any effect on your metabolism, the same way, short term fasting will not slow down metabolism .. metabolism is the main function of your BMR and the cost of your activity levels, so eating food or not food doesn't make a difference.

5. Fasting causes muscle mass loss...... absolute myth... fasting for as long as 72 hours does not cause an increased breakdown in your muscle, nor does it slow down protein synthesis.

6. Fasting can cause a blood sugar drop...... your blood sugar is automatically regulated when food is not provided for long stretches of time. The average person without an underlying condition does not have to worry about getting low blood sugars when they are fasting.

Intermittent Fasting Benefits

1. You eat less overall with intermittent fasting: - it leads to overall calories restriction which then not only leads to weight loss but also reduces inflammation potentially reducing the risk of cancer and better glycaemic control.

2. Hunger is good: - intermittent fasting helps recognise between emotional eating and real hunger. When you wake up in the morning and within an hour or so feel hungry, this is not hunger, it is a habitual reaction to eat. It is emotional eating. We

eat because we crave sweet or fried foods. We eat because others are eating the doughnuts etc. bottom line is that we eat because we are addicted to eating. The food industry spends billions of dollars to promote food.

3. Helps improve insulin sensitivity and increases human growth hormone. If you eat too many carbs, more insulin is release, and over time you become insulin resistance. Elevated fasting insulin us the single greatest marker for assessing a person's risk for cardiovascular disease and diabetes. Intermittent fasting leads to improved insulin sensitivity. There are many studies that confirm an increase in human growth hormone during periods of fasting. The only way to increase your growth hormone naturally is through deep sleep, high intensity activities, and through fasting,

4. Saves time, a lot of it.... There is no point eating a few small meals every day.

5. It helps suppress inflammation, and helps improve your brain, and may help maintain a healthy heart and fight cancer. It can also help prevent cognitive decline and help with growth of nerve cells.

Fasting pattern number 1: - lean-gains
- After eat dinner, before 6pm. Fast for at least 16 hours. Black coffee, lemon juice, tea. No calories. So, 16-8 fast. Or 18-6. Or 20-4 fast. So, starting from fast end to 6pm eat 2,3 meals if you want.

Fasting pattern number 2: - eat stop eat
- Eat stop eat recommends for you to fast for 24 hours 1-2 times a week.
- For example: - Monday dinner at 7pm, can only eat after 7pm Tuesday.
- Benefits are immense.

Fasting pattern number 3: - warrior diet
- The warrior diet triggers and unleashes primal instincts within us, many of which have been dulled or inhibited. It endorses virtues such as feeling a sense of freedom, alertness, and physical strength.

- Warrior diet is highly instinct based. 1 meal a day always at night. Without any restrictions of calories or macronutrient content. 1 feast a day. This activates the sympathetic nervous system. Undereating phase. This helps significantly with your daily detoxification and manipulate your hormones to reach maximum metabolic efficiency and prime your body to lose fat and build muscle. Overeating phase: - this helps significantly to stimulate parasympathetic nervous system, digestion, activates carious metabolic processes and helps us to relax.

<u>Fasting pattern number 4: - 5 :2 diet</u>
- Eat normally for 5 days a week, then 2 days you eat 500 calories if you are a woman and 600 calories if you are a man.

Chapter 12

Diabetes Reversal

Diabetes is the 6th leading cause of death in the word. Around 1.6 million people die every year through diabetes. A staggering 422 million people have diabetes in the world. That means 6% of the global population is already infected with diabetes. This number is increasing all the time, and that doesn't include all the people who have not tested for diabetes

Today, type 2 diabetes is affecting children and adolescents. According to reports from UNICEF, the number of children suffering from obesity is rising by 10-12 times since the mid-1970s

Why should you be worried?

- Diabetes may not lead to a life and death situation, but it is the leading cause to a lot of the complications that make the quality of life extremely poor and also lead to death in the longer term.
- The Heart, kidneys, nerves, eyes, and skin are some of the most common organs that get damaged because of diabetes. To avoid all these complications, it is extremely important to control diabetes.
- By taking medicine for diabetes, you are only delaying the inevitable, because even though you are taking this medication, your blood sugars will eventually worsen.

How do you say goodbye to diabetes?

- You need to make changes in your lifestyle. These may be overwhelming at first but are quite easy once you stick to them.
- Many people have reversed their diabetes by following these changes in their lives.

- There is ZERO cost and NO side effects with these lifestyle changes.

The 4 pillars of diabetes control and reversal
- Diet
- Fitness
- Sleep
- Stress

The HEAL Strategy stands for
- Healthy diet,
- Exercising regularly
- Adequate sleep
- Low stress.

What is Diabetes? And why does it happen?

Diabetes is a disease where the person's body cannot control the level of sugar or glucose in the blood. We need glucose because it provides us with the energy to perform all body functions and day to day activities. Our stomach converts the food we eat into glucose by breaking down the carbohydrates.

This glucose then gets released into our bloodstream, and then it gets consumed by the cells in our body, and this gives energy to the cells to perform day to day functions. Once glucose enters the cells, the blood sugar levels in the body declines. Cells cannot automatically absorb glucose. Another hormone is needed to unlock the cells so that glucose can enter. This hormone is called insulin, which is released by the pancreas. Insulin acts like a key to open the inside of a cell, such as muscle, fat, or other cells for the entry of the glucose.

Insulin is responsible for controlling the glucose in the blood. As more glucose is absorbed by the cells, the lower the blood sugar level will be. Besides being the key that lets glucose into the cells, insulin also helps in the formation of fat and muscles and blocks the breakdown of protein. Another important function is that insulin stores glucose in the form of glycogen for times when there is a shortage of glucose in the body.

For healthy people, the sugar or glucose amount in the blood is maintained by releasing adequate insulin and absorption of glucose by our body cells. The blood sugar levels rise when the glucose does not get absorbed by our cells. This happens when either the production of insulin is inadequate or when cells resist absorption of glucose despite the availability of insulin in the blood. In many cases both these cases both these conditions can happen together.

Hyperglycaemia

The condition when excess glucose stays in the blood stream, leading to high blood sugar levels, is also called hyperglycaemia.
- For people without diabetes the normal range for the haemoglobin A1c level is between 4% and 5.6%.
- People with prediabetes, A1c levels are between 5.7% and 6.4%
- People with diabetes have an A1c level of 6.5% or higher.

Lack of insulin production and insulin resistance.

Diabetes is caused when excess glucose stays in the bloodstream.
- Physiologically: - this is caused by; low insulin secretions, insulin resistance or in some cases it can be both. If the pancreas does not produce enough insulin to manage sugar levels, this is caused because the insulin production reduces due to the beta cells in the pancreas being damaged. This is due to an auto-immune disease, where the body's immune system fights itself to damage the cells in the pancreas. The high blood sugar in the blood stream further damages the pancreas as it gets pressurised to generate more insulin. As the beta cells become damaged, the pancreas stops producing enough insulin to meet the body's needs. This condition is mostly prevalent in TYPE 1 DIABETES.
- The 2nd condition is insulin resistance in the body, where, although sufficient amount of insulin is present, it gets rejected by the cells. Insulin resistance occurs when the cells in

the muscles, liver or fat, do not efficiently respond to the insulin that is being produced by the pancreas. The cells are not able to take up the glucose from the blood. The insulin is like a key to unlock cells, only after which the glucose can enter the cells.

- Insulin resistance happens due to the fat deposits on the cells. These fat deposits do not allow to unlock the cells. As a result, the glucose levels rise in the blood. As the cells are starved of glucose, they keep sending signals to the body to release glucose, the liver responds by releasing the glucose it has stored.
- To respond to the rising blood sugar from digestive food and the liver, the pancreas is further burdened with insulin's demand due to high blood sugar. This eventually leads to the situation where the pancreas gets damaged and stops producing insulin. This form of diabetes is called TYPE 2 DIABETES, and 90% of total diabetes cases globally are type 2.

Symptoms of diabetes

- Frequent urination and thirst. When you have high blood glucose levels, you are kidneys are working overtime to function. They are constantly working to help get rid of that excess glucose in the blood. Then your kidneys are totally over worked, the excess sugar gets out through urination. This causes excessive urination. So your urine actually contains sugar or glucose. Along with glucose, the kidneys also drag other fluids from the tissues. This makes the person feel dehydrated, because of this, people drink more and more drinks. The cycle of excessive thirst leads to more consumption of drinks, which then leads to excessive urination.
- Fatigue: - feeling weak, lazy and not having the energy to do anything is a common symptom of people suffering from diabetes. This is because glucose doesn't enter the cells, the cells are deprived of energy. As glucose is the fuel for our muscles and our body to be able to perform day to day activities. Because glucose can't enter cells, it cannot produce energy and cannot facilitate many other chemical reactions.
- Weight loss: - people with diabetes tend to lose weight despite an adequate diet, as the glucose cannot enter the cells to

give them the necessary energy. The cells keep sending signals to the body asking for glucose, and this constant demand makes the body burn fat and muscles to get the required energy. Also because of excessive urination, and loss of bodily fluids, people with diabetes often experience weigh loss.

- Persistent vaginal infection amongst women: - With diabetics, all the fluid in the body contains high glucose levels including sweat and genital area discharge. Bacteria and Fungi thrive in a high glucose environment, which is why women with diabetes experience itching, burning, abnormal discharge from the vagina
- Blurry vision: - Due to high blood glucose levels, the shape of the lenses in eyes change, which cause blurred vision, which is another common symptom of diabetes.
- Dry skin: - High glucose levels are the cause behind most of the skin problems. High glucose levels in the blood leads to poor blood flow, and blood circulation which then causes the skin to become dry. In addition, high blood sugar levels pull fluid from the cells so that enough urine can be produced to get rid of this excess glucose. This removal of fluid from the cells then leads to dry skin.
- Slow wound healing: - proper blood circulation is a crucial factor to heal the wounds and for cells to repair themselves. With diabetes, high blood glucose levels obstruct the blood vessels leading to low blood circulation, which leads to less flow of oxygen to the cells, causing delayed healing of wounds.

These symptoms would appear simultaneously over a short period of time in type 1 diabetes. However, in type 2 diabetes, these symptoms would come one after another, with some delay in between.

Type 1 Diabetes
Type 1 diabetes occurs when the body fails to produce any insulin completely. It is an auto immune condition where the body's immune system itself attacks the pancreatic beta cells this completely stopping the production of insulin.

This condition where the body attacks its own healthy cells may be due to a genetic or environmental condition, like contracting a virus, caesarean delivery or use of antibiotics. This failure to produce insulin by the pancreas causes the glucose to stay in the bloodstream resulting in high blood sugar levels. About 10% of the total cases of diabetes are type 1. This type of diabetes is most common among young adults below the age of 30 years old.

Type 2 diabetes

Statistics show that 9 out of 10 diabetics globally suffer from type 2 diabetes. In this form of diabetes, while the pancreas is producing insulin, the cells reject the insulin and are not able to absorb the blood sugar.

This condition appears due to fat deposits that hinder the unlocking and absorption of glucose by the cells. This makes the cells insulin resistant. If we continue to have foods with carbohydrates, the excess sugar stays back in the bloodstream causing blood sugar levels to rise.

Obesity is the main cause of insulin resistance. However, normal weight people can have type 2 diabetes, having a sedentary lifestyle with no exercise and a high carbohydrate diet can increase the risk of type 2 diabetes. Other causes of insulin resistant diabetes are

- Smoking
- Lack of proper sleep
- Hereditary
- Hormones
- Use of steroids
- Old age

Prediabetes

Although this is not diabetes, this is the stage before type 2 diabetes, prediabetes occurs when the blood sugar level is high but not high enough to be classified under diabetes.

People with type 2 diabetes, usually have prediabetes first. It is more likely to occur in people over the age of 45 years old, who have high cholesterol and obesity, and who consume a lot of red meat and processed foods. Women with polycystic ovarian cancer can also be susceptible to pre-diabetes.

Gestational diabetes
This type of diabetes is diagnosed for the first time during pregnancy, the high blood sugar levels in the body is harmful for both the mother and the foetus. Women who have gestational diabetes normally go back to their normal blood sugar levels after pregnancy. But they are at risk for type 2 diabetes. Gestational diabetes can be kept under control with a healthy diet, exercise and taking required medication, and the regular testing of blood sugar levels is very much required.

Medication induced diabetes
This is a condition when certain medications, or side effects of certain medications, lead to the development of diabetes. Some of the patients with medication induced diabetes have got rid of diabetes completely by stopping that medication while others nothing can be done.
Corticosteroids, thiazide diuretics, statins and beta blockers may induce diabetes. Psychotic drugs sometimes have side effects that can lead to diabetes.
While these are the major types of diabetes, there are some more less common ones.

Harmful effects of diabetes
Diabetes is often called the silent killer, because the high blood sugar levels effect the body slowly. The damage caused to the body parts is permanent and can even lead to death.
- Loss of vision: - diabetes causes damage to the retina, leading to problems like blurred vison or loss of vision. People with type 2 diabetes are 2-5 times kore likely to develop cataracts.
- Damage to nerves: - diabetes is a major cause of peripheral neuropathy, which is a result of damage to the nerves outside the brain and spinal cord. This often causes weakness, numbness and pain, usually in your hands and feet. It can also

affect other areas of the body. People may lose the sense of cold, heat, and pain. It also slows down the healing of wounds. In extreme cases even silent heart attacks occur as it may go unnoticed as the person may not feel any pain at all. This is a lifelong condition and cannot be cured.

- Gangrene: - death of tissue due to lack of blood flow or serious bacterial infection. Blood sugar decreases the elasticity of blood vessels and causes them to narrow, which eventually leads to lowering the blood flow. As the high blood sugar levels affect the blood flow, blood may not reach all the body parts and reduce its ability to fight with bacteria. Gangrene affects the arms and legs including the toes and fingers, but it can also occur in the muscles and in organs inside the body such as the gallbladder. It can easily develop wounds and infections. Gangrene may cause doctors to amputate a finger or toe, or extreme cases an entire limb.

- Heart problems: - High blood sugar levels increase the formation of fatty deposits in the walls of the blood vessels. This restricts the blood flow to the arteries, and can lead to hardening of the artery walls, also called atherosclerosis.

- Kidney failure: - Around 20% high blood sugars damage millions of cells in the kidneys, which can lead to kidney failure. The arteries in the kidneys become narrow and hardening, this is called artery stenosis. So around 20-30% of diabetics develop diabetic neuropathy or kidney disease due to being diabetic.

- Slow healing wounds and skin infection: - when it comes to healing wounds, proper blood flow and circulation are extremely important, wounds heal better with good blood flow. In diabetics, due to the narrow blood vessels, there is an inadequate flow of blood and low level of oxygen reaches the tissues and this it takes a longer time for wounds to heal and in some cases, it may not heal at all. Diabetics are also susceptible to many skin and bacterial infections.

- Impotence and sexual disfunction: - erectile disfunction is commonly seen in males with type 2 diabetes due to high blood sugars damage the nerves that control sexual stimulation and response. Reduced blood flow from damaged blood vessels can

also cause erectile disfunction. In some cases, it may also decrease libido.
- Digestive problems: - high blood sugar levels cause damage to the nerves. The vagus nerve is damaged due to high glucose levels in the body. The vagus nerve is extremely important for the process of digestion, as it runs from the brain to the face thorax and abdomen. It is responsible for moving food in the digestive tract. Because of damage to the nerve, movement of food is slowed down or even stopped. This leads to a condition called gastro peritus. This means the stomach takes a long time to empty the food content in it. Some of the symptoms include, bloating, nausea, heartburn
- Hair loss: - due to the damage cause to blood vessels with high blood sugars, this provides the cells with less oxygen and nutrients
- Weakness and exhaustion: - people with diabetes often experience tiredness, and feel lethargic during most of the day, this makes it difficult for them to carry out and manage daily tasks. They may often take more naps than usual and feel drowsy. This all happens because the cells of the body are deprived of energy because glucose is blocked or restricted.
- Loss of productivity: - loss of energy and lethargy, difficult to carry out everyday tasks efficiently, necessary to nap after lunchtime, experience problems with their memory.

Diagnosing and testing in diabetes

- FPG: - Fasting Plasma Glucose Test: - this is done after completing 8-12 hours of fasting. Except for water, the person should not have consumed anything during that period. This test is usually done in the morning and used to check for prediabetes and diabetes. When the blood glucose levels after fasting is less than 100mg /dl the blood sugars are normal. If it is between 100-126 mg/dl this is prediabetes. If it is more than or equal to 126 mg/dl this means diabetes.

- Oral Glucose Tolerance test: - this is a test which is done to check the body's tolerance to glucose. For this test a person is given 70 75 grams of glucose in 200ml of water. After 2 hours, the blood sugar levels are checked. This test looks at the body's ability to metabolise glucose from the bloodstream. The test requires the person to drink a liquid syrup solution after fasting. After this the blood sample is taken to see if glucose is metabolised. If the person's blood glucose levels are less than 140, the blood glucose levels are normal. If it is more than 140 and less than 200mg/dl the person has prediabetes and can later develop type 2 diabetes. If glucose levels are equal to 200ml/dl or more, diabetes is diagnosed. The OGTT is used to test prediabetes diabetes, and gestational diabetes.
- Random or casual plasma glucose test: - This measures the amount of glucose in the blood. It is called random because the blood is tested at any time, irrespective of whether fasting or food was eaten. If the test results are less than 140 it indicates normal blood glucose levels. Blood glucose levels higher than 200mg/dl along with body experiencing excess urination, hunger or thirst indicate diabetes.

Haemoglobin A1c Test

This blood test is used to diagnose diabetes and monitor the progress of a treatment plan. A1C test provides information on the average blood sugar levels over the past 3 months. People with diabetes take this test to see if their blood glucose levels are fluctuating and then medications are changed and altered accordingly.

A1C is a type of glycosylated haemoglobin which is a haemoglobin bound to glucose. A protein found in blood is haemoglobin which gives the blood its red colour and transports oxygen to the cells in the body. In diabetics, due to excess glucose present in the blood stream, the glucose binds with the haemoglobin in the red blood cells.

As these red blood cells live for around 3 months, this test shows the average glucose levels in the blood for this period. If the blood glucose level is high, the HbA1c test will be higher, normal range of glucose levels are less than 5.7%. levels between 5.7 and 6.5 indicate prediabetes, and levels higher than 6.5% on the HbA1c test indicate diabetes.

<u>Myths about diabetes: - My diabetes is because of my genes, and I can't do anything about it</u>

Yes, your genes do count. If all family members suffer from diabetes, you are more likely to develop diabetes or other chronic health issues that are lifestyle related. However, this does not mean that you must suffer from it for the rest of your life. You can reverse your diabetes.

One of the main factors that contributes to the development of diabetes is your lifestyle and habits. The 4 most important lifestyle habits are your Nutritional habits, Physical activities, Sleeping habits, Stress management habits

Getting enough sunlight, getting enough emotional support, hobbies etc are also important factors too. However, when it comes to diabetes specifically, unfortunately these lifestyle habits are also closely associated with your family. You inherit bad habits from your family and generally continue them through your life. But the control is all on you, you can control your diabetes by changing your lifestyle.

<u>Myth 2: - if you are working out you can't get diabetes</u>

Some part of this myth is true, as we understood as said before, fat deposits are one of the major reasons for insulin resistance, so people who are obese have a higher chance of getting diabetes.

<u>Addressing the root problem</u>

The key to treating type 2 diabetes effectively is to eliminate excess sugar, not just redistribute it within the body

Oral hypoglycaemics
- As of 2012, a staggering statistic reveals that more than half of the American population is grappling with diabetes or pre-diabetes.

Glucose control and health outcomes
1. Lowering blood glucose: - the primary goal in treating type 2 diabetes has been to lower blood glucose, which is associated with improved health outcomes.

The disappointing impact of exercise
- Expectations v reality: - exercise is expected to be an ideal way to burn calories, but the actual benefits are often less than anticipated due to increased appetite and decreased non exercise activity.
- Compensation effects: - intense exercise can lead to compensatory behaviours such as eating more, or reducing other activities with diminished the effectiveness of the exercise program
- Root cause: - type 2 diabetes is not caused by lack of exercise, but by excessive dietary glucose and fructose, which exercise alone cannot effectively address

The flawed logic of low-fat diets
- The logic behind lo-fat diets for type 2 diabetes is fundamentally flawed. Type 2 diabetes is characterised by high blood glucose levels, and refined carbohydrates, which are often emphasised in low diets, raise blood glucose more than any other foods.

Why eat healthy fat
- Monounsaturated fats: - monounsaturated fats are recommended for heart health, with avocados and nuts linked to better health outcomes.
- Omega three rich fish: - fatty cold water fish rich in omega 3 oil are considered extremely protective against heart disease.

- Full fat dairy: - high blood levels of trans palmitoleic acid from full fat dairy are associated with a reduction on the incidence of type 2 diabetes,

Reducing refined carbohydrates
- High glycaemic load in the diet raises blood glucose and the risk of type 2 diabetes, which increases the risk of heart disease
- Certain diets provide superior glycaemic control, specifically low carbohydrate and Mediterranean diets.

Reducing carbohydrates and embracing fats
- mediterranean diet benefits: - studies prove that a reduced carbohydrate higher fat mediterranean diet using olive oil, reduces the need for medication by 59%
- natural fats: - by recognising the potential benefits of eating natural fats and reducing added sugars and processed carbohydrates, we can reduce and reverse type 2 diabetes.
- Insulin stimulation: - remember that of the three macronutrients, dietary fat stimulates insulin the least, making it a key component in managing diabetes.

Get rid of sugar – get rid of diabetes
1. Too much sugar: - we know that the very essence of type 2 diabetes is too much sugar in the body, not just in the blood.
2. Natural solutions: - if the problem is too much sugar, two treatments will work, stop putting sugar in and burn remaining sugar off.
3. Drug free solution: - a natural drug free solution to type 2 diabetes, now lies within our grasp, focusing on dietary changes that eliminate sugar

Caloric restriction and liver decompression
- Caloric restriction depletes liver glycogen stores, forcing the body to burn fat for energy, preferentially from the liver and other organs. This process removes the ectopic visceral

fat that causes metabolic syndrome, reversing type 2 diabetes before any substantial reduction in overall fat mass.

Removing beta cell dysfunction
- By removing excess fat from the pancreas, beta cell dysfunction is resolved, leading to the normalisation if insulin secretion and the drop in blood glucose levels, effectively reversing type 2 diabetes.

Insulin resistance and the liver
- Deflating the liver from its overinflated state by burning the excess fat reverses insulin resistance, addressing the dual defects of type 2 diabetes and leading to the remission of the disease.

Type 2 diabètes:- a réversible diseuse
- The succès stories in bariatric surgery demonstrate conclusively that type 2 diabetes is a fully reversible disease, contradicting the belief that it progresses inevitably. This revelation points to the incorrect treatment of the disease as the reason for its epidemic status.

Standard treatments and progression
- With standard treatments of low calorie, reduced fat diets and medications, type 2 diabetes often progresses, highlighting the need for a re-evaluation of these methods in favour of more effective alternatives.

Caloric restriction and disease remission
- The sudden severe caloric restriction that bariatric surgery enforces, prompts the body to burn off the excess sugar and fat that causes type 2 diabetes. Leading to the remission of the disease without the need for surgery.

Low carbohydrate diet as a solution
- As an alternative to the cost and complications of surgery, a low carb diet can offer a way to burn off ectopic fat, and reverse type 2 diabetes, providing a non-surgical solution to the disease.

Intermittent fasting
- This is recognised for its potential to reverse type 2 diabetes. This is not only about weight loss, but also about improving insulin sensitivity and overall health.

Fasting impact on diabetes
1. Glucose reduction: - abstaining from food naturally leads to a drop in blood glucose levels, aiding in diabetes management,
2. Weight loss: - weight loss associated with fasting can contribute to the reversal of type 2 diabetes.
3. Insulin sensitivity: - fasting improves insulin sensitivity, addressing the root cause of type 2 diabetes.

Understanding intermittent fasting
1. Caloric deprivation: - intermittent fasting creates periods of severe caloric deprivation, which can reverse type 2 diabetes.
2. Caloric restriction: - continuous mind caloric restriction does not produce the same beneficial hormonal responses as intermittent fasting
3. Hormonal responses: - intermittent fasting triggers hormonal changes that maintain a high basal metabolism crucial for diabetes reversal.

Caloric reduction versus intermittent fasting
- constant caloric reduction: - constant caloric reduction is often recommended for weight loss and diabetes management but fails to produce lasting results.
- Intermittent fasting: - intermittent fasting with its profound hormonal changes, is more effective than constant caloric reduction.

- Success versus failure: - the difference between intermittent fasting and constant caloric reduction is the difference between success and failure in diabetes management

The starvation myth
- Caloric restriction: - caloric restriction diets can lead to a compensatory decrease in the body's metabolic rate often referred to as starvation mode.
- Fasting advantage: - contrary to the starvation myth, actual fasting does not trigger starvation mode and maintains a high basal metabolism.
- Survival mechanism: - fasting is a survival mechanism that allows the body to utilise stored fat for energy without reducing basal metabolism.

Fasting versus caloric reduction
- Caloric restriction: - basal metabolism decreases and insulin levels plateau
- Intermittent fasting: _ basal metabolism increases, and insulin levels there is a continuous reduction

Preserving lean mass
- Fasting is 4 times more effective at preserving lean mass compared to portion controls
- Lean mass percentage increases by 2-2% with fasting, compared to only 0.5% with portion control.

Overcoming the starvation myth
- The starvation myth suggests that fasting leads to a lower metabolic rate, but studies show that intermittent fasting maintains or even increases basal metabolism. This is crucial for sustainable weight loss and diabetes management, as opposed to the starvation mode triggered by constant caloric restriction, which leads to a decrease in metabolic rate and eventual weight regain.

Fasting or reducing carbs: - which is better?
- Intermittent fasting: maximally lowers insulin, offering a quick and efficient method for weight loss and diabetes reversal.
- Low carb diets: - these also effectively reduce insulin and can be combined with fasting for maximal benefits.
- Combining strategies: - incorporating both fasting and a low carb diet can provide the greatest advantages in managing type 2 diabetes.

Fasting for type 2 diabetes
- Fasting allows the body to naturally deplete its sugar stores, leading to a reversal of type w diabetes. Historical accounts and modern studies alike have demonstrated the effectiveness of fasting and managing diabetes, with patients experiencing significant weight loss and normalisation of blood glucose levels. The process and duration of fating required to reverse diabetes can vary, but the underlying principle remains consistent, be reducing insulin levels, and improving insulin sensitivity, fasting can be a very powerful tool in the fight against type 2 diabetes.

Fasting and medication management
- When incorporating fasting into a diabetes treatment plan, it is essential to consult with a physician and adjust medications accordingly. Certain diabetes drugs such as insulin and sulfonylureas, can cause hypoglycaemia if not managed properly during fasting periods.
- Monitoring blood glucose frequently with a home monitor is crucial to ensure safety and effectiveness. The goal is to reduce and eventually stop all medications while maintaining normal blood glucose level s through fasting.

Adjusting to fasting
- Starting a fasting regimen can come with an adjustment period, where individuals may experience hunger pains, headaches, or other side effects. These are often signs that the

body is releasing its stored sugar and adapting to the new dietary pattern. Over time, these symptoms will lessen or disappear. But it is important to discuss any concerns.

The dawn phenomenon
- This is a natural occurrence where blood glucose levels rise in the morning due to hormonal changes. In individuals with type 2 diabetes, this can result in a noticeable spike in blood glucose, however, this is not a cause for concern. It simply indicates that the body is releasing stored sugar from the liver into the blood. Monitoring and understanding this phenomenon is an important part of managing diabetes through fasting.

Preventing type 2 diabetes
- This is possible through lifestyle interventions that focus on dietary changes and increased physical activity. It is a reversible and preventable disease. With a deeper understanding of its causes and effective treatments, we can eradicate the condition. Lifestyle interventions such as a low carb, high fat diet and intermittent fasting have been proven to reverse type 2 diabetes without the need for medications. By focusing on lowering insulin levels, these dietary treatments offer a path to a diabetes free world.

Intermittent fasting and low-carb diets
- Both intermittent fasting and low carb diets effectively reduce insulin levels, leading to weight loss and the reversal of type 2 diabetes. While fasting provides the quickest reduction in insulin, low carb diets offer substantial benefits without the need to fast. Combining these strategies can provide the best of both worlds, allowing for a flexible approach to managing diabetes.

The power of dietary treatment
- Type 2 diabetes is a dietary disease, that requires dietary treatment. The key to preventing and reversing this condition lies in lowering insulin levels through dietary changes.

Embracing a new health paradigm

- As we conclude our exploration of intermittent fasting and its role in reversing type 2 diabetes, we are reminded of the power of dietary change. By embracing fasting and a lo carbohydrate, high fat diet, individuals can embark on a transformative journey towards better health this new health paradigm offers a path to a future free from the constraints of type 2 diabetes, empowering people to take control of their wellbeing.

Mediterranean diet

The mediterranean diet is rich in foods that can help reverse insulin resistance, the mono and polyunsaturated fats in foods like extra virgin olive oil, nuts and seeds have two effects that sensitise cells to insulin and clear sugar from the blood. Foods to eat on the mediterranean diet are

- Olive oil, especially extra virgin oil
- Unsalted nuts and seeds including walnuts, almonds, and pine nuts
- Oily varieties of fish including sardines and mackerel
- Seafood such as prawns, squid, mussels
- Poultry
- Chickpeas, lentils, peas and beans

- Wholegrain wheat, rice, oats and pasta
- Fruit including avocado, tomatoes, pomegranate, berries
- Greek yoghurt.
- Eggs,
- green leafy vegetables as well as courgettes
- vegetables such as sweet potatoes and sweetcorn
- herbs such as basil, oregano, dill and rosemary

foods not to eat

- butter, margarine, lard
- biscuits, cakes, pastries
- confectionary

- white refined versions bread, pasta, rice
- processed food and meats, sausages, bacon, burgers
- cut down on red meats
- high fat cheese, cream and milk

what is the Pegan Diet

the Pegan diet lowers blood sugar, reduces inflammation in the body, reduces diabetes type 2 and heart disease. It focuses on plant based and sustainable foods. It also focuses on nutrient rich foods and minimises or avoids unhealthy choices. Like the paleo diet, the Pegan diet focuses on foods that early humans would have hunted or gathered. But the twist is that most of your daily food intake will be plants, you eat much lower amounts of animal-based foods than you would on the paleo diet.

Eating Pegan

- 75% of your diet is plants, including fruits, vegetables, nuts and seeds
- 25% of your diet is meats, poultry, eggs, fish (grass fed) organic or sustainably raised

Pegan foods you can eat

- All fruits, with an emphasis on low glycaemic fruits such as cherries, strawberries, pears, apples
- All vegetables
- Dairy alternatives without added sugar, such as raw milk, nut milk or coconut yoghurt, eggs
- Nuts and seeds (except peanuts which are legumes)
- Oils rich in healthy fats like avocado or olive oil
- Meats and poultry (organic, grass fed)
- Sustainably caught fish, especially low mercury options like anchovies, salmon, sardines.
- Very minimal amounts of black rice, legumes like beans lentils (up to 1 cup per day) and quinoa

Foods can't eat or to avoid
- Bread and most grains like barley, oats, and wheat (except black rice and quinoa
  - Dairy products including cheese, ice cream and yoghurt
  - Foods with added sugar or a high glycaemic index
  - Processed foods like packaged, boxed, junk foods

Chapter 13

Autoimmune solution

There is a natural solution to any illness. Consistency is key. It will require dedication. In general, most diseases, but autoimmune disorders, and any digestive disorders are caused by two main factors, and that is deficiency, and toxicity. It is as simple as that. In fact, it is scientifically proven that 70% of health issues, are caused by environmental factors such as medication overload, the standard 'American diet', chronic infections, chronic stress and anxiety, and exposure to chemical and heavy metals found in food, water, air, cosmetic and household cleaners. And these environmental factors cause excess inflammation in the body, nutritional deficiencies, weakened microbiome, intestinal permeability, oxidate stress, food sensitivities and adrenal fatigue.

All these factors are the main contributors to autoimmune disorders, digestive disorders, and in fact, all chronic illness such as cancer, diabetes, candida, high blood pressure, and many more.

Triangle of health

Imagine your health expressed as a triangle. At the base, it's all your genes, all 23,000 of them. Each of these is inherited by your parents in your whole life. Genes can be turned on or off much like a light switch, by what we can visualise as the points of the health triangle. These points are the chemical self, the physical self, and the mental self. This triangle of health represents the components of the autoimmune matrix. It is understood that autoimmune diseases are caused by chemical, physical, or mental influences turning on certain genes. In other words, autoimmunity is spread by lifestyle choices and behaviour. It is important ot note that each of these elements can interact with one another.

If we are not tending to our physical self, our chemical self-reacts and vice versa. Fortunately, this means they can also be addressed in the same way. Our influences chemically, physically, and mentally, can determine our health to either compromise or optimise. While that may sound scary, it is equally empowering and can instil a lot of hope in those suffering from autoimmune conditions.

Most conventional doctors today will solely focus on chemical components using medication. There are endless ways to influence the body using the standard care, using artificially manipulating inflammation by the hormones and many other chemical processes in the body. This is all done with one common goal, which is to cover up the symptoms. On the other hand, natural medicine addresses the origin of the disease to ensure comprehensive and effective treatment is done. Covering up the symptoms should never be considered or disguised as a cure.

Chemistry refers to anything that enters the body. So this refers to food, vitamins, minerals, water, pesticides, preservatives, dyes and much more. Other environmental factors that you may have control over how much you get exposed to include, bacteria, parasites, toxins, allergens, and other microorganisms. The common theme throughout the triangle of health is your control. Your chemical self is influenced by what can enter your body, and in turn, the chemical influence and your gene activation.

<ins>Top nutrient deficiencies</ins>

Essential nutrients found in food such as vitamins, minerals, amino acids, carbohydrates, proteins and fats are all necessary for the proper functioning of the body. Each have their own job, and everyone's needs are specific to their own unique health. One thing to consider, is the why, behind these deficiencies. It may be due to not consuming enough foods that contain them, or it could be impaired function of your gut, or the result of an existing autoimmune issue. The most common nutrient deficiencies seen in practice include but are not limited to: - Vitamin D, Vitamin B12, Zinc, Omega three fatty acids, and believe it or not water. Unfortunately, the conventional procedure for measuring these levels is serum testing.

Most immune cells have specific Vitamin D receptors, which help modulate immune activity and response. It is no surprise that clear connections have been found between autoimmune diseases and Vitamin D deficiency. A few of the most prominent include Type 1 diabetes, rheumatoid arthritis, an multiple sclerosis. Some common foods that are high in Vitamin D include wild cuts of salmon, tuna, eggs and mushrooms. The most abundant source of Vitamin D, however, is from direct sunlight. Yet we are advised to limit our time in the sun and wear UV blocking protection. However, Vitamin D is IMMUNOMODULATING, otherwise known as an aid in proper immune system function. This in turn helps to prevent autoimmune disorders. This doesn't add up, does it?

Common medications used to treat autoimmune diseases can cause vitamin and mineral deficiencies, and in turn hinder the immune system. You can see how this is truly counterproductive.

- For common blood pressure medication, the following deficiency may occur, Vitamin B1, B6 and C, magnesium, calcium, potassium, zinc, sodium, coq10, and melatonin.
- For common cholesterol medication, the following deficiencies may occur, vitamin A, B2, B6, B12, D, E, K, folate, beta carotene, iron, and coq10.
- For common diabetes medication, the following deficiencies may occur. Vitamin B12, folic acid, COQ10.
- For anti-inflammatory medication, the following deficiencies may occur, Vit A, C, D, B12, folic acid, potassium, iron, magnesium, and zinc.
- For common heartburn medication the following deficiencies may occur, Vitamins D, B12, folic acid, beta carotene, calcium, Iron and Zinc.
- For common hormone replacement medication, the following deficiencies may occur. Vit B2, B.B6, B12, folic acid, magnesium, zinc and selenium.

Toxic overload

We are exposed to toxins regularly and many are often unavoidable. These include but are not limited to:- pesticides, GMOs, air pollutants, heavy metals, chemical contaminants, Toxins can be the cause of many health complications such as fatigue, muscle aches, joint pain, sinus congestion, post-natal drip, headache, bloating, hormone imbalance, cancer and autoimmunity. To reduce and prevent this toxic overload, there are many ways to minimise exposure such as: - eat organic and non-GMO foods, air purification systems, water filters, and using toxic free household items.

Lab tests
- Iodine loading test: - this measures your iodine status and possible deficiency.
- 25 OHD: - This test is an effective way of measuring Vitamin D,
- CBC: _ also known as the complete blackout, this is the most comprehensive blood test for assessing anaemia, and the functioning of many systems within your body.
- Homocysteine: - this is an indirect marker for the nutritional status of Vitamin B2, B6, B12, folate
- Haemoglobin A1C: - this detects the average blood sugar
- C Reactive protein: - this is an identifiable marker of inflammation
- Insulin: _ insulin affects the body in several ways, this test measures the amount of stress on the pancreas based on the amount of sugar found in the bloodstream
- Intestinal microbial health test: -

The gut – aka the gateway to health

To properly diagnose nutrient deficiencies or most health complications in general, it is important to rule out any issues associated with gut function. If your gut is not functioning properly, it is unlikely that your body will be able to absorb the proper nutrients. Therefore, eating the right foods or taking the right supplements will go unnoticed, and you may become frustrated with the lack of improvement.

Some of the major functions of the gut include digestion, immune response, nutrient absorption, hormone regulation, vitamin production, detoxification, mood management. Above all the gut's sole purpose is to ensure you are absorbing the good and excreting the bad. If this balance is disrupted, major health complications occur. There is ten times the number of bacteria in your body than our own cells, and most of them are housed within your digestive system. Gut health is truly the gateway to health for several reasons

The gut firewalls

Fortunately, our gut has defences or firewalls that help it properly do its job. These include: -
- gastro associated lymphoid tissue, which is also known as GALT. This is the guts immune system, and in fact 70% of our entire immune system.
- Tight junctions, these are small proteins that are responsible for holding the gut cells together,
- mucosal IGA, which is otherwise known as immunoglobin A, and it is the antibody considered our first line of defence against toxins.
- Friendly bacteria, we have more bacteria in our bodies than we do have our own cells, and these bacteria can communicate with the adult, warning of potential danger.
- Stomach acids: - this is essential for the digestion and absorption of nutrients. All these barriers together combine to promote a healthy gut, and in turn, a healthy immunity.

Damaging the gut

The following components have been proven to significantly damage the gut: -
- the standard American diet,
- chemicals such as pesticides, preservatives, heavy metals, food dyes, GMOs, Glycosides, and microbial trans glutamates.

- Infections such as bacterial, viral, parasitic or yeast overgrowth,
- gluten and other grains, food allergies,
- excessive medications, aggressive exercise and chronic stress.

All of these are some of the main proponents for the cause of leaky gut syndrome, a harmful condition that causes a plethora of health complications,

How the gut gets leaky

Leaky gut is when the tight junctions between the intestinal cells begins to open due to the proteins breaking down from agitation. When this happens, bacteria, chemicals and toxins can leak outside the digestive tract and eventually enter the bloodstream. This signals a flood of immune antibodies and can increase allergic reactions. This cycle continues and ultimately leads to autoimmunity. That is why it is super important to test your gut, to make sure that your microbiome and your gut lining are healthy.

Medications damage

If you are on medication, it is crucial to be aware of the potential risks and some include antibiotics.

- Antibiotics can destroy the good bacteria needed for digestion, it can cripple vitamin synthesis and increases your risk of yeast overgrowth.
- Common pain medication has been found to erode the mucosal lining of the stomach and small intestine, which contributes to intestinal permeability, otherwise known as leaky gut.
- Acid reflux medications block stomach acid production. In turn this hinders digestion and absorption, often leading to nutrient deficiencies.
- Anti-depressants: - they negatively affect the neurotransmitters in the gut.

Allergies

Some of the most ignored allergies include food allergies, medication allergies, surgical allergies, chemical allergies, mould allergies, and allergies in the additives of any of the above. All untreated allergies can cause serious health complications, including autoimmune diseases.

Fortunately, there are many ways to test for allergies, including, skin test, blood test, lung function test, pass testing, food challenges which are often in the form of elimination diets

Heavy metals

Common heavy metals and elements include lead, mercury, cadmium, arsenic, fluoride, bromine and chloride. These are all incredibly dangerous to your health and immunity. Unfortunately, we are exposed to all of these in the air we breathe, the water we drink, and even the food that we eat.

The most alarming way toxic metals affect our health is by competing with an official mineral for binding sites. This leads to deficiencies regardless of your daily intake. Your exposure to many of these toxins is often gradual, and therefore the accumulation can be left unnoticed for extended periods of time.

Fluoride

Fluoride consumption has become an increasingly more prominent issue, it is often put in public water and encouraged in our dental routines. Yet research suggests that this mass exposure can contribute to autoimmune thyroid disease, brain damage, and the displacement of iodine.

Note that iodine is especially important for thyroid functioning and the production of T4. The thyroid hormone thyroxine: - inhibiting the production and maintenance of essential thyroid hormones have truly dangerous and disabling consequences. Note that iodine is especially important for thyroid functioning and the production of T4, the main hormone produced by the thyroid. If the thyroid does not operate properly, many health complications occur, such as adrenal dysfunction, fatigue, depression, weight gain, muscle aches, brain fog, low libido, and you guessed it autoimmunity.

Chemical wrap up

Our health is truly a combination of all the things we put in our bodies. Between the quality of the food we eat, our exposure to toxins and our body's ability to detoxify efficiently, our chemical makeup is directly affected. You need a comprehensive healing strategy, to take control of your chemical health.

Physical self

The physical component of health is a bit more straightforward. There is a common misconception that as we age, our health naturally declines. We hear it all the time from doctors that the ageing process is synonymous with our bodies breaking down and becoming sick. However, this is very, very wrong. Instead, our choices are what facilitate this breakdown. As we age, we begin to exercise less, this is not due to inability to exercise, it is a choice we make because we get busy, and it is justified to not be as active as we were before.

A sedentary lifestyle breeds a dangerous cycle of health issues, including muscle atrophy. Muscle atrophy increases joint pressure, decreases flexibility and escalates pain. Pain then causes us to continue not to exercise, which leads to more muscle loss and further joint restriction and pain.

Emotional self

This is just as important as the rest of the triangle. You are what you think. If you do not believe that you can recover, that will become your reality. Feed your passions, spend time with people you love. Find things that make you relaxed, manage your stress, and don't forget to love yourself throughout your healing process.

Being In a chronic state of stress truly breeds disease, especially autoimmunity and inflammation. Everyone manages their stress differently, but to add a little relief into your life, deep breathwork, meditation, qi gong.

How to heal autoimmune disorders

The good news is that by taking some simple and inexpensive measures such as consuming high-quality supplements, and watching what you eat, drink and think, all chronic illnesses are preventable, treated, and in many cases 100% reversed. The 5-step blueprint to health consists of
1. Gently cleanse while nourishing the body with foods
2. Restore your gut and immune system
3. Eliminate environmental toxins,
4. support your nervous system and adrenals
5. Improve your emotional health and manage stress

Autoimmune 101

Autoimmune disorders are diseases of the immune system. They manifest in different ways, but all behave very similarly in the sense that the immune system become confused and begins attacking the body's healthy tissues, mistaking then for foreign invaders.

Due to the lack of understanding of these diseases, conventional medicine works to treat the origins affected, rather than viewing them all for what they are. Diseases of the immune system... therefore there is no unified branch of medicine for these autoimmune conditions. Instead, patients are given referrals to specialists that are trained in specific organ systems. This strategy of course brings patients further away from treating their body's immune system, resulting in a vicious cycle.

It is common for those who suffer from autoimmune challenges to see several specialists for each of their symptoms. Some of the specialists they tend to see are, dermatologists, endocrinologists, neurologists, nephrologists, haematologists, gastroenterologists, and physical therapists. While these professionals provide an important service and are adequately knowledgeable in their speciality, there is a good chance they are not equipped to address the need for truly supporting the immune system.

Unnecessary categorization
Autoimmune disorders come in all different forms including type 1 diabetes, rheumatoid arthritis, lupus, multiple sclerosis, Hashimoto disease, inflammatory bowel disease, Gillian Barr syndrome, psoriasis, graves' disease, thyroiditis, vasculitis, SPS. All these autoimmune disorders have two things in common.
1. The immune system is not functioning properly.
2. Formal diagnoses are required to receive conventional medicine treatment.

Fortunately, natural medicine practitioners do not wait for the label to begin combatting the autoimmune challenges.

Common causes of autoimmune conditions
According to natural medicine, the most common root causes of autoimmune disorders include: - excessive inflammation, a weakened microbial intestinal permeability, chronic infections, oxidative stress, food sensitivities, exposure to toxins and many others.

With these identified, it is easier to assemble an approach to combat these challenges naturally and holistically, rather than just temporarily masking the symptoms.

The fight against autoimmune
Various natural medicine strategies used to battle autoimmune imbalances include, addressing the inflammation, dietary changes, gut healing, supplementation, detoxification, physical activity, infection treatments, stress management, relaxation techniques, hypnotherapy and many more.

Inflammation spotlight
To best be prepared to combat autoimmune complications, it is important to understand the role of inflammation in the body. Inflammation is a vital immune response, it is the body's attempt to defend itself against pathogens, heal from injury and repair damaged tissue. Chronic inflammation, however, can worsen the body's ability to recognise foreign invaders and put your body on high alert for prolonged periods of time. This can cause lasting damage in the autoimmune response that leads to the body

attacking its own healthy cells. Inflammation can be caused by a number of things, many overlapping with factors thought to cause autoimmune issues.

Heal your gut with the 4Rs

The gut microbiome is an ecosystem of organisms including bacteria, yeast, fungi, viruses and protozoan throughout the digestive tract. Most importantly it is home to 70-80% of your immune system. An imbalance in the gut bacteria or increased permeability of the intestinal walls, also known as leaky gut, are both primary causes, if not a prerequisite to the development of autoimmune conditions.

These issues contribute to inflammation and in turn worsening autoimmune responses.

The 4R program provides an effective and complete way to address and treat gastrointestinal dysfunctions while achieving optimal health and digestion.

1. Remove all possible irritants: - including inflammatory foods, toxins and low-grade infections. There are many ways to recognise the culprits of your discomfort. The first and most effective way is to do a microbiome test. Then you can test for food allergies, and those can be determined by skin and blood testing. Food sensitivities are best identified by taking part in a comprehensive elimination diet. It is also recommended to avoid common gastric irritants including caffeine, alcohol, and non-steroid anti-inflammatory drugs. Stool analysis can uncover potential infections caused by parasites, yeast or bacteria. Also testing for heavy metals in the body can be done via blood, urine, or hair and nail analysis.

Once you are aware of the things irritating your body's natural digestion, you can begin gradually removing them to allow your body to regain its natural rhythm. Once you are confident that the antagonising foods are no longer part of your diet, infections are identified, and various toxins are removed.

2. Replace: - replacing the factors needed to optimise your digestion such as digestive enzymes, essential fibre, vitamins, minerals and acids. Digestive enzymes are often found in pill form and work to enhance digestion, nutrient absorption and

intestinal repair. Your nutrient needs are determined by lab testing and provide you with personalised results regarding vitamin and mineral excess or deficiency, that can be addressed by diet change or supplementation.

3. Re-inoculate: - this is all about restoring the balance of your gut bacteria. A proper balance of healthy bacteria flora in the gut is crucial for immune activity, mood stability, weight management, disease prevention, and communicating bodily changes. A way to repopulate the much-needed healthy bacteria is by including probiotics and prebiotics into your diet.

- Probiotics are the live bacteria found in foods such as yoghurt, kefir, sauerkraut, Thampi, miso, kimchi, and kombucha, they promote a healthy balance of bacteria throughout the digestive tract and aid in the battle against many gut related chronic illnesses.
- Prebiotics are a type of plant fibre, and act as food or fertiliser for the probiotic bacteria. In short prebiotics are needed to help probiotics stay alive and thrive within our systems. Prebiotics can be found in many different foods such as artichokes, garlic, onion, asparagus, apples, and some legumes.

4. Repair: - chronic inflammation and stress can severely compromise the lining of the gut. When not addressed, this leads to further autoimmune challenges and nutrient deficiencies. Eating foods high in zinc, L Glutamine, Vitamins A, D and E, fatty acids and antioxidants support immune functioning and restoration of your gut. Also, herbs are a wonderful option to restore the lining of your gut.

Supplemental nutrition

The most important nutrients for those suffering from autoimmune issues include

- Vitamin D. most immune cells have Vitamin D receptors that can help adjust the balance of the immune response. Additionally, Vitamin D can activate over 1000 genes in the body.

- Zinc helps support the thymus glands and the inflammation regulation cells. Proper zinc levels play a huge role in coordinating the immune system's reaction
- Glutathione: - is a powerful antioxidant that especially promotes healthy detoxification of the many irritants that breed inflammation. It also protects the body from oxidative stress and immune dysfunction.
- Omega three fatty acids: - an excess of omega six fatty acids in the body promotes inflammation. Therefore, it is important to counteract this build up by taking in the proper amount of omega three fatty acid as well/ an imbalance has been proven to be a leading cause of systemic inflammation and possible autoimmune complications.

Maintenance stage: - a whole foods diet.

Autoimmune complications develop over a period, just as the healing process is not completed overnight. As you begin to uncover the causes and make the appropriate lifestyle changes, it is important to implement dietary adjustments to ensure you sustain your optimal health.

If foods such as gluten or dairy were found to be causes of your inflammation, these may need to primarily stay out of your long-term eating habits. However, if once you have combatted the inflammation and strengthened your immune response, your body may react very differently to some foods that were once bothersome. It is imperative to remain on the elimination diet for at least 21 days and work to repair your gut before beginning to introduce possible food irritants. You should test your gut microbiome, as it will tell you exactly what foods are good for you and which ones are not.

Detox your toxins

We are exposed to so many toxins daily, whether it be pesticides in our food, pollutants in the air, water contamination, or the chemicals in our household products. Our bodies are absorbing, breathing, and ingesting these toxins constantly. To reduce this toxic buildup, you must prevent exposure and detoxify regularly. Some prevention methods include water filters, air purification systems, organic non-GMO foods, toxic free household items, and herbal supplements that detoxify your body. Detoxification methods include proper nutrition, ample hydration, fasting, sweating, exercising, and herbal supplements

Stress management
Stress and disease go hand in hand. When stress is not managed properly, the body takes the load, it becomes inflamed and often develops or worsens autoimmune conditions. Everyone manages their stress levels differently, but here are some ideas that you can use to manage your stress. Deep breathing, exercise, yoga, qi gong, massage, meditation,

Action steps
Get the proper testing done to identify your body's unique needs and treat accordingly. Luckily there are other things you can do to amplify your health now.

Herbs and supplements
Herbs and supplements are a key component in healing any chronic illness such as adrenal fatigue, autoimmune disorders, and digestive disorders. Without the help of herbs and supplements, healing is more difficult, and in some cases, it is almost impossible. That is why herbs and supplements are such a big component of this program. You get the nutrition from the food that you eat. If you have a chronic illness or taking medications, you are not only deficient in nutrients, but your gut is also not able to absorb all nutrients efficiently. Therefore, it is going to be very important for you to take supplements while you recover.

This will include herbal supplements that can return your body to a state of balance, so it can start healing itself and speed up recovery. Herbal supplements do work and are highly effective, but only if you are using high quality ingredients that are given in the right quantity. Also, the formulas have to be designed correctly, and the product has to be extracted correctly as well. They are an excellent alternative to the toxic medications that exist today with none or very minimal side effects. A lot of herbs you find in stores, the dose is very low, it must be the right quantity and quality.

For supplements to work you need to take them at least 3 months, if not longer. It just depends on your body, constitution, how long you have been sick. If you are doing everything you can to heal yourself or are still contributing to your illness.

STEP 1: - Gently detoxing and cleansing your body

One of the main contributors to any disease is toxic overload. Hence one of the main steps in the protocol is to cleanse your body. However, it is important to gently cleanse your body whilst you also nourish it. Because when the body is weak and malnourished, it does not have the strength, and capacity to easily bring about health and symptom relief. In fact, you can stress your body even more by cleansing too fast.

A gentle cleanse is recommended, using foods like basil, cilantro, leafy greens, and using cleansing and liver support herbs that you can take daily. They will accelerate the detoxifying process, whilst also supporting your liver and kidneys and flushing out any ingested environmental toxins from the body

These herbs include but are not limited to dandelion root, schisandra, yellow duck, milk thistle, burdock, red clover, and many other herbs. Remember the quality of the herbal supplement that you take is directly correlated with its effectiveness.

Toxicity is one of the main contributors to developing most diseases, including adrenal fatigue, and autoimmune disorders. Toxicity is the degree to which a substance, either a toxin or a poison, can cause harm. Heer are two medical distinctions of toxicity. Acute toxicity involves harmful effects in an organism through a single or short-term exposure. Chronic toxicity, is the ability of a substance or mixture of substances to cause harmful effects over an extended period, usually upon repeated or continuous exposure, sometimes lasting for an entire life of the exposed organism

The body's natural process for detoxification is done by removing impurities from the blood in the liver, where toxins are processed for elimination. The body also eliminates toxins through the kidneys, intestines, lungs, lymphatic system and skin. We are continuously bombarded with various chemical and environmental toxins which can slow down the body's elimination process. Detoxification is about resting, cleansing, and nourishing the body from the inside out. Detoxing can help prevent and reverse disease by removing and eliminating toxins, then feeding your body with healthy nutrients.

The goal of any detox program, is to help boost the body's natural cleansing process by resting the organs through fasting, stimulating the liver to draw out toxins from the body, promoting elimination through the intestines, kidneys and skin, improving circulation of the blood, refuelling the body with healthy nutrients. The detox program focuses on gently clearing toxins with food and herbs while at the same time nourish your body. You do not have to suffer from an autoimmune disorder or a chronic illness to detox. We are all exposed to toxins daily, so to prevent getting sick, it is good to detox a quarter or every 6 months.

Some of the common symptoms of toxicity include but are not limited to: - unexplained fatigue, sluggish elimination, irritated skin, allergies, low grade infection, puffy eyes or bags under the eyes, bloating, menstrual problems, and mental confusion. Anyone who experiences one or more of the above regularly can benefit from even a small detox to help alleviate the stress on the body.

Detoxing isn't a new discovery, for centuries, cultures around the world have practiced detoxification as part of religious rituals. And have been rewarded with health benefits. After a detox people report clearer skin, weight loss, increased immunity, lessened cravings, food intolerance relief, improve clarity and sense of well-being, elimination of excess waste and more energy.

Aside from the obvious external factors such as the chemicals in clothing, furniture and cleaning supplies, many of the foods we eat are not really food. They are merely made with food-like substances. Even the fruit and vegetables we eat are grown with pesticides and heavily covered with poisons. Here are some of the top offenders when it comes to toxic foods.

- Sugar, and sugar substitutes, GMO, gluten, caffeine, dairy, meat, alcohol, processed foods, and soda. There are several adverse health outcomes associated with a diet containing the foods previously mentioned. These foods are also associated with poor overall dietary intake, which has been linked to many diseases and chronic conditions including the following. Cardiovascular disease, type 2 diabetes, obesity, some types of cancer, osteoporosis, autoimmune disorders, adrenal fatigue, and hormone imbalances.

Every time a population adopts a western diet high in processed foods, they get sick. The processed foods I am referring to are those that have been chemically processed and made solely from refining ingredients and artificial substances. Detoxing from processed foods results in a lower intake of the following. Sugar and high fructose corn syrup, artificial ingredients such as preservatives, colourants, flavour enhancers, chemicals, texture and finally refined carbohydrates, the ones responsible for rapid spikes in blood sugar and insulin levels. Processed foods are engineered for overconsumption and can lead to addiction. In short, our bodies aren't designed to handle massive amounts of salt, sugar, and unhealthy fats found in processed foods.

Refine your palate

Some amazing results have been reported by people who detoxify, who significantly cut sugar intake. Weight loss is noted as the most noticeable outward sign. Followed by a clear complexion, and internal benefits include an increase in sustained energy levels and experiencing less bloating and gas. Refined sugar is one of the most harmful things you can put in your body, which is not classified as a narcotic or poison.

Emerging research suggests sugar causes our cells to degrade faster, leading to DNA damage and accelerated ageing. Once you have broken the cycle of sugar dependency, and cleansed your system of its effects, sugary snacks like doughnuts and cakes won't have the same irresistible appeal they once had. And foods you never thought as particularly sweet, like bell peppers, carrots and beets will start tasting very sweet to you. Something very sweet like an apple will taste like candy.

By ditching the refined sugar, your palate, will become more attuned to the natural sweetness of real foods. When removing animal products from the diet, the body goes into cleansing mode to rid itself of the accumulated toxins. Noted benefits of detoxing from meat and dairy include reduced inflammation, lower blood cholesterol levels, and a rebalancing of healthy gut bacteria. Even if you are not ready to take the plunge and go full on vegetarian, it is recommended to avoid meat and dairy while going on a detox, because meat slows down digestion, clogs up the bowels, and breeds harmful bacteria in your gut. Milk, cheese and other dairy products are acidic to the body, leading to a reduced cell function and the slowing down of detoxification. In general, even when detoxing, the recommended amount of meat products is 4 ounces per meal. Meat should become a side dish in your meals, not the main course.

Detoxing is all about diet. Not counting calories. Just removing the known food offenders and increasing your intake on non-toxic foods. Non-toxic foods include, stevia, greens, a little bit of fruit not too much, water, vitamins, a little bit of legumes and all grains, no more than half a cup a day. Nuts and seeds, and herbal teas. When it comes to detoxing, many different options are available, depending on your need. Detox programs can last anywhere from 3 days to a month and even 3 months. Fasting programs should be done with extreme care, and for only a small duration of time.

<u>3–7-day juice fast</u>
- This means only drinking fresh fruit and vegetable juices and water, this can be effective way to release toxins from the body.

There are many beneficial herbs that are incredibly detoxifying to the body, and they also help to support all the organs of elimination such as the liver, the kidneys, the blood, lungs etc. Cleansing and liver support herbs taken daily, purify the blood and gently accelerate the detoxifying process while supporting the liver and kidneys and flushing ingested and environmental toxins from the body.

Some of the herbs that you can use to detox and cleanse are, burdock root, dandelion root, dandelion leaves, yellow dock, chassandra, milk thistle, red clover, sassafras, nettle and many other. Select a few of these herbs and create an herbal tincture formula for yourself. To make your formula more effective, add a little bit of synergistic herb like ginger or liquorice to the formula.

Start every morning with a glass of warm lemon water. This water will stimulate digestion for the day and clear the body of any toxins that may have settled in the digestive tract overnight. And then you can drink chilled lemon water throughout the day. Drinking lemon water supports the immune function, alkalises the body, aids digestion, clears the skin, and promotes healing. Smoothies are packed with nutrition and can make a great meal. Plus, you can have all kinds of healthy additions in a smoothie. You can add to your smoothie, aloe water, spinach, chia seeds, strawberries, protein.

Eat plenty of fibre, including brown rice, and organically grown fresh vegetables in a little bit of fruit such as beets, radishes, artichokes, cabbage, broccoli, spirulina, asparagus, and seaweeds. They are all excellent detoxifying foods. Cleanse and protect the liver by taking herbs such as dandelion root, burdock, and milk thistle, drinking green tea. Take Vitamin C, which helps the body produce glutathione, a liver compound that drives away toxins. Drink at 2 litres of water

STEP 2: - the basics of good nutrition

In addition to chronic stress, nutritional deficiencies is one of the main causes of any chronic illness. The consumption of food and liquid gives us the energy and the necessary nutrients to sustain life and to meet our bodies needs for growth, development and function. Without proper nutrition, our bodies are more prone to disease, infection, fatigue and poor performance. Every cell in the body depends on the right quantity and continuous supply of the following five nutrients. From the food we eat to stay healthy and productive,

- Proteins: - these are needed to build, maintain and repair muscle, blood, skin, bones, hormones and other tissues and organs in the body. That is why protein is an essential component of a healthy diet, especially if you are suffering from a chronic illness such as adrenal fatigue.
- Carbohydrates: - these provide the body with glucose, which is then converted into energy, that is used to support bodily functions and physical activity. Unlike most fad diets, like the keto diet, carbohydrates are also an essential component of a healthy diet. However, we need to eat the right type of carbs in moderation. Carbs should make up to 30% of your diet, and they should be mostly from non-starchy vegetables.
- Good fats: _ they are the body's secondary source of energy and provide more energy, per gram, than any other nutrient. They are difficult to burn, but they are good for your heart, brain.
- Vitamins, minerals and enzymes; - They are all needed in small amounts but are essential and good for your health. They control many functions and processes in the body and in the case of minerals, they also help build body tissues such as bone and blood.

Proper nutrition is essential for achieving optimal health because our organs and tissues need adequate nutrition to work effectively. Extreme diets that emphasise eating one type of nutrient over another may help you lose weight, but in the long run they set you up for life threatening medical conditions. Because so many foods are excluded from these diets, they are unbalanced and not recommended. For example, overeating saturated fats like butter, and large amounts of red meat, increases the amount of cholesterol in your blood, thereby multiplying the risk of developing heart disease. Overeating protein can also hurt your body.

Instead of avoiding meat altogether, eat grass fed meat, and only eat 4oz instead of 12 oz. instead of avoiding carbs altogether, eat plenty of non- starchy vegetables and a small amount of starchy carbs.

One of the two most common diets used to avert any chronic illness, such as leaky gut, candida, adrenal fatigue and other immune disorders is a whole food plant-based diet. As much benefits as this diet have, it also has its limitations. Whole foods describe natural foods that are not heavily processed. That means whole, unrefined or minimally refined ingredients.

Plant based means food that comes from plants and doesn't contain animal ingredients such as meat, milk, eggs, or honey. A whole food plant-based diet is a lifestyle that is based on eating mostly plants, it also eliminates processed, highly refined foods such as bleached flours, refined sugars, and oils.

The term vegan describes a lifestyle that excludes, as far as possible, all animal products for food, clothing or any other purpose.

Vegetarian is a more widely known lifestyle and excludes foods that consist of or have been produced with the aid of products composed of or created by any part of the body of a living or dead animal. This includes meat, poultry, fish, or insects. Vegetarians typically eat dairy and eggs

An omnivore is a person that eats food of both plant and animal origin. A carnivore follows a lifestyle that includes consuming meat. You may be thinking that a whole food plant-based diet is going to be hard work or boring, and that avoiding animal ingredients limits your options.

Trying a plant based whole food diet is your opportunity to explore and expand your palate. Many chronic diseases can be controlled, reduced or even reversed by moving to a whole food plant-based diet. A recent study called the China study, is one of the most comprehensive studies of nutrition ever shown that a plant-based diet can reduce the risk of type 2 diabetes, heart disease, certain types of cancer, and other significant illnesses. Three categories of whole food plant-based benefits have been identified.

1. Easy weight management: - people who eat a plant-based diet tend to be leaner than those who don't. and the diet makes it easy to lose weight and keep it off without counting any calories.

2. Disease prevention: - whole food plant-based eating can prevent, halt or even reverse chronic diseases, including heart disease, and type 2 diabetes.

3. A lighter environmental footprint: - a plant based det places much less stress on the environment. Increased heart health and reversing heart disease can be done through a plant-based diet.

Anything that has been processed or refined, plant based or not, will create disease in the body.

The Big C

- Research suggests that following a plant-based diet may reduce your risk of certain types of cancer, particularly organic plant-based diets. The non-organic plant-based foods contain pesticides which are also contributed to cancer. There are 2 important factors to know when discussing cancer.

1. Cancer cells thrive in a high sugar environment. When the cells are starved by reducing sugar, they cannot flourish

2. While DNA can play a role in the risk of developing cancer, diet, lifestyle and environmental factors are modifiable conditions that contribute to cancer

Vegetarian diets are associated with a significantly lower risk of gastrointestinal and colorectal cancer. A whole food plant-based diet can help reduce inflammation, boost your immune system and decrease your body weight, all of which are attributed to reducing cancerous growth. Adopting a whole food plant-based diet may be a useful tool in managing and reducing your risk of developing diabetes.

Plant based eating is associated with many health benefits and the brain is no exception. Plant based diets appear to influence both mental health and cognitive function positively. Higher levels of antioxidants in the blood from plant sources have been associated with a significantly lower risk of depression and lower suicide rates.

Vegetarians show fewer symptoms of depression, anxiety, stress and mood disturbances than omnivores. The higher levels of antioxidants are also attributed to slowing the progression of Alzheimer's disease and reversing cognitive deficits. A meta-analysis, which is a review of several different studies of similar subjects, found that eating more fruits and vegetables led to a 20% reduction in the risk of developing cognitive impairment or dementia. Foods in the whole food plant-based diet include

1. Vegetables: - peppers, corn, avocados, lettuce, spinach, artichokes, kale, peas, collard greens etc
2. Tubers: - root vegetables like potatoes, carrots, parsnips, sweet potatoes, beets etc. tubers are starchy vegetables so they can increase your blood sugar, o eat about half a cup a day only.
3. Whole grains: - only eat grains and cereals in their whole form. And only about half a cup a day. Quinoa, brown rice, millet, whole wheat, oats, barley etc. even popcorn is a whole grain
4. Legumes: - beans of any kind, plus lentils, pulses, and similar ingredients.
5. Fruits: - these should be eaten in moderation as well, as any type of fruit, including apples, bananas, grapes, strawberries, citrus fruits etc,

The paleo diet

The paleo diet can also be used to reverse any chronic illness such as leaky gut, candida, Siegel, adrenal fatigue and autoimmune disorders. The paleo diet has many benefits, and has healed many people

The paleo diet is often called the caveman diet, primal diet or stone age diet. The premise is that all the food that you consume it will be directly sourced from nature as your ancestors had hunted and gathered during the palaeolithic era. before the birth of agriculture about 10,000 years ago humans did not eat grains, beans, starchy vegetables, potatoes, and added milk and sugars. Yet today approximately 61% of human calories are from foods that were unknown to us and our bodies prior to the start of food processing. Meats, fruits and vegetables, equal natural. Processed foods of any kind equal unnatural. The modern diet of refined foods is completely different from the way early humans ate.

    The paleo diet recommends avoiding all dairy products, grains (rice, wheat, corn, oat, barley, millet, rye), beans & legumes, starchy vegetables such as potato and squash varieties, sugary foods and artificial sweeteners, high salt foods such as processed or smoked meats, soft drinks and fruit juices, refined vegetable oils. There are many things you eat on the paleo diet

- chicken, turkey, fish, shellfish, eggs, fruits and berries, most vegetables, nuts and seeds, honey in limited amounts, healthy oils like olive, walnut, flaxseed, macadamia, avocado and coconut.

The paleo plate consists of most lean meats, a close second of vegetables, a serving of healthy fats, and some fruits and nuts. And water. When you eat a balanced paleo meal you are providing your body with natural energy sources from all natural sources. This is the way our bodies are meant to be fuelled. Not to mention our quality of sleep incredibly. This is done by organically from cutting out typical additives in our FAD food sources. The serotonin in our brain signalling when it is time to sleep, is no longer drowned out by the chemicals in our food. So proper sleep equals natural foods.

    The structure of the paleo diet naturally promotes weight loss between cutting synthetic chemicals from processed foods, increasing our daily intake of fruits, vegetables, and healthy fats, and providing ourselves with ample protein for muscle growth. While there are foods you can't eat, you are NOT counting calories, seeking for cheat days or staying hungry. The paleo diet promotes eating when you are hungry. The catch is, when you do it correctly, you will not be as hungry as often.

The emphasis on calorie dense, healthy fats, whole foods and plenty of fibre creates the perfect equation for not feeling hungry. Since we have altered our consumption of a lot of harmful additives such as trans fats, MSG, refined sugar, and excessive caffeine, we are inherently giving our bodies the rest. Additionally, our antioxidant, phytonutrient and fibre intake increase aiding in the detox process.

Many diseases can be traced back to a single word, inflammation. Luckily, the paleo diet is structured around anti-inflammatory diseases, while cutting out many of the known inflammatory food sources.

The quality of our food is of the utmost importance considering trying to lose weight. Unfortunately, it is a common misconception that eating less is the answer to the weight loss epidemic. It is more important to focus on quality over quantity, The paleo menu is full of towering rich animal products, omega 3 and fibre rich carbohydrate sources. Taurine helps propel fat cells into weight loss mode. This is done by reducing inflammatory signals to the fat cells and improving fat tissue insulin sensitivity. Omega 3's also aids in pushing fat cells into a weight loss mode by improving our metabolic health, and overall lowering inflammation. Lastly, fibre. The paleo friendly carbohydrate sources are jam packed with fibre. Carbohydrates that feature a healthy amount of fibre do not cause those blood sugar spikes mentioned earlier.

For athletes, the paleo diet can potentially provide the following athletic benefits: - improved muscle recovery, improved digestion, allowing more efficient absorption of essential nutrients, improved glucose control, improved cognitive abilities and focus,

Overall, the paleo diet provides the nutrition needed to have sustained energy, ability to grow and maintain muscle, and strengthen the immune system and cognitive ability. A paleo diet is highly influenced on preventing disease. The prevalence of autoimmune diseases has been rising for some time now.

An autoimmune disease is basically a condition where the body cannot decipher between our own healthy tissue from foreign invaders, such as bacteria and viruses. Because of this our immune system goes into attack mode too often, even attacking our own bodies. These attacks can go unnoticed for years, until an identifiable autoimmune disease develops.

There are 80 different known varieties of autoimmune diseases as of right now, but more are being discovered. So, what will be the best thing combatting this? You guessed it, to reduce inflammation.

That is where the autoimmune protocol or autoimmune paleo diet comes in. making these dietary changes helps to heal the immune systems communication system with our bodies, and our gut healthy flora, which is essential to an accurate immune response.

Paleo + vegan diet – the Pegan diet.

Both the paleo and plant-based diet can be used successfully together, to help many people heal from chronic illnesses such as diabetes, candida, adrenal fatigue, and autoimmune disorders. Both diets are very clean and reduce inflammation in the body, making them a huge benefit to our health. However, both also have some significant limitations that may cause health issues in the long run, and that is because they are both restricted in one way or another.

Research shows that a plant-based diet helps with weight loss, reverses diabetes, and lower cholesterol. Nevertheless, research also indicates that a paleo diet seems to do the same thing. So how can those two different diets work to reverse chronic illness? What happens with nutritional research is that each side of the vegan versus meat arguments, is that each side clings to its diet with near religious ideals, and each one can point you to studies validating their point of view. In order to understand the research, you must read the research in detail and not just read between the lines or just read the headlines.

To stay healthy, it all comes back to a few dietary principles, and these are, eat foods as close to nature as possible. This way of eating means letting go of refined, processed food, and consume foods that are sustainably, natural grown if animal foods. This also means eating clean food free of pesticides, and other toxic chemicals. Eat low sugar glycaemic food. Eat lots of plant food, not necessarily a plant based.

- 75% of your plate should be non-starchy vegetables. And this way of eating, meat becomes the side dish, not the central part of your meal.
- Eat good fats such as those that come from nuts and seeds. Also, omega 3 fats that are found in fish, olive oil, avocado oil, and coconut oil.

As you can see these principles are universal, and to one degree or another, both the plant based, and paleo diet follow these principles which is what makes them anti-inflammatory and clean. We should take the best of both diets. You take the benefits of each and discard the disadvantages of each, and that is how you eat.

What are the disadvantages of each of these diets

- The plant-based diets disadvantages are that you do NOT get all your nutrients from plants such as Vitamin B12. Collagen is a must if you have leaky gut or an autoimmune disorder, and it only comes from animals. If they are not careful with how they eat, vegans will lack iron and other minerals in the long run. Both animal protein and omega oils are more bioavailable in animal sources, especially as you get older. It is harder to process both protein and fat from plant sources.
- Most vegetarian protein comes from products that are also rich in carbohydrates, such as beans, and you need to eat a large quantity of them to meet the daily needs of protein, making it a high carb diet. The exception is nuts, but you will need to eat a lot more of them to get the same amount of protein than in a minimal amount of animal product, and protein is essential to stay healthy. It is the foundation block for every cell of your body. To be the healthiest vegan possible, it takes extra vigilance to get

proper nutrition. This topic is critical if you have a chronic illness because you are already deficient in some nutrients, and you do not want to make things worse.

- The Paleo disadvantages are: - many people often interpret as a meat centred diet, and some use the paleo philosophy as an excuse to overeat meat and very little plant-based food. For these people, the paleo diet can put them at risk of an increased risk of developing cardiovascular disease and in the long run, increase a toxic load in their bodies. Toxic overload is one of the contributors to autoimmune disorders and chronic illnesses.
- Any drastic reduction in carb intake can cause heath issues. Carbohydrates are also an important part of a diet. We can't just eliminate them. Eliminating entire food groups can mean essential nutrients, and vitamins are not included in your diet. People in the palaeolithic era did not eat large amounts of animal products because it was not readily available. And they also exercised more. This is the reason who the paleo diet should NOT be a meat centric diet. Eating just a meat-based diet can lead to not eating enough fibre and carbs, which can lead to inflammation, constipation, and many other diseases. It seems that each of these two diet's disadvantages get compensated by the advantages of the other. These diets have more in common than they are different. For example, they both focus on natural, whole, fresh food that is sustainably raised.

<u>What does the Pegan diet look like</u>
- Eat foods low in glycaemic load, low in sugars, starches, flour and refined carbohydrates.
- Focus on eating primarily non-starchy vegetables, and more protein and fat such as nuts (except for peanuts), seeds like flax, chia, hemp, sesame, coconut, avocados, sardines, etc.
- Eat mostly vegetables, and very little fruit.
- Everything you eat should be low in pesticides, antibiotics, hormones and no or low GMO foods. No chemicals, no additives, preservatives, dye, MSG, artificial sweeteners, and other chemicals that you will never have in your kitchen.

- Include good quality fats from olive oil, nuts, seeds and avocados. Do not eat most vegetable oils such as canola, sunflower, corn or soybean oil,
- Eat adequate protein for appetite control and muscle synthesis, especially in the elderly.
- If animal products are consumed, they should be sustainably raised or grass fed. If you eat fish, choose low mercury and low toxin containing fish such as sardines, herring etc
- Avoid dairy. Its purpose is for growing calves into cows, not for humans. Remember unlike what we have been told, milk does not make a body good, however, if you are craving a little bit of milk, products or dairy, try goat products, and only as a treat and always organic.
- Avoid gluten: - gluten is mostly made from wheat that has been altered somehow. If you are going to eat gluten, herlom wheat. Eat gluten free whole grains sparingly. They raise blood sugar and they can trigger autoimmunity. they are also high in carbohydrates, so limit your intake to half a cup per day
- If you do eat legumes or starchy vegetables, eat them in moderation, only half cup to one cup a day.

What to eat
- Eat a nutrient dense diet. To function well, the human body needs 52 or so minerals. And it is essential to keep a proper mineral balance to keep the body's self-defences.
- These minerals can be found in natural, fresh, organic foods such as vegetables, nuts, seeds, good fats, pasture raised meats and fruit.
- Some cleansing foods include lemon, miso soup, beets, carrots, brussels sprouts, leafy greens, dandelion leaves, avocados, seeds, nuts, garlic, onions and other pungent spices.
- There are also foods that hinder healing including dairy, alcohol, gluten, some grains and legumes, soy, eggs, refined foods. Processed foods, GMO foods, non-organic foods, artificial colourings and flavourings.

Step 3: - restore your gut an immune system

There is no doubt that health starts with a healthy gut. Many scientific studies have shown that the gut interacts with the immune system, and that the health of our gut is directly correlated with the health of our immune system. When this interaction fails, autoimmune or autoinflammatory diseases occur. It is very common for people with adrenal fatigue or autoimmune disorders to have what is called a leaky gut, or intestinal permeability.

This is a condition where the lining of the small intestine becomes unhealthy, and may have cracks or holes, causing undigested food particles, toxic waste products, or bacteria to leak through the intestines and flow into the blood stream. Contributors to a leaky gut are: - a junk food diet, medication overuse, infections or gut imbalances, toxic overload, inadequate digestive enzymes, eating too much raw foods, chronic stress, anxiety, depression and other chronic negative emotions. Therefore, it is imperative to restore the lining of the intestines to be able to regain our health. Fortunately, food, probiotics and herbs such as slippery elm, marshmallow, liquorice, chamomile and peppermint can help us do this.

The leaky gut solution

The gut or gastrointestinal system is truly a gateway to overall health. The gut microbiome is a ecosystem of organisms including bacteria, yeast, fungi, viruses and protozoan, throughout the digestive tract. Far beyond just digestive health, the following organ systems are closely related to gut health, and they are the immune system, endocrine system, nervous system, circulatory system, integumentary system, respiratory system, and reproductive system. That means that if your gut is not healthy or out of balance, all these other systems may get impacted, causing many diseases that are not really related to gut symptoms. A few key points to consider are

- There are 10 times the number of bacteria in our body than there are cells. And most of the bacteria is found in our digestive tract. The gastrointestinal system contains 90% of the body's happy hormone, serotonin. Most importantly, approximately 70% of our immune system is housed in the gut. As you can tell, gut health doesn't stop at digestion.

- The health of our gut affects nearly every system in our bodies

Leaky gut is a term that refers to intestinal hyper permeability. It has become an increasingly more common health problem today. Leaky gut causes major health problems, including autoimmunity. How though?

Intestinal hyperpermeability is exactly what it sounds like. The digestive tract is no longer able to ensure the good stays in, and the bad stays out, instead, the tight junctions or the proteins holding the intestinal walls together are loosened. This leaves sizeable gaps for undigested food particles, digestive fluids and toxins to enter the bloodstream. Then the body reacts to these foreign particles in the blood by producing immune antibodies or pro inflammatory cells to fight them off. This breeds chronic inflammation, food allergies, and various health complications. Of course, there are no signs of improvement until the gut's permeability is addressed. Fortunately, we now have a better understanding of the causes, obstacles, and treatment methods for leaky gut. So, there is a stop to this cycle.

Several factors have proven to negatively affect the gut's intestinal integrity. The most prominent include the standard American diet., exposure to chemicals, chronic infections, gluten and other greens, food allergies, excessive medications, and believe it or not, poorly managed stress.

The standard American diet

The standard American diet, rightfully known as the FAD diet, is one of the leading causes of the chronic health issues that we see today. According to a 2009 study conducted by the USDA. 63% of the calories Americans are consuming come from processed foods containing preservatives, refined grains, dairy and added sugars and oils. None of these foods have any business being part of our diets at all.

You can call it what you want, Frood, Frankenfood, Frood like substances, fake food, but you most definitely can't call most of our food supply real food. When most of our diets are packed meals, with paragraph long ingredient list in labels we can't understand, we are NOT eating real food. Here are a couple of alarming facts. The United States Food and Drug Administration, otherwise known as the FDA, has approved approximately 3,000 different food additives, preservatives and colourings without adequate research on safety.

The average person ingests over 150lbs of additives each year. The magnitude these chemicals are allowed into our lives is incomprehensible. We are becoming more and more aware of the consequences from this fake food lifestyle. This is only one factor in this leaky gur epidemic, but it is a big one.

Inflammation is a vital immune response, and it is the body's attempt to defend itself against pathogens, heal from injury and repair damaged tissue. Chronic inflammation, however, is not beneficial to our bodies in any way. In fact, it can worsen the body's ability to recognise foreign invaders and puts the body into a state of stress for extended periods of time. This can cause lasting damage, increasing food allergies and eventually autoimmunity. This type of inflammation can be caused by a number of things, but largely seen as a result of leaky gut syndrome and poor dietary habits. If chronic inflammation goes untreated, leaky gut is worsened, and the body ultimately loses its ability to repair from the damage.

Much like the additives and preservatives flooding our food supply, pesticides are also a big part of what is on our plates. There are 3 million tons of pesticides used worldwide each year, and more than 16,000 chemicals involved in the production of these pesticides. Studies to show their safety on humans have been very limited, whereas some have no documented research at all.

There are strong links between pesticide exposure and nervous system disorders, immune system suppression, reproductive damage, hormonal imbalances, thyroid issues, type 2 diabetes and obesity, asthma, migraines, attention disorders and developmental delay in children. The magnitude of pesticides along with steroids, hormones, antibiotics, that show up in our food supply is truly frightening.

Medication is severely overprescribed in the current medical model used today. Medical programs train doctors to medicate symptoms, even when they are unsure of the cause. This in the short term seems to work, as patients experience temporary relief from their discomfort. But what isn't taken into account is how these excessive prescriptions have affected our bodies. For example, statins, drugs used to lower cholesterol have shown to lower vitamin D. While it may be lowering cholesterol, it is simultaneously causing nutrient deficiencies, muscle fatigue, increased blood pressure, and a weakened immunity.

- Painkillers like ibuprofen, Lexapro, and aspirin, contribute to Vitamin C and iron deficiencies, leaving one vulnerable to disease and eroding the mucosal lining of the stomach.
- Acid reduction medications hinder the digestion of protein, calcium, and Vitamin B12, often causing chronic pain problems
- Long term use of anti-depressants too significantly affects the gut motility and cause digestive issues

It is important to know that almost all medications are unable to differentiate between the good bacteria in our gut and the illness that it is trying to attack, and that results in an altered microbiome, and much greater risk of infections. There are very FEW situations where drugs should be your solution, such as a life-threatening infection, or surgical situation without an immediate emergency need of medication.

Our gut has 4 critical elements or defences that it truly needs for healthy gut function. In order from the most outer layer of defence they include.

1. Mucosal IGA otherwise known as immunoglobin A. This antibody found in the mucous membranes is considered your guts first line of defence against toxins
2. Tight junctions: - these are small proteins that are responsible for holding the gut cells together. This is the part that is mostly directly affected when you have a leaky gut
3. Gastro-associated lymphoid tissue, otherwise known as GALP. This is the guts concentrated immune system, and in fact 70% of our immune system altogether. This is the guts last and most powerful layer of defence. The guts accessory defences include friendly bacteria. These bacteria can communicate with the GALP system warning of potential danger.
4. Stomach acid: - this is absolutely essential for the digestion, absorption of nutrients, and defence against infections. If there is any dysfunction throughout your guts line of defence, these primary barriers need to be evaluated to heal and be treated properly.

The first step of healing is ruling out the fundamental causes of leaky gut. It is important to recognise that it is very rarely only one cause, but it is a combination of several issues causing the damage. You must first rule out or begin to recognise the following.

- Vitamin deficiencies: - by functional nutrition testing or using the biome test
- Infections, pathogens: - by blood and GI tract test
- Heavy metal toxicity by urine or hair testing
- Gluten sensitivity through HLA-CQ genetic testing
- Environmental allergies via skin or blood test and test your microbial health.

If any of these come back positive, you have your first set of instructions. ADDRESS THE DEFICIENCIES. Implement dietary changes, limit exposure to allergens, and consider the detox methods outlined in program, including taking herbal supplements. Once you have a better understanding of your body's unique needs, you can begin the formal natural medicine protocol.

The 4R program is administered to help you heal from digestive distress, reverse gut complications, and rebalance your gastrointestinal microbiome. It is an incredible tool to acknowledge and treat health issues, dysfunctions, imbalances and personal health needs. It is done in the following order.
1. Remove: - eliminate problem foods, toxins, low grade infections, and oxidative stress.
2. Repair: - begin to re-introduce a clean diet with essential nutrients that your body needs.
3. Restore: - repopulate your gut with healthy bacteria to restore the proper balance of gut flora.
4. Replace: _ replace digestive enzymes, antioxidant and immune boosting vitamins to promote a sustainable and healthy digestion.

You will need to remove much of the chemicals burdening your daily life. This includes pesticides in your food, genetically modified organisms, unnecessary medications, unnatural housework cleaners, and unnatural cosmetics. Repair, restore and replace is done by calming the chronic inflammation and reintroducing nutritious foods, digestive enzymes, probiotics, essential fibre, vitamins, minerals, and acids. One of the best supplements for a leaky gut is L Glutamine, as well as the herbal supplements. TEST YOUR MICROBIOME.

Probiotics

Probiotics are well known for their therapeutic use in the management and treatment of gastrointestinal diseases, immunity and ultimately autoimmune disorders. These live microorganisms help to improve the microbiome of the gut, which can have positive system wide effects.

Probiotics are an important component of healing a leaky gut, autoimmune disorders and any other chronic illness. Our bodies contain trillions of microorganisms, in fact some scientists estimate that bacteria cells outnumber human cells by 10:1. While this sounds scary, you should note that many of these microorganisms help our bodies function properly.

Bacteria helps break down food, destroys disease causing microorganisms, and produces vitamins. Many of the microorganisms in probiotic supplements are like the microorganisms that naturally exist in our bodies.

Probiotics contain a diversity of microorganisms, but the most common ones belong to groups called lactobacillus and bifidobacterium. Each one of these groups include many types of bacteria. Probiotics have a diversity of effects on our bodies and can affect different people differently. However, these are some of the ways probiotics might work.

1. By maintaining a more desirable and balanced community of microorganisms, by stabilising the digestive tract barrier against undesirable microorganisms, or produce substances that inhibit their growth.

2. They outcompete undesirable microorganisms. Generally, in healthy individuals, probiotics have a good safety record.

Probiotics reduce the risk of traveller's diarrhoea by 8% and lower the bacteria from other causes by 57% in children and 26% in adults. An increased number of studies link gut health to mood and mental health. Both human and animal studies have shown that probiotic supplements can improve mental health disorders, such as anxiety, depression, autism, OCD and more. Certain probiotic strains may reduce the severity of eczema in children, and in infants. Because probiotics can inhibit the growth of harmful bacteria, it may also help give your immune system a boost. An extensive review found that taking probiotics reduces the likelihood and duration of respiratory tract infections, and another found that children taking lactobacillus GG reduced the frequency of respiratory infections by 17%.

Taking probiotics might help with weight loss, through several different mechanisms. Some probiotics prevent the absorption of dietary fat in the intestine, excreting it to faeces rather than storing in the body.

Some can help you feel fuller longer, resulting in more calories burned and less fat stored.

In one study, dieting women who took lactobacillus for 3 months lost 50% more weight than women who didn't take the probiotic. Prebiotics are the food source for beneficial bacteria that probiotics bring to the table and can help them survive and thrive in the gut microbiome.
- Kombucha is made from black or green tea that has been fermented by friendly bacteria and used.
- Yoghurt is one of the best forms of probiotics as the process of making yoghurt consists of fermenting milk with friendly bacteria.
- Kefir is a fermented probiotic drink that contains both friendly bacteria and yeast.
- Fermented cabbage has been eaten for centuries all over the world, both sauerkraut and kimchi can bring tons of health benefits. Sauerkraut, a European staple is a probiotic rich in fibre as well as vitamins C, B, and K. it also contains iron, manganese, and antioxidants such as gluten
- Kimchi, is a spicy Korean condiment, made of a mix of seasonings such as red chilli peppers, garlic, ginger etc, and it contains lactic acid and bacteria lactobacillus kimchi.
- Tempeh is a fermented soybean product that is formed into a patty and is used worldwide as a protein meat supplement. Through the fermentation process, soybeans are broken down to lower the amino phytic acid, a compound that impairs the absorption of iron and zinc to provide the body with probiotics as well as vitamin B12.
- Miso soup contains probiotics, protein and fibre, as well as vitamins, minerals, and plant compounds such as Vitamin K, manganese and copper.

Antibiotics kill all the bacteria in your body, be it beneficial or harmful. This includes the microbes that are helping your body operate. How? Because in addition to killing disease causing bacteria, antibiotics destroy healthy bacteria too, which drastically affects the amounts and types of bacteria that you have. In fact, only one week of antibiotics can change the makeup of the gut microbiome for up to a year.

Chapter 14

Adrenal fatigue

The main cause of adrenal fatigue is experiencing chronic stress, and stress is not limited to emotional stress. It also includes physical stress, such as an illness, aches and pains, exhaustion, or trouble sleeping. In general, most diseases, but in particular adrenal fatigue are caused by three main factors. And they are: -
1. Stress
2. nutritional deficiency
3. toxicity.

It is scientifically proven that 70% of health issues are caused by environmental factors such as medication overload, the standard American diet, chronic infections, chronic stress, anxiety, exposure to chemicals and heavy metals found in food, water, air, cosmetics, and household cleaners. These environmental factors cause excess inflammation in the body, nutritional deficiencies, a weakened microbiome, intestinal permeability, oxidative stress, food sensitivity, and adrenal fatigue. All of these are main contributors to adrenal fatigue, and other chronic illnesses, like autoimmune disease, digestive disorders, cancers, diabetes, high blood pressure, candida and many more.

What is adrenal fatigue

This syndrome is a collection of related symptoms caused by insufficient adrenal gland function. When the adrenal glands operate inadequately, complications arise, and adrenal fatigue syndrome can develop. Usually, the onset of adrenal fatigue is attributed to prolonged stress and chronic infections, hormonal changes, immune response and metabolic changes. Those suffering may not present any physical signs of illness, but we still feel generally fatigued, have trouble cognitively, and experience strong food cravings. Sleep does not solve this exhaustion, so it is common to see an increase in intake of coffee, sugar, and other stimulants to sustain energy throughout the day. Unfortunately, this is counterproductive for adrenal fatigue.

What do the adrenal glands even do?
The adrenal glands are two glands located above the kidneys and are made up of two different parts. Both are responsible for hormone production but differ greatly.

1. The adrenal cortex produces hormones such as cortisol and aldosterone, that are essential for life. Cortisol works to regulate our metabolism, immunity, and stress response, while aldosterone helps control blood pressure and proper cardiovascular function.

2. The adrenal medulla produces non-essential hormones or ones that are not vital for life. This does not mean that this component of the adrenals is not important. The adrenal medulla is incredibly valuable for dealing with physical and emotional stress and contributes to the fight or flight response of our parasympathetic nervous system. The most noticeable chemical messenger produced in this part of the adrenals is adrenaline.

The adrenal glands also produce the sex hormones estrogen and progesterone, as well as various neurotransmitters such as dopamine. When the proper production of these hormones is disrupted, adrenal fatigue can develop. Because of the multitude of responsibilities that these little glands have, adrenal fatigue can manifest very differently depending on the individual.

Stress and cortisol
When a person is under chronic stress or anxiety, the hypothalamus, that is a tiny region at the base of the brain, sets off your body's alarm system. This alarm system triggers a combination of nerve and hormonal signals that prompt your adrenal glands to release a surge of hormones, including adrenaline and cortisol. Adrenaline increases your heart rate,

elevates your blood pressure, and boosts energy supplies, while cortisol increases sugars, that means glucose into the bloodstream, enhances your brains used of glucose and increases the availability of substances that repair tissues.

Cortisol is a glucocorticoid type of steroid hormone that the adrenal glands, that is the endocrine glands on top of your kidneys produce and release. This hormone is the primary stress hormone and is elevated when we experience heightened stress or anxiety. Glucocorticoid steroids such as cortisol, suppress inflammation in all bodily tissues, and control metabolism in your muscles, fat, liver and bones. Glucocorticoids also affect the sleep and wake cycles. Cortisol is an essential hormone that affects almost every organ and tissue in your body. Even though cortisol is widely known as the stress hormone, it also plays many vital roles in your body, including regulating your body's stress response, helping control your body's use of fats, proteins, carbohydrates, or your metabolism, suppresses inflammation, regulates blood pressure, regulates blood sugar, and helps manage sleep and wake cycle.

Cortisol is not always bad. Especially when you produce it in the right amounts. It is only harmful to the body when it is overproduced or under produced. Cortisol also curbs functions that will be nonessential or harmful in a fight or flight situation, such as altering your immune system responses, and suppressing the digestive, reproductive and growth processes. This complex natural alarm system also communicates with the brain regions that control mood, motivation, and fear. These are supposed to be temporary effects that will help you focus your body to survive in a dangerous situation. Unfortunately, when stressors are always present in your life, and you are constantly feeling under attack, even if it is imagined, that fight or flight reaction stays turned on, which causes high levels of cortisol to be released on a consistent basis.

Almost all tissues in your body have glucocorticoid receptors. Because of this, cortisol can affect every organ system in your body, including but not limited to your nervous system, immune system, cardiovascular system, respiratory system, reproductive system, musculoskeletal system and your skin, nails, hair and nerves.

Imagine what happen to your digestive system when it is consistently suppressed because you are constantly under perceived stress. In that case you are unable to digest food properly, which eventually leads to malnourishment, and being overweight, regardless of how good your diet is. If your body is malnourished, it cannot restore itself or function properly. So, the long-term activation of the stress response system and over exposure to cortisol and other stress hormones, can disrupt almost all of your bodily processes.

This puts you in an increased risk of many health problems, including anxiety, depression, digestive problems, hormonal imbalances, headaches, muscle tension and pain, heart disease, heart attack, high blood pressure and stroke, sleep problems, weight gain, memory and concentration impairment.

More specifically, cortisol affects your body in the following ways. Blood sugar regulation. Under normal circumstances, cortisol counterbalances the effects of insulin, a hormone that your pancreas makes to regulate your blood sugar. However, cortisol raises blood sugar by releasing stored glucose, while insulin lowers your blood sugar. So chronic high cortisol levels can lead to persistent high blood sugar, this could cause type 2 diabetes, or insulin resistance.

Cortisol also helps regulate your metabolism. Therefore, cortisol helps control how your body uses fats, proteins, and carbohydrates for energy. As the high levels of cortisol course through your blood stream, the hormone increases your appetite, causes insulin resistance and slowdowns your metabolism. This leads your body to store fat and calories to help you cause with stress. If you are overweight and are having issues losing weight, it might not be your diet causing you to gain weight, instead, it could be high cortisol causing the problem, and it will be for your benefit to manage your stress.

Cortisol also suppresses inflammation. Cortisol can boost your immunity by limiting inflammation in short spurts. However, if you have consistently high levels of cortisol, your body can get used to having too much cortisol in your blood, leading to the opposite, which is inflammation and a weakened immune system. And inflammation is the toot of most chronic illness such as autoimmune disorder, heart disease, diabetes etc.

Cortisol also helps regulate blood pressure; the exact way cortisol regulates blood pressure in humans is unclear. However, elevated levels of cortisol can cause high blood pressure, and lower than normal levels of cortisol can cause low blood pressure.

Cortisol can also raise your cholesterol. When cortisol and adrenaline are released, it raises your cholesterol level, specifically, the release of cortisol raises blood sugar levels, or the body's use as energy, as it locks away fat, so it is not used in this state as energy. Studies suggest that high levels of cortisol from long term stress can increase blood cholesterol, triglycerides, blood sugar and blood pressure.

Cortisol can also impact vision, when cortisol levels become dangerously high, it can reduce blood flow from the eyes to the brain, potentially leading to vison problems. Too much cortisol in your body can result in stress related macular degeneration.

Cortisol helps control the sleep wake cycle. Under regular circumstances, you have lower cortisol levels in the evening when you go to sleep and peak levels in the morning right before you wake up. High cortisol levels have been linked to insomnia, waking up during the night, and less sleep time overall. When cortisol levels are normal, the hormone helps us wake up in the morning and drift off at night.

Optimal levels of cortisol are necessary for life and maintaining several bodily functions. If you have consistently high or low cortisol levels, it can negatively impact your overall health. Both the hypothalamus and the pituitary gland are involved in hormone regulation. So, to have optimal levels of cortisol in your body, your hypothalamus, pituitary gland and adrenal glands must all be functioning properly.

In addition to chronic stress, other factors that impact cortisol levels in the body are: - taking large amounts of corticosteroid medications, such as prednisolone, tumours in the adrenal glands, neuroendocrine tumours in other parts of the body, such as your lungs. The symptoms of high cortisol depend on how elevated your cortisol levels are.

Common signs and symptoms of higher-than-normal cortisol levels include, rapid weight gain, especially in your face and abdomen. Fatty deposits between your shoulder blades. Wide, purple stretch marks on your abdomen. Muscle weakness in your upper arms and thighs. High blood sugar. High blood pressure. Excessive hair growth, in people assigned female at birth. Weak bones, skin changes, mood swings, anxiety, irritability, depression. Increase thirst and frequency of urination.

The adrenal fatigue theory suggests that prolonged exposure to stress will start with high levels cortisol, but as it progresses, it will drain the adrenals, leading to the opposite, which is low cortisol. Adrenal depletion will cause brain fog, low energy, depressive mood, salt and sweet cravings, light-headedness.

Chapter 15

Thyroid Imbalance

Ok, let's start with this statement.... Thyroid dysfunction is a consequence not a cause! Your thyroid hormone gets disrupted when you have an overburdened liver + insulin resistance + Stress. This leads to fatigue, weight gain, feeling cold, reduced concentration, puffy face, bloating, brain fog, infertility. As in every section in this book, it is about taking back control of your health and energy. The way to do this is to balance your hormones, detox your liver, and optimize your thyroid function.

So, the secret to getting your thyroid back on track and beating thyroid related problems such as hypothyroidism, hyperthyroidism, Hashimoto's etc, is the liver and how your body regulates glucose, insulin and cortisol. The blood test that all the doctors keep coming back to, TSH, is false, and it doesn't tell you the full picture of what is actually happening with your thyroid health.

There are many people with classic hypothyroid symptoms, that are simply not tested beyond the TSH test. The fact is that you can be suffering from a compromised thyroid even if your TSH keeps coming back normal. And even when people have been diagnosed with thyroid problem, most people on synthetic thyroid medication actually never even find relief from their symptoms until the detox their liver.

Hashimoto's Disease

Hashimoto's thyroiditis is an autoimmune disease of the thyroid, and it is the leading cause of hypothyroidism. When we have an autoimmune disease, the body produces auto antibodies, that attacks our own tissue. This happens because the immune system has been overactivated in some way.

Antibodies are proteins that guard against substances or antigens such as bacteria, fungi, viruses, and toxins that enter your body like foreign invaders. The problem is when you have an autoimmune disorder which attacks our own cells, you are then producing autoantibodies which attack our own cells, tissues and proteins. The reason for this is that your immune system does not distinguish between your own healthy tissue and potentially harmful antigens.

There are different autoantibodies which then result in different autoimmune diseases such as rheumatoid arthritis, lupus, multiple sclerosis, Crohn's disease, Celiac disease, fibromyalgia, and even skin disorders such as eczema, psoriasis are all autoimmune diseases.

In the case of Hashimoto's, the body attacks its own thyroid tissue, and the problem is standard lab tests may not reflect this tissue destruction for some time. The problem is TSH can take a long time to become elevated, even though underneath there is destruction of the thyroid gland, and that is why a lot of the symptoms someone is having is actually pointing to thyroid problems, but the tests say otherwise. It is so important to get a full thyroid lab panel done when you visit your doctor. You need to test for thyroid antibodies, as well as get a thyroid ultrasound.

Helpful lab tests to test for Hypothyroid problems include: -
- Free T3, Free T4, TPOab, TGab, TSH, reverse T3, reverse T4.
- Vitamin D, Ferritin, Iron, B12
- Estrogen, progesterone, DHEA, Prolactin,

Another problem is that thyroid antibody levels fluctuate so you might need to get tested periodically for a more accurate picture. Elevated thyroid antibodies are a sign of an autoimmune disease. Once you have one autoimmune disease, you are susceptible to developing others. When you have Hashimoto's, you must address the underlying autoimmune component and not just the thyroid.

- There are many symptoms of Hashimoto's disease, and they include heat and cold intolerance, unexplained weight gain, dry skin, constipation, leaky gut, general inflammation, brain fog, thinning hair, low blood pressure, infertility, miscarriages, PCOS, histamine imbalance, gluten insensitivity, fatigue, Vitamin D deficiency, skin problems, anxiety, backache, insomnia and much more.

The problem is that the symptoms keep coming back with diagnosis of depression etc because the tests come back as normal, and this is wrong. So, there needs to be more in-depth testing.

When you have compromised thyroid function, a complex and system wide reaction occurs, and things in your body start to happen such as slowing down of functions, such as digestion, energy production is low, fatigue, and liver detoxification can slow causing rapid weight gain and insulin issues. The adrenal glands then become compromised because the cortisol production becomes elevated to compensate lower thyroid function.

It then can spiral into things like food allergies, joint pain, skin problems such as hives and rashes. Nutrient deficiencies them become more and more which further exacerbate the symptoms.

There can be many factors that cause Hashimoto's/ / thyroid problems and some are listed below.

- Extreme stress such as bereavement, work problems, family life, money problems
- Heavy metal toxicity such as dental fillings, lead/aluminium at home
- Exposure to endocrine disruptors such as BPA's. Pesticides and fluoride.
- Breast implants
- Pregnancy
- Gluten sensitivity
- Vitamin D and nutrient deficiency
- Overuse of antibiotics and other drugs
- Latent viruses in your system such as Epstein Barr, Lyme disease,

- Intestinal permeability
- Genetic disposition

No pill or drug is going to cure autoimmune disease, it might mask symptoms, but they won't cure it. What can help is a combination of diet, lifestyle, and clearing out the waste and toxins in the body and detoxing can let you regain control of your health and take your life back.

Conventional medical treatment for hypothyroidism is usually a synthetic T4 drug. T4 is the inactive form of the thyroid hormone. Your body must convert it to T3 Which is the active form of thyroid hormone, for you to feel better. However, up to 80% of T4 gets converted in the liver, and up to 20% gets converted in a healthy gut.

Many people do not find relief in conventional standard treatment because Hashimoto's is the leading cause of hypothyroidism, and when you have Hashimoto's both the liver and gut are already compromised, making it, which makes it virtually impossible for your body to convert these synthetic T4 drugs to the active and usable T3 form. To add to this, some of the synthetic thyroid T4 hormone drugs also contain fillers that can irritate the system even more.

This is why diet and lifestyle changes can help you condition more and your underlying autoimmune condition as well as helping you improve thyroid function naturally.

What you do need to do is eliminate inflammatory foods, and evaluating the right supplements, and weaving in tools such as deep breathing, stress management and hypnosis. It really is up to you and whether you are prepared to make those lifestyle changes that can help you regain your life and health. How important is your health to you?

As we have discussed in a previous chapter, 70 to 80% of our immune system lies in our gut, but focused gut healing comes after we have set up our bodies to be able to heal. There is no point taking a prebiotic if you are still eating inflammatory foods or highly stressed or not sleeping well.

Lab tests
- free T4: - free T4 measures a level of the main thyroid hormone that circulates in the blood (thyroxine) which is not bound to proteins. It is able to enter and affect the body's tissues. Optimal free T4 should fall in the upper half of the lab range. Remember T4 must be converted to T3 in the body, which is the active and usable form of thyroid hormone. The thyroid only produces roughly 20% of T3. The rest converts via various ways, one is by the liver.
- Free T3: - Free T3 measures a level of thyroid hormone (aka triiodothyronine) that is not bound to proteins. It is able to enter and affect the body's tissues. T3 controls how your body stores and uses energy |along with other functions. This more accurately shows how the thyroid is functioning. This should fall in the upper quartile of the lab range.
- TSH (Thyroid stimulating hormone):- this measures how much of the stimulating hormone is in our blood, and many endocrinologists will say a TSH between o.4 and 4.0 mu/L is normal, but most people feel optimal when TSH is below 2.5 TSH is not an indicator of the tissue bioavailability of active T3, so basically a normal TSH can still mean that a patient feels sluggish and with hypothyroid symptoms.
- Reverse T3 or RT3 this is an inactive thyroid hormone. There is a percentage of T4 which also converts into Reverse T3, which is the inactive form of T3. What it actually does is it competes with T3 at a cellular level and is considered a natural buffer against thyroid overactivity. The problem is when RT3 production increases relative to T3 levels, thus may cause a problem and produce hypo like symptoms. It is normal to produce RT3, but it should be in a healthy ratio to T3. RT3 over production can happen when stress levels are high, or if there is poor regulation of sugar or insulin resistance or nutritional deficiency.

Here is a quote from the American Thyroid Association *"the immune system of the body normally protects us from foreign invaders such as bacteria and viruses by destroying these invaders with substances called antibodies, produced by blood cells known as lymphocytes. In many patients with hypothyroidism and hyperthyroidism, lymphocytes react against the thyroid (thyroid autoimmunity) and make antibodies against the thyroid cell proteins. Two common antibodies are thyroid peroxidase antibody and thyroglobulin antibody. Measuring levels of thyroid antibodies may help diagnose the cause of the thyroid problem. For example, positive and anti-thyroid peroxidase and pr anti-thyroglobulin antibodies in a patient with hypothyroidism results in a diagnosis of Hashimoto's thyroiditis"*

So, there are two more tests that are crucial to finding out if you have a problem with your thyroid glands.
- TPOab (Thyroid Peroxidase antibody): - should be within the lab range. 0 is best
- TGab (thyroglobulin antibody):- should be within the lab range
- Remember that lab levels can fluctuate in pregnancy and should be checked regularly.

It is important to also get a thyroid ultrasound, and also other tests include estradial, testosterone, prolactin, DHEA, Vitamin B12, Vitamin D, and Iron.

<u>SIBO (Small intestinal bacterial overgrowth</u>

SIBO is a disorder that causes bowel irritations and also intolerance to carbohydrates. The symptoms for SIBO can include bloating, abdominal pain, diarrhoea, abdominal distention, fatigue and constipation. To determine whether you may have this, you can go to your doctor or even find them online, and this is a SIBO breath test (hydrogen Methane breath test) which is a simple non-invasive test, which evaluates your digestion of particular sugars by measuring the gas you exhale, and then you are given a sugar testing solution to consume and will repeat breath samples at intervals. SIBO untreated over time can lead to leaky gut syndrome and autoimmune issues.

SIBO happens when the bacterium from the colon gets misappropriated into the small intestine and the bacteria multiplies and then there is major overgrowth. If SIBO is left untreated, various nutritional deficiencies can occur. What basically happens with SIBO is that the bacteria which should be there eats your food before you do and releases gas as a result. This causes gas and bloating in your belly.

SIBO may need to be dealt with through a protocol called FODMAP diet, which is an elimination of foods for a period of time that contain certain types of sugar that are fermented in your gut. If you do have SIBO you need to be careful before you start probiotics because probiotics may make the problem worse, because you are literally adding strains of bacteria to your small intestine with probiotics.

Food and your thyroids

Have you ever asked yourself why the foods we grew up with all of a suddenly off limits? Sometimes it is not the food alone which causes us to be ill. There could be several triggers, but one of the major reasons is that food in our modern world is NOT made the way it used to be. Many things go into many of the foods we eat nowadays, include fillers, chemicals, hormones, artificial colours and dyes, pesticides, and preservatives to name but a few pollute our food system.

FACT: - Most food which is produced in factories is NOT really food. They are food-like substances made from the mulch of modified corn and soybean that contain NO vitamins or Minerals, even if the package says they are fortified with iron, B12, folic acid, magnesium. Your body DOES NOT process these added synthetic vitamins in the same way it would if it was getting them from real food sources or a high-quality supplement. What is also important to understand is that supplements don't work if we have a poor diet because supplements require two things to actually work, Cofactors and Enzymes, which are only found in real, nutrient dense, whole foods.

When you eat a whole bag of crisps (potato chips), crackers or a few cookies, you will still feel hungry, because your body knows it has acquired ZERO nutrients eating them, and it is still searching nutrient dense food which is required for healthy cell and brain function.

The more worrying problem to this is that the corn, potato, soybean mulch which they use to make the highly processed foods cause highly inflammatory responses in the body, and not only that the body then releases hormones that only make us hungrier.

Even the fruits and vegetables that we are growing are being grown in depleted soils, many of which no longer contain anywhere near the amounts of minerals and nutrients that they once did. Added to this, many fruits and vegetables are sprayed with known CARCINOGENIC (yes cancer forming) insecticides, including glyphosate, which has been scientifically shown to cause cancer, disrupt our thyroid function, but also decimate the gut microbiome.

If you want to keep getting sicker, and your body turning more into a dis-eased state, then keep eating the processed foods, the fast food, the takeaways, but if you want to regain your health, it's time to start looking at what you eat, and eat more nutrient dense, organic, whole foods. You should be eating fibre from colourful vegetables, protein, and good fat, and remove all processed foods, unstable oils, and refined carbohydrates,

We are told as we grow up that fat is bad, this is false, as we need fat to function, and it is good for our brain health, as our brain is made up mostly of fat. Fat fills us up, and very importantly, it does NOT cause insulin and glucose spikes like simple carbohydrates do.

Did you know that eating fat can keep us feeling full for up to 4 hours, whereas consuming carbohydrates can make us hungry again in as little as 45 minutes. When you think about fat, think about avocados, olive oil, whole olives, coconut, walnuts, ghee, grass fed butter, etc

You do need to eliminate the PUFA oils such as canola oil, corn oil, soybean oil, sunflower oil, safflower oil, and vegetable oils as they are not good fat, they clog up your liver, then burden the liver and cause cellular damage. The fact is that putting good fat on your plate instead of pasta or a pile of white rice can be a game changer.

There is also a problem with the containers or packaged foods that state low fat on the side of them, as they are far from low fat. The fat that they say is removed, is replaced with sugar to make it taste better. Sugar turns into fat when it is not burned off, and then this sugar causes lots of hormonal responses which make us hungrier and ultimately lead to issues such insulin intolerance.

Protein

Protein is essential in our diet as it contains collagen that has amino acids, which are the building blocks for a healthy gut. In a nutshell, collagen is the glue that holds your body together, including your muscles, skin, tendons, bones and the lining of your digestive system. Collagen contains the amino acids that are needed to rebuild and repair the tissue in your digestive system. It also helps tight junctions remain tight in your gut, so that nutrients and water can get in, but also so that the toxic particles stay out. Another important use collagen has is to promote water absorption within the intestines, which helps us with bowel movements.

We get collagen into our bodies from bone broth, gelatine, pork skin, salmon skin, chicken skin, and non-muscle meats such as tendon, oxtail, knuckle, organ meat and egg yolks. If you are vegan, certain fruits and vegetables can also increase collagen production in the body especially berries. You can also get collagen supplements such as hydrolysed collagen or collagen peptides. There are many other good forms of protein for the body and gut including free range poultry, wild caught fish, and grass- fed meats, and they all contain omega 3 fats, which are anti-inflammatory.

There is a problem when we eat too much protein, and that is why the so-called carnivore diet, or caveman diet is not sustainable long-term. There is a reason for this. Excess protein that is not digested, can make its way to the colon, where it can ferment, and this can be there for a long time, and fermenting protein produces ammonia that is BAD for gut health. Another problem that occurs from this is that it also rapidly changes the species of bacteria in the gut from good to bad, stimulating the growth of dangerous pathogenic species in our gut, which then produces even more ammonia which then inflames the bowel and then damages the lining of the gut. There are some pro-inflammatory amino acids which are contained in meat that can turn on our cancer pathways when in abundance, and this is why you can link cancers such as colon cancer etc to meat.

Vegetables and plant foods

Plant foods and vegetables are your greatest source of prebiotic foods, and these help to feed probiotics in your gut. Prebiotics are specialised plant fibres that act as food for the good bacteria in your gut. They help to stimulate growth amongst all the good bacteria in your gut. The probiotics such as Kimchi, kombucha, kefir, sauerkraut, contain the live specimens of good bacteria. So, the fibre from plant-based foods are essential for good gut health and your overall health. The different vegetables you eat feed different microbes via something called phytonutrients and polyphenols.

So, what does a healthy plate look like? fifty percent of your plate should be non-starchy colourful vegetables, 20% good fat, 20% grass fed protein, and no more than 10-15% complex starch vegetables.

Supplements

- Vitamin D3: - This is a hormone, and this may help reduce the risk of obesity, depression and certain types of cancer. It also helps slow the progression of autoimmune diseases such as Multiple Sclerosis. It strengthens your immunity, and as there are so many people being diagnosed with autoimmune diseases, it is no surprise that learn this is due in many cases to a deficiency in Vitamin D.

Vitamin D is especially helpful for people with hypothyroidism and autoimmune diseases. Vitamin D can be acquired in two ways, by the sun of course, and through diet. If you are taking supplements you should start with 8,000 to 10,000 IU of Vitamin D daily.

- Vitamin B Complex: - This should include B1, B2, B3, B6, B9 and B12, and this can make a huge difference to your energy levels, mental function, depression levels. Vitamin B12 supports nerve function and also healthy blood cells. Mental illness and other neurological disorders can be caused by a serious lack of B12. Vitamin B6 is essential for metabolism of protein and is also involved in different enzymatic reactions throughout your body. The Vitamin B1 which is thiamine is a deficiency which obviously affects Hashimoto's and people with thyroid issues such as hypothyroidism. A lot of women with hypothyroidism are carbohydrate intolerant, which means that their glucose spikes very high, even after having a little portion of carbohydrates, or they will experience rapid weight gain after eating carbohydrates. The B Vitamins can help with metabolism of carbohydrates. The Vitamin B9 is folate. B9 should NOT be consumed as folic acid, you need to be taking it as folate, and the methylated forms of B vitamins so that your body can process them.
- Selenium: - the thyroid has the highest concentrate of selenium in the body, and it has been shown that selenium can reduce thyroid anti-bodes, and it also assists the conversion of T4 to T3. Selenium is crucial, as it also reduces inflammation in the body, and it does that by influencing glutathione levels and helping with thyroid inflammation.
- Digestive enzymes: - so many people with thyroid disorders and hypothyroidism, lack digestive enzymes, and lack sufficient stomach acid in order to break down food properly. The thyroid gland can have massive influence on the Gastro-intestinal system and also digestive symptoms of a slow underactive thyroid can manifest as low stomach acid, acid reflux, constipation, anaemia, poor nutrient absorption, bacterial overgrowth. The symptoms of poor digestion include fatigue, food sensitivities, hair loss. What you want is digestive enzymes containing pepsin, bromelain and protease
- Magnesium is essential for over 300 critical functions in your body. It helps with so many things such as stomach regularity, mood disorders, muscle relaxation etc, and plays a

vital role in things such as metabolism, replication of DNA, protein synthesis etc. Magnesium citrate can help with constipation, insomnia, and anxiety levels. Magnesium Glycinate is good for working alongside neurotransmitters to promote calm, better sleep and inflammation. Magnesium chloride helps with detox of cells and kidney function,

The liver
Improving your liver health is one of the most important tools for women and men, and thyroid function. The liver is so critical to our well-being and the overall everyday functioning of our body. It is the largest solid organ in the body. The function of the liver is to remove toxins from the body's blood supply, maintain healthy blood sugar levels, it metabolises fats, and performs hundreds more vital functions such as creating essential nutrients and helping convert inactive thyroid hormone into its active and usable form. Up to 80% good liver function is essential for good health. Many people who suffer from thyroid problems and thyroid disease suffer from an impaired detox pathway in the liver. When this happens, the liver can become clogged up and become prone to non-alcoholic fatty liver disease.

The main reason for non-alcoholic fatty liver disease is NOT too much fat consumption, but because of too many sugars and carbohydrates. The reason is that too much sugar signals for the liver to produce more fat.

Sometimes when a person has a clogged liver, they can experience reactions to benign supplements because the liver can longer metabolise them and becomes overburdened. When a liver is impaired, it does not allow the body to detox estrogen or chemicals that we are exposed to in our everyday environment, and then even the Vitamin D synthesis gets compromised, and many other things. The root causes for autoimmune thyroid diseases are excess estrogen, and exposure to chemicals and pesticides. Excess estrogen in your system is kinked to even more scary consequences. Our liver governs cholesterol levels, weight and our hormonal balance. There are several symptoms of liver imbalance, and they include headaches, hot flashes, PMS, fibroids, impatience, hip pain, irritability, anger, thyroid issues, and feeling restless.

When you do a liver detox, you do this slowly, and this is done by incorporating the right herbs and supplements, eating the right foods that help liver function, and removing harsh chemicals and toxins including alcohol as much as possible from our daily lives. Letting go of your negative emotions from the past and letting go of stress can dramatically help liver function and detox.

Balancing your hormones

Many people with hypothyroidism will have to deal with insulin regulation issues or full-blown diabetes. Blood sugar and thyroid function are closely related together, and how the body regulates and uses glucose determines how well our body will use the thyroid hormones and vice versa.

As you will probably already know, sugar is stored as glycogen in the liver. Glycogen is used as an energy source by your body when blood sugar drops. Blood sugar drops in between meals or at night when we sleep. When you have hypothyroidism, your liver loses its ability to produce glycogen, as a result you are not balancing your blood sugar the healthy way, which is via the liver.

What happens next is that your body produces stress hormones like adrenaline because this hormone and other stress hormones break down healthy muscle tissue into sugar. This happens because your brain needs sugar to function. Stress hormones inhibit thyroid function by blocking your liver from converting thyroid hormone from T4 into the active T3 form. The problem is exacerbated with the stress hormones increase the production of reverse T3 which is a hormone that inhibits the conversion of inactive thyroid hormone to its active form.

This compounds again as you have increased stress hormones from your liver that is not doing what it is supposed to do, from the stress itself, and from what you are eating, and then to add to this your cortisol levels get elevated which means you don't sleep. Excess weight inhibits blood sugar regulation, one way is excess weight does not allow for our cells to use sugar effectively as glucose entry and usage is hindered by the surrounding fat around the cell. Glycogen can also play an important role for the detoxification of estrogen which can be thyroid suppressive when in excess. This is why hypothyroidism sufferers can't detoxify estrogen. Excess estrogen can build up in your tissue and can further suppress your thyroid function,

When we have an impaired liver, we are not able to detox everyday things we are supposed to in our environment. When we talk about alcohol, you need to understand alcohol is a toxin. The more we drink, the more our liver goes into overdrive to clear out those toxins. When you drink alcohol, your body is unable to burn fat for 24 to 48 hours. Another area which exposes your liver is through toxic chemicals which we come into contact daily. This could come from dyes on our food, pesticides, Parabens, chemicals, Mold, fluoride, and these toxins are going through the largest organ in our body, the skin, and the liver must detox these toxins, and this overloads the liver and puts the liver under so much pressure.

You also need to think about limiting your exposure to plastic and stop storing in plastic containers. These are toxic. Change your fluoride toothpastes and soaps full of chemicals, to natural toothpastes and soaps. All the chemical listed on your shampoos, make-up, suncreams, conditioners, toothpaste are toxic and put your liver and your body under pressure and contribute to the symptoms and dis-eases you start to develop.

It is important to also think about eating foods that are going to help your liver, such as fresh ginger, cruciferous vegetables, lemon water in the morning, apples, parsley, Cilantro etc.

There are also many herbs that are amazing for detoxing your liver including Milk Thistle, Dandelion Root and aloe vera.

<u>Simple program to help heal your thyroids</u>

First of all, I want to point out how important breathwork is on your journey. Both meditation and breathwork can help relax your body, help you sleep better, it can help with digestion, calmness and balancing hormones. So, let's look at a sample 4-week program of elimination and healing

Week 1
- Order supplements: - Vitamin B complex, magnesium, Vitamin D, selenium
- Incorporate things like Himalayan salt, Warm lemon water drink first thing in morning when you wake up, think about your meal plan and nourishing meals
- Eliminate the following from your diet: -
1. Gluten: - cereals, breads, pasta, bagels, orzo, barley, rye, ramen, breadcrumbs, wheat products
2. PUFA oils: - canola, corn, safflower, sunflower, vegetable, seed oils
3. Alcohol;- all wine, beer, spirits etc

Week 2
- Order digestive enzymes, and continue with Vitamin B complex, Magnesium, Vitamin D, selenium
- Continue with Himalayan Salt, nourishing meals, hot lemon water
- Eliminate the following this week to add to elimination foods from last week
1. Dairy: - cheese, yoghurt, butter, ghee, milk, ice cream, kefir,
2. Soy: - soy sauce, tofu, miso, imitation meat, energy bars, cookies,
3. Nuts: - almonds, walnuts, hazelnuts, peanuts

Use lentils, sweet potato to help with gluten elimination

Week 3
- Continue with all supplements
- Start with positive affirmations, positive neural pathways, breathwork,
- Add the following items to the elimination list
1. Coffee (limit to 1 cup per day with food before 12pm)
2. Corn: - fructose corn syrup, popcorn, tortilla chips, wraps, packaged foods

Week 4
- Continue with all the supplements
- Add this list to the other eliminations
1. Grains: - rice, wheat, barley, pasta, quinoa,
2. Legumes: - kidney beans, chickpeas, beans, lentils etc
3. Nightshades: - tomatoes, white potatoes, eggplant, cayenne pepper, goji berries, pimentos, black pepper, gooseberry

What you have done over the last 4 weeks is that you have removed inflammatory foods and oils from your diet, and replaced them with colourful vegetable, fruit, and protein, and good fats. Continue with this until you feel a marked improvement in how you feel, and yes eventually you may be able to incorporate certain foods back in even if this is on odd occasions or as treat. But remember, if you want to rebalance your hormones, and get your life back without dis-ease, then you need to keep away from sugars, and all the other foods mentioned throughout this chapter. Look after your body, treat it right, and you will find other parts of your health returning back to normal in no time.

Chapter 16

The Immune System and Inflammation

It is very unlikely that you woke up one morning and there you are, inflammation in your body. It is very likely that it has been a slow build up over many years. Everything you are exposed to from one end of your life to the other, and every stress you go through, every bit of food you eat, they all contribute to your state of health and wellness. There is a word for this and it is called exposome.

"The measure of all the exposures of an individual in a lifetime and how those exposures relate to health. It's an individual's exposures from beginning of life to the end and includes all insults from environmental and occupational sources"

Every single thing from how long you hold your mobile phone beside your head, to the soil your food is grown in, to how much stress you deal with alters your exposome, which alters your position on the spectrum of health.

People are different to each other, as to how certain things affect them, but let's say doesn't affect someone in the same family the same way. This is called your epigenetic characteristic. Your epigenetic characteristics are basically your genetic constitution.

"Epigenetic characteristics is basically your genetic constitution. These characteristics are written into your genes, they are part of what makes you...you" or are they? As we discuss in epigenetics.

So, what this means above is that maybe you don't produce enough of a certain type of enzyme or perhaps you store metabolic byproducts, or maybe you can't metabolise caffeine efficiently. These characteristics are written into your genes.

This is the reason most diets fail, because they don't take into consideration each person's unique constitution.

"This concept of epigenetics and exposome work together to create bio-individuality"

Whenever we are exposed to an environmental trigger which are different for everyone and are determined by our genetics and our epigenetics as well as our exposome, your immune system is activated to protect us from what it sees as danger. Allergens and antigens are the two terms used for these dangers. This is happening all the time in your body, but if there is enough of a trigger, you might start to notice some symptoms such as bloating, headaches or brain fog, stuffy nose etc, and this is a sign that your immune system is doing what it should be doing. If your system is being exposed more regularly or by increasing amounts of these environmental triggers eventually will step itself up further. And this is when the adaptive immune system kicks in, and this is where things can start to go bad.

when you get inflammation, this causes damage at both molecular and cellular level, and when enough cells get damaged then we start to see tissue damage. When enough tissue has been damaged, then the organs start to get damaged, and eventually we start to see symptoms/ so this is where the problem comes in, as it is quite further down the line when damage has been done, that we start to see symptoms. Symptoms are sign that your body is already overwhelmed.

Your immune system can deal with toxins, bacteria, viruses, poisons, and it does this 24 hours a day 7 days a week, and we don/t notice this. To break down this further, there are two main parts of your immune system. The Innate immune system that is also called the non-specific immunity, and the adaptive immune system, which is also called specific immunity.

The job of the innate immune system is to stop any intruders from entering the body, and of they do get past this system, aspects of the innate immune system neutralise the intruder. There are 3 different lines of defence within the innate immune system, the first one is the physical barrier, i.e. the skin, and the mucous lining of our stomach. The second barrier is the chemical barriers such as stomach acid or the microbiome. The third line of defence of our innate immune system is inflammation. So, luckily your skin forms a barrier that prevents most invaders from entering the system, the mucous membranes hold onto any invaders that made it past there into respiratory tract or your stomach acid and your gut bacteria prevent any of this bacterium entering the digestive system/ if these defences fail then that is when inflammation happens.

When an invader or antigen enters the body, a type of cell called a mast cell releases histamine. Histamine is the first step in the inflammatory process, and it is largely responsible for first signs of inflammation, the swelling, pain, redness, heat when the histamine is released. When it is released, it tells a white blood, which is called a phagocyte, to come to the area and eat the invader. After this process it releases something called a cytokine, which is a chemical messenger, which send an alarm where other types of white cells come to area and help deal with invader.

The adaptive immune system has two different primary cells, and they are called B-Cells and T Cells. The T Cells have a few main functions, they cause an increase in inflammation, the activate macrophages, and they stimulate other T Cells into action. When the T Cells are exposed to bacteria, they then from effector and memory T Cells. The effector cells travel throughout the body, and their job is to destroy specific bacterium. The memory T Cells remember every single detail about this certain type of bacteria, which means that if you ever come across this kind of bacteria again, your body can produce an immediate effector T Cell. In this way the immune system responds much faster and more effective.

When a B Cell is exposed to bacteria it creates a special weaponised protein called an antibody. B Cells throw these antibodies out like a net, which then targets a specific invader, and then the antibodies latch on to the invader and prevent it from doing any harm.

Antioxidants & Free radicals

Inside every single cell in your body there are some organelles which are called mitochondria, The mitochondria are the powerhouse of the cell, and there are different numbers of mitochondria in different cells. In a liver cell there are between 1000-2000 mitochondria.

So these little powerhouses called mitochondria take oxygen and glucose and they produce energy in the form of ATP. This actually happens millions of times per second throughout the entire body as each mitochondria does its work, it produces exhaust, and this is a type of oxygen molecule, but not the type that can be used in the body. It is called a free radical. When a molecule is stable it has all its molecules, the problem with a free radical is that it is missing an electron, and what it does is wander around your body looking for an electron so it can take from another molecule. When it takes this electron from a different molecule, then that molecule is then a free radical of its own, and then this does the same thing.

The problem with this process if it left alone, is that eventually it will lead to cellular damage, and this is what causes inflammation. This type of damage is called oxidate stress.

Antioxidants is fix for this, as it has an electron to give away. Our bodies are incredible and made in such a way that we produce antioxidants at almost the same rate as we produce free radicals. Well, it did. The problem is that we are exposing ourselves all the time to more and more free radicals, such as chemicals, antigens, junk foods, processed foods, radiation, then our body can't keep up with the production of free radicals, and more and more oxidative damage is done.

The main causes of free radical production are things like cellular respiration, inflammation, chemicals and medicines, radiation like UV light and X-Rays, build-up of copper and iron, refined and processed foods.

When the liver has to work overtime to process the junk we put in our body, it eventually produces more free radicals than it can manage and the inflammatory process begins, now the oxidative damage causes inflammation, and it is also the result of inflammation.

While your body can deal with certain amounts of free radical formations, there is a point where it cannot keep up. Now can you see where dis-ease and the break-down of your body begins, and you start forming cancer cells etc? This is why we should be eating antioxidant food to sway the odds in our favour.

The immune system

In modern society, our modern lifestyles throw a lot more at our immune system than it has evolved to handle. There are thousands of chemicals daily which affect us, genetically modified foods, herbicides, pesticides, superbugs, heavy metals, and we also live lives with far more stress than we are able to cope with at times. Our bodies see's all of these above as foreign invaders, and something it has to respond to. All of them trigger the immune system into a state of action and an increased level of antibodies. Ever wondered why cancer, diabetes, autoimmune diseases, neurological disorders, and so many other conditions have got so out of control in the modern world|?

When the body is under this amount of pressure, all of this leads to inflammation, and inflammation leads to antibodies. As this gets more out of control, sometimes we get these nagging symptoms that we just pass off normal, or simple part of ageing, and then end up in a state of sub-healthy where you go to doctors, the tests come back normal, but you feel off and something isn't quite right. As this process continues, and the body keeps becoming overwhelmed and we keep allowing the free radicals, and the junk food, and mistakes to keep adding up, eventually the immune system starts to attack itself, and this is called an autoimmune condition.

Allergies, sensitivity and intolerance

An allergy is an immune response that is determined by our genetics. An intolerance is not mediated by your immune system, but often due to a lack of certain digestive enzymes. Food sensitivities are immune mediated, but there are a different set of antibodies involved in sensitivities than in allergies. A food sensitivity involves an IgA and an IgG antibody, and the problem with this is because when you go to the doctor for an allergy test, they only look for IgE reactions, so if you have an allergy to say peanuts you will have elevated levels of IgE antibodies.

But, if you have an immune response and symptoms that are due to other forms of antibodies such as like skin issues, body aches or runny nose, you may well be told there is nothing wrong with you, and the problem is that there are 5 different types of antibodies, and IgE is only one type of the antibodies. When you develop sensitivity to foods you produce IgA or IgG antibodies which still cause systemic inflammation. If you expose yourself to what you are sensitive on a regular basis, you will have chronically elevated levels of antibodies in your system. We don't always feel the symptoms of increased level of antibodies, but they are without a doubt doing damage.

Genetics

While Genetics can be part of development of disease, your genes can be turned on and off. This is called epigenetics as we have discussed. Genes themselves are rarely the cause of disease itself, your genes may say that gluten is bad for you, but it is not the gene that is the problem, it is the environment that the gene is in. Which means the gene is there, but it is harmless until the environment changes. Your genetics influence your health to a degree, and the possible potential for developing disease, but they are not your destiny. What you need to do is adjust your exposome, basically the environment your gene is in, so it really is in your hands. You are the master of your ship.

Exposome

"The exposome is the measure of all the exposures of an individual in a lifetime, and how those exposures relate to health. An individual's exposure begins before birth and includes insults, from environmental, and occupational sources"

While some factors of the exposome are unalterable such as during gestation or what has happened in your past, we can in fact adjust the exposome in the present.

"This is really important because it is the exposome that creates the environment that turns genes on or off (both healthful and harmful) as well as taxes our immune system"

There are quite a few things that affect us and our exposome. Sugar, wheat, dairy, bad fats, processed foods, gluten, dairy, and these are dietary factors that lead to significant amount of increased inflammation and activation of the immune system. All these foods are pro-inflammatory for everyone.

Sugar

Let's get this out there right away, too much sugar is bad for you, and certain types of sugar are bad for you. You need to try and eradicate from your diet the refined sugar, and the added sugar. Added sugar is found in so many things from ketchup, raisins, cereals, etc. Any sugar that has come from a refining process, creates the same response in your body, inflammation.

Refined sugar is one of the most addictive substances on the planet, and it does lots of things to our system that make us feel good. Once we exceed the amount of sugar in our bodies it starts to cause serious damage, and this starts in the early stages as insulin resistance and later type 2 diabetes, what happens is that the excessive sugar is absorbed into your body, and if there is already enough glucose to feed your metabolism, the excess sugar gets stored as fat, and eventually your cells won't be able to store any more sugars and that is when the body becomes resistant to insulin.

What this basically means is that you have glucose floating around your cardiovascular system, and this is when the damage really begins, as the glucose adds fuel to the fire of inflammation.

Did you know that sugar is an immuno-suppressant? Yes, added to the above, sugar suppresses certain aspects of your immune system which of course means you heal more slowly. Sugar is also the primary cause of tissue damage inside the cardio-vascular system.

Gluten

Gluten is a protein, and it is found in many different grains such as wheat, rye, barley, quinoa, rice and corn. Not all gluten is bad for you, it is only certain types of gluten that are bad for you. The type of gluten found in grains that compose of the vast majority of the Standard American Diet are the toxic type. Wheat and other grains make up to around 50% of all calories eaten worldwide. The problem is that we as humans do not possess the enzyme required to digest the type of gluten found in wheat, rye and barley. Research has shown at Harvard University has shown that gluten found in wheat products leads to leaky gut syndrome in 100% of humans,

the process of genetic modification has led to the increase of gluten in wheat. Remember this, no human can properly digest the gluten protein found in wheat, rye and barley.

Dairy

With dairy products we must be mindful of two ingredients, and these are casein and lactose. With lactose, your body simply does not produce the enzyme responsible for breaking lactose down. Casein is a protein found in dairy products, and it is a similar protein to the gluten protein. Milk that you buy in a store, has been through a refining process, where it is heated up to kill any bacteria, and homogenised to give it better texture. The heating up process denatures and destroys much of the healthy vitamins and enzymes found in milk, and the modernisation process breaks the fat molecules down into something your body just doesn't recognise as food.

The vast amount of dairy cows are now injected with hormones and antibiotics, and when we consume the dairy products from the cow's we consume the hormones and antibiotics. The issue with this is that it damages your healthy gut bacteria, your microbiome,

Fats

Fats are essential to hormone production, nervous system production, protection of organs, chemical messengers, energy production and manages inflammation.

Ther industrialised grain oils such as canola, corn oil, vegetable oil, sunflower oil, seed oils are all pro-inflammatory. They are highly processed, cooked at high temperatures and soaked in petroleum solvents to remove the oils. The are BAD for your body and your immune system. There are other things added to these oils such as colouring and chemical to make them smell better,

Fats and oils such as cod liver oil, olive oil, coconut oil, grass fed butter and ghee are all anti-inflammatory, and while they are not antioxidants, they have properties that help stop inappropriate inflammation. Processed foods cause problems due to chemical loading. When foods are refined, they are changed, and chemicals are added.

Dysbiosis

We have four distinct immune systems, we have one in the brain, one in the gut, one in the liver and one in the blood. The largest of those immune systems is in the gut, which constitutes about 70% of your entire immune system. There are many specialised immune cells in your digestive system, and they have different functions. There are B cells which produce antibodies, T Cells that fight invaders, and dendritic cells and white blood cells. The digestive tract has the highest vulnerability to foreign invaders alongside the respiratory tract. So, while the innate and adaptive immune systems do so much to protect us, they need help, and that comes from our microbiome.

Both the large and small intestines are populated with hundreds of species of trillions of bacteria, in fact we have 10 times more bacteria cells on our body than human cells. So, normally our cells in bacteria live in a state called symbiosis, they help each other thrive. The opposite to healthy is dysbiosis. This is when the bad bacteria look for new home, and this is normally in the micro villi in the intestine. When the bad bacteria start to populate the digestive system, it leads to all sorts of problems, and if you end up with more bad bacteria than good, this leads to dysbiosis. When you feed the good bacteria, the food they like, which is food high in polyphenols, like fruit and vegetables, they produce a chemical called butyric acid, and which helps keep the cells of your intestines healthy.

So, what leads to dysbiosis? The main culprits are antibiotics, poor diet and stress. When we expose ourselves to high levels of antibiotics, they kill off the good bacteria as well as the bad. Unfortunately, though, the bad bacteria tend to repopulate the gut much faster than good bacteria. A poor diet can lead to dysbiosis in different ways, the microbiome like to eat are vegetables, so if we feed them a wide range of vegetables, the reproduce and they are happy, if we starve them, they begin to die off and bad bacteria begin to take up residence.

Stress is one of the worst things you can expose yourself to. Your microbiome like a clean home, but when you have chronic stress, you have persistent activation of the Sympathetic Nervous System, and when this happens your digestive system stops functioning the way it should. When the digestive system isn't working optimally, then the microbiome becomes sub-optimal, and the good bacteria begin to die off.

Foods that cause inflammation

So, let's look at some of the foods that cause inflammation: -
- Dairy: - milk, eggs, cheese, yoghurt
- Sugar and artificial sweeteners
- Vegetable oils (soy, corn, sunflower, palm, safflower,
- Fried foods: - fried foods, fried chicken, French fries, chips,

- Refined white carbs: - bread, rice, pasta, cereals
- Highly processed foods: - if it is found in a box on a shelf, it's very likely processed
- Grain fed meats: - beef, chicken, pork
- Processed meats: - bacon, hot dogs, sausage, deli meat.

Foods that reduce inflammation
- Vegetables, fruits, greens, mushrooms,
- Beans and legumes
- Nuts: - walnuts, cashews, almonds etc
- Healthy oils: - olive, virgin olive oil, coconut oil
- Wild caught fish: - salmon, mackerel, oysters
- Grass fed meat
- Herbs and spices: - turmeric, ginger, cinnamon
- Nut milk: - almond milk, coconut milk

So, here is the question. If there was some sort of medication that would help you lose weight, feel better, improve your wellbeing, decrease your pain and increase your libido, and give you better mental clarity, would you take it? Well, there isn't any medication like that, but you can do all this above and doing this yourself. There are two steps to it. Maintaining a healthy diet and exercising regularly. We do this through small wins, and make sure consistency is key.

The fix

Giving up something we like is sometimes harder for us than getting something we like, such as our health back and feeling better within ourselves. So, during the phases of cutting things out to reduces inflammation and heal your immune system, you need to focus more on what you are getting instead of what you are losing. You will notice some improvements as we go along, and may notice some symptoms, but remember in the end you will feel so much better. So, here we go: -

Week 1: - remove gluten: - Gluten is harmful to your body and it is also incredibly addictive. Gluten is a type of exorphin. Gluten makes you feel good, and it's a chemical, but we put it into the system from the outside, and anything that taps into the feel-good receptors of your brain are highly addictive, and your body is going to crave more of it. You will need a supplement to help with this detox and Milk thistle is excellent to help with this. Another supplement is N-Acetylcysteine, is also great to support the detox pathway alongside Milk thistle.

- Wheat, wheat derivatives, rye, barley, pasta, couscous, noodles, ramen, soba, breads and pastries, croissants, pita, naan, bagels, flatbreads, doughnuts, pies, muffins, crackers, pretzels, cakes, cookies, brownies, cereals, granola.

Week 2: - remove Sugar: - after removing gluten, when you remove sugar, you have got rid of the last food source for those bad bacteria and yeast. You will need to eat more fibre, and fibre comes from vegetables. Avoid starchy vegetables such as potatoes, and we want more insoluble fibres. You may feel fatigue when you cut out sugar, but this won't last, and you will feel much better if you stick this out. Alcoholic beverages are pretty much just liquid sugar, and they don't offer any good health benefits.

- Agave syrup, all-natural sweetener, aspartame, beet sugar, brown sugar, cane sugar, caramel, concentrated fruit juice, confectioner's sugar, cornstarch, corn syrup, fructose, fruit juice concentrate, glucose, glycerine, granulated sugar, grape sugar, modified food starch, polysaccharides, saccharine, soy, Splenda, sucrose, white sugar,

Week 3: - Remove Dairy: - once you have removed gluten and sugars, you have really got rid of 90% of the problem. What we need to do though is make sure your body is able to recover and fully heal, we need to get rid of pro-inflammatory foods, so now we are going to get rid of dairy, don't worry you don't have to get rid of it forever, if you don't want. You can begin to re-introduce certain types of dairy into your diet later down the line. We also need to remove all forms of refined seed oils and replace them with high quality fresh pressed oils such as virgin oil.

- Butter, buttermilk, cake mixes, casein, cereals, cheese, chewing gum, cottage cheese, cream, curds, custard, gelato, ice cream, lactose, lactulose, margarine, milk (condensed, dry, evaporated, goat's milk, low fat), malted milk, nisin, nougat, pudding, salad dressing, sour cream, tagatose, whey, yoghurt.

Week 4 is about adding certain herbs and supplements which are going to help healing your body.

- Add: - Turmeric (curcumin) is anti-inflammatory, anti-bacterial, anti-fungal, and antioxidant
- Add: - black pepper (piperine) anti-inflammatory and increases absorption rate of curcumin.
- Add: - Green tea:-(L-theanine), it's good for the brain, and has positive effect on the cardiovascular system. Rich in antioxidants, also anti-inflammatory.
- Add: - Omega 3 oils: - anti-inflammatory. EPA and DPA are found in animal sources such as cold-water fish, salmon, sardines, herring, mackerel, anchovies. Also take an omega 3 supplement.
- add: - garlic: - packed full of vitamins and minerals, helps regulate blood pressure. it is anti-inflammatory, anti-bacterial.
- add: - Ginger: - anti-inflammatory
- Add: - Vitamin D: - 2,000-3000 IU daily.

WEEK 5: - Protein. Vegetables are the most important things to eat as well as fruit. But cooked animal proteins contain the highest quality proteins we can consume. A normal protein offers a complete range of proteins, but it also contains nutrients that are either absent or very difficult to extract from vegetables. Animal protein must be grass-fed or free range.

After week 5 you can start to reintroduce certain foods but remember you will be feeling great by this time, and don't reintroduce sugar, gluten, processed foods and junk food. Look after your body and keep it in that healthy state now.

Chapter 17

Functional medicine and precision health

Functional medicine looks at a body as kind of machinery with lots of cog wheels, when everything works well as a machine, all these cogwheels run smoothly, then everything works well. If something falls in there such as a pebble, or rust, then everything else starts to not work optimally anymore. Initially it might still work, but eventually it all comes to a halt. In functional medicine, we say what is that sludge, what has fallen in there, such as inflammation, gut microbiome, stress.

In functional medicine we look at mental health, metabolic health/weight, structural health, energy, digestive health, immune system, cardiovascular health, hormone health, brain health. And look at the things that may affect these cogs such as inflammation, nutrients and building blocks, purpose and community, stress response, genetics and epigenetics, food intolerance, inadequate autophagy and apoptosis, free radical damage, insulin sensitivity, mitochondria, gut microbiome and infections.

Most of our health trajectory comes down to something called epigenetics, meaning around our genes. We all have a certain set of genes from birth, but depending on our lifestyle, environment, pollution, nutrients, stress levels, all these different things decide which genes we turn on or off. Which is quite empowering, as we can make very educated choices to decide what genes to turn on and which to turn off. How to support these things. You can do a genetic test to discover if there are anything we are deficient in: - Precision health = lab testing + science backed tools.

What your body shape can reveal about your hormones and inner health status

There are three shapes: - apple shape, pear shape, rectangle or hourglass shape.

Hormones are basically messenger chemicals that go throughout the whole body, through the bloodstream. We have glands in the brain, thyroid, ovaries, The hormones are produced, and they are sent everywhere in the body. Wherever the boy has receptors it has an effect.

The apple shape / muffin top

This is where there is excess amount of belly fat, that just doesn't seem to budge. Sometimes people have skinny limbs and trying to do everything right but have excess amount of belly fat. Research shows that if someone has the apple shape an excess amount of belly fat, there are usually 3 main culprits for this.

1. Insulin resistance: - insulin helps to shuttle glucose into our cells for energy or storage. So, if we eat something with sugar or carbohydrates that turn into sugar, our body will then pump out insulin, so that the sugar goes into the cell, for energy use. Once we have had enough of that, and we don't need it anymore, and there is excess amount of sugar still there, it will put it away for storage.

2. Cortisol imbalance: - cortisol is our main stress hormone. Normally we have a spike of cortisol in the morning, which gets us going and out of bed, and should taper off throughout the day,

3. Inflammation: - our bodies and immune system produces inflammation when there is a virus, or bacteria, infection. The problem if it stays to long, and then will signal our brain for us to become more insulin resistant, and will create that belly fat and bloating around waistline

If there is insulin resistance, cortisol imbalance or inflammation, our brain will signal to the body to accumulate belly fat around the waistline, even if we are eating the same amounts of food, it will still basically send the wrong signals, it will think we need a layer of belly fat to support ourselves. It will redistribute fat from the lymph's to the abdominal and dorsa cervical (thoracic region).

Han-gry:- when you get like this, it means your blood sugar has dropped, and that usually comes after your blood sugar has had a spike. If we do this for too long, our cells stop responding to sugar and insulin and become insulin resistant. A problem with blood sugar spikes, is that if the blood sugar spikes too often, then something called advanced glycation end products happens. When we have a blood sugar spike, sugar is in our blood stream, and it attaches itself to our protein. Most of our body is made of protein, when sugar attaches itself to protein, and this makes us rust from the inside.

When sugar attaches itself to our protein, then it causes advanced glycation end products, causing rusting and wrinkles inside. It also damages immune system, joints, creates free radicals, feeds the wrong kind of gut microbiomes. When we have a lot of blood sugar spikes, and our body must constantly release insulin, at some point we become insulin resistant. If you are constantly having too much sugar, our cells at some point stop responding to insulin. They just say we are tired; you are constantly making us work, we don't want to respond to insulin signals anymore.

If we are insulin resistant, our brain will signal to the rest of the body to redistribute that weight to around the waistline and create what is called visceral abdominal fat. If that stays for a long time and it becomes excessive, it can contribute to something called metabolic syndrome.

Metabolic syndrome is associated with lots of ill health trajectories such as PCOS, cancers, cravings, binge eating, immune system, mood swings, ADHD, perimenopause symptoms, Alzheimer's disease, cardiovascular disease, glycation, wrinkling, rusting of cells

When there are Cortisol imbalances and stress hormone imbalances, that has been shown to contribute to metabolic syndrome, lowered immune resilience, other immune issues (PMS, fertility problems, sleep disturbances, lowered digestive health, worse perimenopause symptoms, frailty, brittle bones, weaker muscles, increased morbidity,

Where there is inflammation, this can cause metabolic syndrome, Alzheimer's, cardiovascular disease, anxiety, autoimmune conditions, cancers.

Pear shape
This is where there is a lot of weight around the butt and hips, is usually more protective from metabolic syndrome. If it is excessive, it can be a sign of estrogen dominance. If there is too much estrogen and not enough progesterone, then we are running into something called estrogen dominance, this can contribute to things like PMS, painful periods, shortened cycles, heavy periods, painful breasts, anxiety, endometriosis, cysts, difficulty conceiving, cancers.

Rectangle shape / potato shape
This Shape has more to do with thyroid issues. Thyroid issues often go hand in hand with apple shape as well. Thyroid issues can contribute to things like Hashimoto's, hair loss, cold intolerance, slowed metabolism, constipation, depression, cholesterol, fertility issues, insulin signalling, kidney and nerve disease.

Which type are you?
- Apple: - cortisol / Insulin
- Pear: - estrogen dominance
- Rectangle: - thyroid
- Hourglass: - balanced

The basics of a healthy diet – 4 cornerstones
1. Carb-cycling: - balance the blood sugar. Goal, a balance steady blood sugar, with periods of ketosis. Carbohydrates and fruits break down into sugars inside the body.
2. No snacking: - 3 or 3 proper meals. Snacking etc causes insulin spiking.
3. Protein: - supports metabolism, blood sugar steady, right building blocks to make serotonin and dopamine.
4. Become a Qualitarian. Colourful veg, protein, fats. No food after 7pm.

Insulin resistance

Insulin is one of our hormones that gets released when there is sugar in the bloodstream, and glucose. Our body releases insulin to take that sugar and put it into our cells to use for energy, and to do that job. The cells have the receptors, and the insulin goes into the receptors, so that the sugar can go into the cell.

If that happens excessively over years, and we are constantly having blood sugar spikes, and the body constantly must pump out insulin, then at some point those receptors stop responding. And then even though you might have high sugar in the bloodstream, the body will not allow the insulin to open the gateway for the glucose to enter the cell. It won't respond. Then you have more blood sugar in the bloodstream. There are also other factors leading to insulin resistance other than eating too many carbs and too much sugar and these are: -

Inflammation and oxidative stress, which is free radical damage, if that is happening, in our brain, it makes our body insulin resistant, even if we are eating good types of food, and right diet, if there is inflammation in the brain, the brain will signal to the cells not to respond to the insulin properly, so we become insulin resistant.

There are also other factors including subclinical hypothyroidism,

- lack of sleep: - lack of sleep has been linked to the cells in the body being more insulant resistant the next day.
- Lack of movement, makes the muscles less insulin sensitive,
- If there is stress, cortisol, makes our body more insulin resistant

Iinflammation

If we already have some white adipose tissue (belly fat) around the waistline, then that has become inflammatory itself. So, it is a cycle, and we need to break it, and address the belly fat, so that it doesn't start producing more inflammation. White fat is the fat we don't want; this is the inflammatory and kind of makes us sick. The brown fat which gets stimulated by cold showers, which is good for us, is anti-inflammatory.

NLRP3 inflammasome activation: -this is part of our immune system and if it is upregulated it makes us inflamed. One of the reasons for inflammation is something called Palmitic acid, and this is a substance that when we eat a lot of saturated fats and sugars, they will increase our bodies production of palmitic acid, and that has been shown to go straight to our brain and cause inflammation. This part of the brain is the hypothalamus, and this then signals to the cells to become insulin resistant, and store that fat around the waistline.

Another thing that causes inflammation is Omega 3 to 6 imbalance. They are both needed for building blocks, our membranes, brain, cells. They need to be a nice balance, if omega three is too low in comparison with omega six, then we become more prone to inflammation because omega three is important when there is inflammation to get rid of that inflammation. When there isn't enough omega three, we are more likely to be inflamed. Omega three is mostly found in seafood. Other causes are: -

- Free radical damage / oxidative stress: - there are many reasons for this, heavy metals (stored mercury, lead, arsenic, aluminium) through exposure over lifetime, pollution etc.
- Excess sugar consumption: - has been shown to increase inflammation in the brain, in the rest of the body, and this causes the insulin resistance, telling the body to store fat around the waistline.

Gut health

Our gut is where everything really starts. If we have the right kind of gut bacteria, the right kind of balance, then our gut lining stays healthy, can absorb the right nutrients, whole system functions well.

A lot of us don't have enough of the good bacteria in the gut anymore, allowing the bad bacteria to take over such as streptococcus, or candida, and if they take over, they make our gut lining more permeable, and what this does is that it allows food particles from healthy foods like almonds or avocados, they can then pass into the bloodstream, when they are bigger than the body is used to, and the immune system doesn't recognise it, and this is when the body develops food intolerances to otherwise healthy foods.

Cortisol and stress

Long term elevated cortisol has been linked to increased blood pressure, insomnia, anxiety, elevated blood sugar, lower levels of progesterone (fertility, PMS), immune system malfunction, lowered gut lining integrity, opposes thyroid hormone function and increase cholesterol levels, high levels of cortisol inhibit testosterone synthesis, more menopausal problems, redistribution of belly fat.

If we start to store weight around the waistline, the adipose tissues is then considered an endocrine organ, an hormone producing organ, and that then secretes more cortisol, it secretes inflammation in itself, and it has been shown to mess with our zinc levels in the blood. Zinc is important for insulin signalling, and also satiety, sex hormones, estrogen, testosterone, our immune system.

Once we have lower plasma zinc levels because we have too much cortisol and belly fat, then that lowers our insulin sensitivity, and that again then leads to layer, and accumulation of belly fat. And then it becomes a vicious cycle that we need to break.

Cortisol also changes our eating behaviour. If you are stressed out, research shows that it changes our eating behaviour, because when we are stressed out, that part of the brain that doesn't really think it's good for you, and its bad for you, doesn't get activated, and the brain switches over to the reptilian part of the brain, the back of the brain. When you are stressed out it becomes hard to make healthy choices. When we are in that reptilian brain, we are more prone to binge eating, bad food choices, fatty sugary foods, substance abuse.

Stress leads to loss of lean muscle, osteopenia, and wrinkles, hepatic gluconeogenesis, decreased glucose uptake and insulin sensitivity, protein degradation of muscle, bone, skin for amino acid substrate, oppose anabolic growth, thyroid, sex hormones.

If cortisol is too high, and stays elevated throughout the day for too long, and for a long time, then at some point that connection between the brain and the adrenal gland might not work as well anymore, and the brain might not send the right signals, or the adrenal gland might not respond as well anymore, and it might start to drop the cortisol in the morning, where we should have a spike to get motivated

If cortisol is low in the morning, it is very similar to if high later in the day, it has been shown to mess with estrogen, and this can lead to conditions such as cysts, MPS, endometriosis etc. if there is low cortisol in the morning it has been shown to link to immune system problems, such as autoimmune disease, cancers, allergies, because it messes with our immune cells. It has been linked to burnout, and increased risk of obesity and weight gain.

The cortisol paradox

If cortisol is high and insulin and leptin are low, then we have increased fat burning. If we are having a cortisol spike in the morning, when we are hopefully still fasted, then that helps us burn fat.

If cortisol is high, and insulin and leptin are both high at the same time, this leads to increased fat storage, especially around the midline. If you are chronically stressed mid-afternoon, had meals, insulin and leptin elevated because you have had food, and satiated, and body metabolising, but also increasing cortisol through having tons of coffee or stressful environment, that is when you start to store the fat around the midline.

If low morning cortisol, as seen in chronic fatigue, burnout, that then leads to fat storage and obesity.

High cortisol later in the day, increased fat storage, especially around the midline

Sleep

Sleep plays into the stress circle, but on its own it has its very important role as well. Sleep is important for memory consolidation, so if we don't have a good night sleep, then our memory from past day doesn't work that well

- Longer term, it has been shown that it can contribute to things like Alzheimer's, because what usually happens is that when we have a good, deep sleep, our brain can start to flush things out, and it only really works when we are in deep sleep. It can clear out toxins, amyloid plaques, as the lymphatic system comes through and sweeps it all out.
- if we have one-night bad sleep, then it is more likely the next day we will make bad choices and food choices, and more likely to eat bad things.
- Lack of sleep has also been shown to mess with our blood pressure, immune system, circadian rhythm, cortisol

Supporting a good circadian rhythm

- Morning: - support a rise in cortisol in the morning with bright light first thing in morning, high intensity exercise, cold showers, Vitamin C, Vitamin D, Omega 3s, coffee, tea
- After 2pm: - avoid cortisol increasing activities, stimulants past 2pm.

Support sleep

- Ain for 7.5-9 hours' sleep
- Move daily and exercise at least 5 times per week
- Relax before bed, crate a room for sleep, set a schedule.
- Reduce alcohol intake, keep blood sugar stable, avoid eating late at night, no coffee's late at night,

Alcohol

Alcohol can lead to insulin resistance. Alcohol can increase estrogen, if we have too much alcohol it can lead to a bad type of estrogen, that then damages our cells more, and there is a higher risk of estrogen related breast cancer, fibroids. Up to 7 units per week for women, and up to 14 units for men.

People in Greece Mediterranean, usually have glass of wine with meal maybe 1 unit per day which is much better for health. If you have lots of units in one go, the body becomes inflamed, research shows body will be inflamed for rest of week, and immune system will be messed up, your inflamed you will be storing weight around belly. Insulin resistance. If someone is healthy and don't have candida problem, stick to natural alcohol, red wine is drier and less sugar. Dry champagne. These don't usually spike blood sugar. Spirits, straight, are ok, vodka, tequila, whiskey,

Supplements
- Vitamin D: - Unless you live somewhere nice and sunny, where you have good exposure to sunshine all year round that's good, but if you are living in the UK, you will need vitamin D supplements. In winter. 5000IU a day. Even in summer if you are working in an office, or spending a lot of time inside, or there are weeks where it is raining, or if you put suncream all the time, then your body can't make enough Vitamin D.
- Magnesium at night: - 350mg. this will help you relax your muscles, help you to relax your brain if you are a little anxious, and never turn off.
- Multivitamins: - 3 x weekly before noon
- Vitamin C: - 1000mg 1-3 x daily. It helps our body get rid of free radical damage, helps the immune system make the right amount of white blood cells to kill of infection, to stay stable. It also helps our cortisol levels.
- Omega 3: - 1500-2000IU on days when not eating fish. Helps with inflammation.
- Glutathione: - our main antioxidant in the body, body can make itself, but occasionally depletion.
- Probiotics: - microbiome, bottle of good probiotics.
- Turmeric: - helps with inflammation
- medicinal mushrooms: - help with our immune system
- resveratrol: - free radical damage.
- ashwagandha: -stress levels.

- Others include: - collagen, B12, zinc, lysine, iodine, berberine. But test and don't need all time.

Chapter 18

Skin problems

When you have eczema on the outside, your gut is screaming for help on the inside. You need to address the root cause of the problem. The real cause of skin problems is inflammation from your diet in 90% of cases, and environmental in other 10%.

When you eat a trigger food, it releases a bunch of inflammatory chemicals like cytokines, histamines, prostaglandins and leukotrienes which are called mediators, and your immune system interprets this trigger food as an antigen or a foreign invader. In response it produces antibodies to fight off these antigens.

One of these antibodies is called immunoglobulin E, or IGE which is responsible for the allergic reaction you are seeing in your skin in the form of eczema.

Another source of inflammation comes from stress. When you are stressed from work or school or having eczema 24 hours a day, your sympathetic nervous system, which is your fight or flight response, is dominant, which means you are on survival mode all the time. Your stress signals your adrenal glands to produce more and more cortisol, which is causing you chronic inflammation in your body.

Now inflammation not only leads to eczema, but it is tied to pretty much every single medical condition that you can think of. One of the inflammatory chemicals called prostaglandins is directly linked to various cancers like breast, liver and lung cancer. Another chemical called leukotrienes causes all sorts of inflammatory diseases including asthma, arthritis, dermatitis, and pulmonary disease. Inflammatory cytokines are not only linked to eczema, but also many diseases such as osteoporosis, colitis, Alzheimer's and Parkinson's disease.

You are accumulating inflammation every time you eat a trigger food, and one of the symptoms is eczema.

Eczema drugs and creams

The most common drug is your typical steroid cream. They range in potency from class 1 which is super potent, to class 7 to class 7 which is the least potent. Many of these creams work by suppressing the inflammatory chemicals that are produced by your immune system overreacting to a trigger food that you ate. Your immune system thinks that the junk food you ate is an antigen, and it should do everything it can to fight it off.

Hydrocortisone is a steroid cream that adds a steroid hormone cortisol onto your skin, to suppress the overeating immune system. Over time this has negative side effects including thinning of the skin and losing its effectiveness the longer you use it. You are constantly adding cortisol to your skin and suppressing your immune system response.

Most of the time your gut is screaming for help and telling your immune system to overreact to fight off the junk food you keep putting in your mouth. when people finally realise the damage, they have done to their bodies and try to get off steroid creams, they experience something called topical steroid withdrawal, or red skin syndrome.

Nour skin has become so addicted to the extra cortisol and the suppressed immune system, it doesn't know what to do without it, so the skin turns bright red and starts burning and stinging.

Food is medicine

You need to take a mediator release test, which is one of the most comprehensive food sensitivity tests in the world. It tests 170 different foods and food chemicals. It is the only blood test In the world that measures the level of inflammatory chemicals released from white blood cells at the end of the digestion process. By measuring their volumetric change from solid to liquid molecules.

Inflammatory foods you should avoid
- Common inflammatory foods: - Dairy, wheat, sugar, gluten, gluten free grains, legumes, corn, soy, eggs, tomatoes, peppers, potatoes, eggplant, citrus, yeast
- Common toxic foods: - sugar, alcohol, caffeine, GMOs, artificial sweeteners, additives, preservatives, dyes, high fructose corn syrup, processed food, junk food, fast food, trans or hydrogenated fats. White carbs. Avoid food with pesticides.
- Your eczema is not skin problem, it is a gut problem.

Anti-inflammatory foods you should eat
- Rich source of sulforaphane: - cauliflower, brussels sprouts, kale, cabbage, broccoli, kohlrabi.
- Red foods: - apples, radish, grapefruit, cherries, melon, strawberries contain phytonutrients lycopene, ellagic acid, quercetin, hesperidin, anthocyanidins
- Purple foods: - berries, onions, blackberries, blueberries etc_ resveratrol, anthocyanidins, phenolics, flavonoids
- Green foods: - broccoli, brussels sprouts, cabbage, spinach, avocados- phytonutrients: - lutein, zeaxanthin, isoflavones, EGCG, indoles, sulforaphane
- White foods: - mushrooms, onions, garlic, cauliflower, nuts, EGCG, allicin, quercetin, indoles, glucosinolates
- Orange foods: - pineapple, peaches, bananas, mango, lemons, carrots: - alpha-carotene, beta-carotene, beta cryptoxanthin, hesperidin. Turmeric.

Apple cider vinegar
Apple cider vinegar has a PH of 2-3. It has anti-glycaemic properties that stabilise your blood sugar levels. Apple cider vinegar has been shown in studies to have anti-bacterial and antifungal properties because it inhibits the growth of harmful microorganisms like E Coli, and staph aureus, and candida based on different dilution levels. It also reduced the pro-inflammatory cytokines and increased the white blood cell potential to fight off these harmful bacteria which helps to boost your immune system.

More than 90% of eczema patients have Staph bacteria on their skin and the staph prevents you from healing.

Additionally, people with acne or eczema have higher PH levels on their skin most likely due to the products that they are using with harsh chemicals that increase the PH level on the skin to make it even more alkaline.

Most of the common cleansers you use are destroying your skin microbiome. You want to use products that are slightly acidic to kill off the staph bacteria that like to grow in higher PH environments which can be cause by you using cleansers, detergents, shampoos

Apple cider vinegar is also a great exfoliant as well because it contains alpha hydroxide acids AHAs, like lactic, malic, and citric acid that exfoliate the top layer of the skin and helps to remove dead skin cells and helps to reveal smoother skin underneath.

Supplements to add to your diet

Remember supplements should not replace real nutritious food. As you know eczema and skin conditions are mainly caused by inflammation in your body. The latest research shows that eating gluten, directly impacts the intestinal lining. This is through zonulin production. Zonulin is a protein that directly causes leaky gut. It is intestinal permeability. This means that the gut lining is damaged, which allows bacteria and toxins to enter the bloodstream, and cause inflammation which is the root cause of skin problems. When you have constant stress, which causes your adrenal glands to produce more cortisol, leading to chronic inflammation, and not getting enough fibre in. Fibre is needed for digestion, and he; move food through your intestinal tract. Without fibre, the junk food you are eating is tearing your gut lining.

Chapter 19

Menopause

There are different stages of midlife that women go through. Many women start perimenopause in their 30s, and this is the stage in life where things can start changing significantly. Some women start having hot flashes and night sweats, and many times these are subtle changes in in the body, that the person may not even be aware of, but is the body preparing to end the childbearing years.

Menopause is a time-period. You can lose your period when you are in perimenopause, for a couple of months at a time, and then it can come back, and lose it again. You can get two periods in one month, and this is basically what perimenopause is. With menopause, when you have reached month twelve of no period, then you go into menopause.

Did you know that you are actually menopausal for just 1 day? After that you are post menopause.

The symptoms for post menopause can last for many years. Everything can get out of control for women in menopause / post menopause as there are so many symptoms.

Symptoms
There are many symptoms which are connected to menopause, and women can experience many different symptoms, and not all women will experience things the same way, and in fact some women barely notice the changes while others have very difficult time going through menopause and post menopause. There are 34 main symptoms reported by most women.

- Physical symptoms: - breast tenderness, fatigue, dry skin, headaches, migraines, weight gain, water retention, hair loss, heart palpitations, hot flashes, joint pain, night sweats, period changes, sleep issues.
- Vaginal/sexual/urinary symptoms (genitourinary syndrome of menopause / GSM):- low libido, painful sex, urinary incontinence, urinary leaks, urinary tract infections, vaginal/vulva dryness, urinary frequency and urgency.
- Cognitive symptoms: - brain fog, inability to focus, inattentiveness, poor word retrieval, forgetfulness, impaired short-term memory.

You need to pay attention to your body, and address the things that can be addressed or managed by exercise, natural supplements, changes in your diet, sleep patterns, and seeking advice and talking to someone if you feel very low in mood and down,

There are a number of things you can do to relieve some symptoms of menopause, and here are just a few pointers: -

- consume more water - but cut off before 6pm so to reduce the need to disturb your sleep.
- Try and switch from coffee to herbal tea, or a caffeine-free coffee replacement, because this will reduce hot flashes and anxiety.
- Avoid all spicy foods, especially for dinner, as this is a sure-fire way to keep you awake.
- Begin an exercise routine, to keep your weight in check, as your hormones are stored in your fat instead of ovaries, and this fat tends to accumulate around the stomach for most women. This is the worst place for it to accumulate as it increases your risk for cardiovascular disease, type 2 diabetes and heart disease
- Wear 100% cotton or 100% linen PJs as these fabrics allows for breathability and less sweating at night.
- Eat regularly if you find your blood sugar is unstable. Complex carbohydrates and protein are your friends,
- Eat more phytoestrogens: - these are plant foods which will decrease vaginal atrophy, improve sleep and mental cognition, and positively affect bone health

- Love yourself: - stop comparing yourself, don't worry about others, allow yourself to make mistakes, remember your value, trust yourself, and be gentle with yourself.

Estrogen

There are three types of Estrogen in your body. There is E1, E2, and E3. Estrodial (E2) is the one that increases our risk of cancer. During menopause, a woman's ovaries stop producing estrogen. This is needed by the body, as it is part of the human makeup. The ovaries are mostly responsible for producing the estrogen. When they stop working the liver does produce a little estrogen as does the adrenal glands. Many of the hormones produced in the human body are produced by the Adrenal Glands on top of the kidneys. But our body is so smart it decides to make the good old fat cell the workhouse estrogen production, so that is why people gain weight all of a sudden. This is a biological function of the body that requires our body to produce the fat cells in order for us to have the estrogen that we need in our body. Unfortunately, sometimes our body gets carried away and produces a lot of fat cells. The key is to get those fat cells of your body and looking a little what it did before menopause came along.

Insulin Resistance

As discussed in a previous chapter, one of the main reasons you are not losing the weight is due to insulin resistance and carbohydrates. Remember carbohydrate is basically anything that is not fat or protein. There are two main sources of carbohydrates, simple and complex.

Simple carbohydrates are things like table sugar, fruit, white rice, honey, potatoes, white bread, pasta. Simple carbohydrates are broken down into sugars in your body, they get broken down very quickly, which is why you get energy from it minutes after eating it. Complex carbohydrates have a lot of processing to do inside your body. And they take a long time to process.

Would you believe that over 50% of women have insulin resistance when they enter menopause. When you eat a carbohydrate, and your body digests it and processes it, those sugars from the carbohydrates end up in your blood stream. Your body knows exactly how much insulin to pump into your system. Insulin is like the messenger, the key to your body that says, hey here is a carbohydrate, this is what to do with it, and it sends a message to the cells, saying this is what we need to do with it. The problem with insulin resistance is that the insulin is not being released at the appropriate times and not being allowed access to the cells. Remember the insulin is the key to open the cells for the glucose to enter the cells.

Nutrition
When you have caffeine, spicy foods, high fat processed foods, food flavourings, are going to increase your menopausal symptoms. Sugar is also going to make your symptoms worse, and this comes in things like white flour, pastries, cakes, crackers, pasta, white bread, white rice, sweets, chocolate etc. So, what should women eat during menopause?

- Cruciferous Vegetables: - these vegetables have a indole phytonutrient, and when it is chewed, they release plant enzymes. These enzymes affect your estrogen levels and significantly help to reduce menopause symptoms. These include: - Arugula, Bok Choy, Broccoli, Brussel Sprouts, Cabbage, Cauliflower, Collard greens, Kale, Radishes, Rutabaga, Turnips and Watercress.
- Healthy fats: - healthy fats are so important in our diet, because not only do they keep us full, but they are also amazing for your joints, hormone levels, brain health, keeping our cholesterol in check and skin. They can be found in Avocado, Coconut Oil, Ghee, Fish Oil, Olives and Flax Seed.
- Protein: - Protein provides your body with nutrients, not just protein to build muscles. It also helps repair and build your body's tissues. Protein is responsible for our metabolic reactions, which helps to maintain our bodies pH and fluid balance. It also helps to keep our immune system thriving. Another important thing it does is to transport and store nutrients and when needed can act as an energy source when our carbohydrates and fat are used up. Essential hormonal proteins such as insulin and oxytocin perform important functions like regulating blood sugar levels.

Ideal sources of protein come from: - Venison, Salmon, trout, eggs, pasture/grass raised chicken and poultry
- Fruit: - fruit has lots of fibre, and if you eat fruit that isn't full of sugar you can include them in your daily diet. Make sure the fruit is organic, as many fruits are sprayed, and these chemicals will force your body to produce fat cells to store the chemicals in to protect your body. Ideal fruits include: - coconut, kiwi, lemons, limes, blackberries, raspberries, strawberries, blueberries, tomatoes, apples, pears and bananas.
- Complex carbohydrates: - complex carbohydrates have a very important job to do along with fibre, protein and healthy fats, and that is to foster a gradual increase and decrease in blood sugar and insulin levels. Ideal Complex carbohydrates include: - brown rice, buckwheat, oats, quinoa, lentils, chickpeas, black beans, kidney beans, Cannellini Beans, peas, sweet potatoes, butternut squash, beets and parsnips etc.

What not to eat during menopause

There are several foods and drinks which will not only increase your menopausal symptoms, but they will also contribute to weight gain, insulin resistance and they will very likely make it very difficult for you to lose weight,
- Spicy foods and caffeine: - if you are struggling sleeping, and having hot flashes and night sweats, then it is common sense that these two will also be contributing to you feeling restless and hot.
- Other things you need to eliminate ideally from your diet include pasta, cereal, yogurts with sugar, soda, candy, alcohol, baked goods, fruit juices, white bread, pastries, white flour, pizza dough, white rice, desserts, whole wheat, sugar, crackers, jam and all processed and junk food.

Dieting and what to eat

There are many different diets out there, such as ketogenic diet. The Keto diet is NOT high protein, the high protein diet is called the carnivore diet. The keto genic diet is low protein, low carbohydrate and high fat diet. You are getting most of your calories from fat. At first with all the fad weight loss diets, you are going to experience great weight loss results in the beginning, but in the long term they are NOT sustainable. The reason for this, is that you are missing essential nutrients, and some of the side effects that you will start to experience might include hair loss, mood swings, anxiety, depression, fatigue.

Did you know that up to 100% of your estrogen production can come from your fat cells when you are post-menopausal? And up to 50% of estrogen production can come from your fat cells when you are peri menopausal. This is the reason why many women gain weight during menopause, and if you combine that with the insulin resistance issues, and the carbohydrate issue, it is no wonder women find losing weight in the menopausal years.

The problem is when you have a big dip and become low in estrogen you then get issues such as brain fog, memory problems, you get emotional, and the biggest problem possibly is that it increases your cortisol levels. Cortisol is another hormone, it is the stress hormone, and what happens when you have really low estrogen levels, prior to your body making the fat cells to produce estrogen, you end up increasing your cortisol levels.

Supplements

There are a number of supplements that can help while you are going through the menopause and these are: -
- Vitamin B complex: - this is very important for stress levels and maintaining energy
- Omega 3: - Brain Health, Heart Health, Joint Health
- NMN (Nicotinamide Mononucleotide): - this increases your NAD, which is responsible for metabolic pathways, DNA repair, chromatin remodelling, cellular senescence, and immune cell function.
- Collagen: - this is good for hair, nails, joint lubrication, gut health, and increased skin elasticity,
- Vitamin C: - this is an antioxidant, helps with immune function and reduces inflammation.
- Zinc: - This is good for immune function

- Quercetin: - This is anti-inflammatory and an antihistamine.
- Moringa Leaf powder: - this is the most nutrient dense food on the planet. It contains polyphenols, vitamins, micronutrients, and antioxidants. It also boosts the metabolism and energy levels by lowering blood glucose levels and it has been shown to helps with mood stabilisation and weight loss.
- Probiotics: - things like Kimchi, Kombucha and Sauerkraut are all excellent for your gut, and believe me your microbiome is responsible for your health.
- Berberine: - This regulate blood sugar, and it is also anti-bacterial and anti – inflammatory.

Xenoestrogens and estrogen

There are some soy products that are good for us which are fermented soy. Such as natto, tempeh and miso. One of the things that fermented soy does is that it actually helps to remove anti-nutrients. They have phytonutrients in them, and this helps to get rid of the anti-nutrients.

Xenoestrogens can be found in thousands of products that you are using in your homes, such as cleaning products, make-up, spray on foods. Xenoestrogens are bad, and these are why you tend to see men walking around with moobs, and fat on chest. When you have fermented soy products it helps you get rid of xenoestrogens. You need to start to remove the xenoestrogens from your life.

Phytoestrogens

On the other hand, Phytoestrogens are so important for your health especially during menopause. Phytoestrogens are a type of polyphenolic compound that naturally occur in plants and have a molecular structure similar to estrogen. It has been suggested that they may behave similarly to estrogen when it is ingested into the body, and that increasing your intake of phytoestrogens during perimenopause and menopause can alleviate symptoms associated with fluctuating estrogen levels, much like HRT (hormone replacement therapy)

So how do they work? Well, phytoestrogens have the ability to attach to estrogen receptors in the body, which may result in a change in hormone and enzyme levels. The compounds can imitate natural estrogen in the body and are recognised by the body's oestrogen receptors in the same way that real estrogen is, but not quite as effectively. Below are some phytoestrogen foods:
- Seeds: - poppy, sunflower, sesame, flax seeds, pumpkin seeds
- Whole grains: - barley, rye, oat
- Beans and lentils: - kidney beans, chickpeas, mung beans, lima beans, pinto beans, split peas
- Fruits: - berries, apples
- Fermented soy: - tempeh
- Vegetables: - Broccoli, Brussel Sprouts, cabbage,

Inflammation

There are two precursor hormones, which means that something else makes then first, and then they do their own thing. They are called DHEA and Pregnenolone. First of all, Pregnenolone is made from cholesterol, which then makes DHEA, which then goes on to make a whole host of other hormones such as estrogen, testosterone, progesterone, and other adrenal hormones such as cortisol, and aldosterone.

Now remember, Estrogen, plays a role in brain health and minimising brain inflammation, and acts as a protector for our brain against degenerative diseases such as MS, Alzheimer's and Parkinson's Disease, as well as things like brain fog.

Pregnenolone, is what they call a steroid hormone, that is produced by the brain, and this regulates mood and memory. When there is a lack of pregnenolone, it can lead to depression, poor memory, and of course fluctuations in hormones such as estrogen. Unfortunately, DHEA has similar effects on the brain. Unfortunately for women, this means that they may lose much of their neuroprotection (the brain inflammation protection), when the precursors to estrogen which are Pregnenolone, and DHEA, decrease, leading to decreased estrogen levels.

You also must remember that the hormone bundle of pregnenolone, DHEA and estrogen are also responsible for protecting our joints against inflammation and protect our muscles from getting stiff.

The positives though are that you can do a lot to help with reducing the inflammation in your body.

1. Start with your diet. Stop eating the foods that are inflammatory. Look at a fasting period between meals. Things like coffee and chocolate, sorry guys are inflammatory during menopause, and you need to cut them down, if not out totally. Chocolate has mould in it and can lead to inflammation, histamine intolerance, swelling, aching joints. Peanuts, coffee beans also have mould in them.

2. Exercise: - Don't do high impact exercise, as this is going to cause your joints to be inflamed, you really do need to be gentle with your body if you are struggling with symptoms of menopause. Make sure you take supplements to aid your body and help your body against inflammation.

Whilst some women may feel they may have start of arthritis, it is just a symptom of menopause, and if you look after your body it will pass. The inflammation and pain in the joints should also settle and go away.

Ghrelin and Leptin

Ghrelin is the hormone responsible for your hunger, and Leptin is the full hormone, the one which says I am good I don't need food. The problem with many menopausal women is that these two hormones get all messed up, and the carbs and cortisol all play a role in this. When we are not sleeping, then it can be a major issue due to these hormones.

When you first open your eyes and wake up in the morning, the first hormone you encounter is Ghrelin, which says 'Hey I am hungry'. And that is the indicator that it is time to eat. There is a problem here though. When you go to bed with food in your stomach, (also remembering that it takes the average person three to five hours to fully digest your food, and of course depending on what you have eaten), then while you are sleeping that food is not going to be digested as quickly as it should, and your motility level is going to decrease. This means that food will start to ferment in your gut, and this could cause problems in your gut and leaky gut etc. because the Ghrelin didn't get the message from the Leptin, this makes you famished in the morning and probably eating quite a bit throughout the day.

If you go to bed and your stomach is empty, at about 2am in the morning, the Leptin is released, and signals that food is not needed. In this way, Leptin can continue to signal that until you decide when you want to eat.

Exercise

The most important thing as you age is maintaining your muscle mass. You need lower body and leg strength, so trying to maintain the muscle mass and your strength is vitally important for you to maintain your independence.

During menopause it is maybe not the best time to be doing HIIT classes, as these raise the cortisol levels in the body, and cortisol levels need to be kept as low as possible. The best exercises that you should be doing during menopause and post menopause are things like nice slow jogs, speed walking, or weightlifting. The best exercise though is a nice walk, or a nice slow jog for about half an hour, and full body work outs at the gym if you want.

Androgens

Have you noticed the increase of hair growing in certain parts of your body. That means you have an excess of androgen in your body. Androgen is a male hormone. Yes, there is such as a thing as Male menopause, and it is called andropause. Women need andropause too, but too much androgen can have hairs sprouting out from everywhere. Androgens in women can be found in ovaries and adrenal glands to a lesser extent. The imbalance of this hormone can lead to issues such as decrease in breast size, increase in body hair such as on the chin, face and abdomen, and even male pattern balding.

Excess androgen in women is often caused by conditions such as polycystic ovary syndrome (PCOS). Other causes include heightened sensitivity to androgen, surplus production of adrenal androgen, elevated prolactin, menopause and the use of hormonal birth control with high androgen levels.

So how do you reduce your androgen? This is a simple solution, you do it by weight training and cardiovascular training. This is the simplest solution to getting your excess androgen under control. If you are on birth control, get off it.

Nuts and flaxseeds are also a good way of reducing androgen in your body. Nuts and flax seeds have monounsaturated and polyunsaturated fatty acids which are the key ingredients needed.

<u>Ageing and your skin</u>

When going through the menopause, you may be shocked at how quickly wrinkles appear over a period time. The reason this happens is because when your estrogen stops being produced, your collagen drops away also, and things start to sag, and wrinkles start to show. The most important thing to help with this is hydration... yes keep yourself hydrated. You also need electrolytes, and you can also add orange juice, and you can also get a lot of water from eating vegetables.

Another good way to help is by sweating. When we sweat, we release toxins from our skin, so when you exercise, you are going to be releasing toxins from your skin, and it is going to be replenishing, and it will help you feel good and look more youthful.

When you think about Botox, or any cosmetic work which you do to your body, you must also remember you will have to pay a price at some point for doing this. There are a few things you can do which are less invasive such as facial sculpting massages, Buccal Massage, and Blepharo Facial Massages. You can use rose quartz roller just to massage areas between eyes and at side of the eyes, gua sha facial massages are also excellent for helping with wrinkles, as is LED light therapy. When you massage your face with gua sha tools, it encourages collagen production, moves fluid, and tightens your face,

Intimacy

During menopause lots of things happen to a woman's body (take note all the men reading this out there). With menopause, sexual desire decreases in many women, and physical changes can make it difficult to become sexually aroused. It can also be uncomfortable to engage in sexual intercourse, and difficult to reach orgasm, many women try to avoid intimacy.

The reasons for this are because the hormone levels decrease, which have a big impact on sexual desire. Estrogen levels decrease rapidly during menopause. If a woman has had their ovaries removed, this can also cause an immediate loss of libido. There are a number of physical menopause symptoms in the sexual region including: --

- Vaginal tightness, dryness and irritation
- Urine leakage or incontinence
- Decreased libido
- Pain during sex
- Less clitoral sensitivity

Interest in sex may also decrease due to things like hot flashes, worries about body shape, headaches, muscles aches and pains, insomnia and fatigue. Other things such as irritability, mood swings, anxiety and depression, stress can also have big impact during menopause, and it is important for partners to understand the number of changes /that can happen during this period and to be mindful of how their loved one may be feeling and be very supportive.

Negative to positive

There are many things you can do to make yourself feel better and go from that negative outlook to a strong positive outlook going forward.

- Remember that you are the same woman inside, the same gifts, talents and heart that lots of people around you LOVE
- Don't ever compare yourself to anyone else, even a younger you.
- Practice gratitude daily, be grateful for the body that has served you well.

- Speak kindly to yourself, your words reflect your self-love
- Try and surround yourself with other women who are going through this stage, support is very important
- Remember to do what you can to minimise the effects physically, like eating well and exercise.
- Try to make yourself feel good every day, pamper yourself, clothes, make-up, hair, spa day.

Each day is an opportunity to love yourself a little more. Ageing is a gift not everyone is blessed to have. You have a lifetime of memories which are shown in every single wrinkle on your face, every laugh line, every tear shed, and every memory made, you are beautiful no matter what the calendar says.

Chapter 20

Forgiveness & Ho'oponopono

You have to forgive yourself and let go of your past mistakes. You can't punish people for their mistakes. True justice is paying once for each mistake. True injustice is paying more than once.

Animals pay once for their mistakes, humans pay 1000's of times, as every time we remember, we judge ourselves and feel guilty over, and over again.

Many times, in our lives we make mistakes, and we must forgive ourselves for these mistakes. Most people have more resentment towards themselves than anyone else. There are two things that our minds unconsciously do when we feel guilty, one of them is to try to repay or make right our mistake, often excessively if we feel that there is nothing, we can do to make something right. The second option we choose (unconsciously), is to punish ourselves.

Take a moment to reflect on your actions towards yourself, or others in the past that you may regret. Are there any mistakes you made that you continue to beat yourself up for?

How are you punishing yourself for it?

Are you directly or indirectly punishing others for it?

Your guilt is not going to undo what has happened. Even more importantly, holding onto this pain is causing further pain in your life.

You are missing out on a great deal in your life, if you don't know what it feels like to forgive. People often struggle to get past painful memories in their lives, and they dwell on the past, creating a downward spiral of pain and disappointment.

Forgiveness is a gift that you give yourself, and the people you love. The problem is people say they have forgiven, but still bring up the past, which just shows that they haven't truly forgiven. If you truly forgive somebody, then the past should remain in the past, and shouldn't be brought up again.

What forgiveness does, is that it gives both you, and the person you feel has wronged you, the freedom to move on. When you carry the burden of not forgiving somebody, you carry it with you for your whole life, which diminishes your ability to experience true happiness.

Forgiveness allows you to lift the burden and to see life from a different perspective.

The true art of forgiveness is when you can look inside yourself, and see no hatred, and feel no negativity, or any strings attached to past bitter experiences.

When people are angry, it is very hard for them to understand that forgiveness works in two ways. On one hand, it lets someone get away with actions that are unacceptable, and this is the side that most people see, but on the other hand, it lets you get away without all the bitterness.

There is ultimately a difference between forgiving someone and condoning their actions.

Forgiveness also opens a path to empathy, and empathy allows you to become more of a complete person who can peacefully co-exist with others whose opinions differ from your own.

Try this... the next time someone hurts you, don't wait for them to apologize, break the ice, and give them a call, to get the relationship back on track. It's not about you forgetting what they did to hurt you, it is about you releasing yourself from it, and moving forward, because it really does not matter who apologizes first, as long as there is forgiveness. If the other person cannot apologize, then they are always going to be in a weaker position.

The fact is that you imprison your heart when you are not able to forgive. You are imprisoning yourself when you cannot forgive, not the person you cannot forgive. You are the one suffering from the anger, negativity, hate, lack of trust, and all the other things, and they may, or may not be feeling anything at all. It does not matter, the only thing that matters, is that you forgive the other person, and free yourself from the hot piece of coal you are holding onto and let go and forgive.

We are all made up of energy. That is all we are, energy, and if we cannot forgive, we give off this negative energy, and other people around will avoid us, and this negative energy.

So many people hold onto grudges and learn nothing from them. Instead of holding onto grudges and hate, tell them what they did wrong, regardless of if they apologize, and move on, let it go.

The art of forgiving others and moving on shows your strength of character, and what you do then is move on, and learn from the experience. The next time something bad happens that gets you annoyed and frustrated, try not to let the emotions control you. Don't react to negative emotions, just take a step back, and look at the situation calmly, forgive others, and look for a positive solution.

To forgive someone, is to put aside all the thoughts of anger, and revenge, and when you can do that, it is called absolute forgiveness.

"The truth is, unless you let go, unless you forgive yourself, unless you forgive the situation, unless you realize that the situation is over, you cannot move forward" Steve Maraboli

"True forgiveness is when you can say, thank you for the experience" Oprah Winfrey

"Forgiveness has nothing to do with absolving a criminal of his crime, it has everything to do with relieving oneself of the burden of being a victim, letting go of the pain, and transforming oneself from victim to survivor" C R Strahan

Today is the day for you to find the freedom in forgiveness.

Ho'oponopono

I would like to tell you about the wonderful ancient practice of Ho'oponopono, which has been practiced for 1000s of years by people in Hawaii, and is truly a wonderful, and it is a very powerful healing process. I only go into this wonderful technique in a little detail in this book, but again on the "awakening workshop" and group sessions we cover this in greater detail.

Ho'oponopono is about the art of forgiveness. It's about solving conflicts and setting emotions free. Ho'oponopono basically means to fix and error or mistake.

(Hawaiian) Ho'o - "cause" pono " –perfection"

Ho'oponopono is a technique which is used to clean and erase memories that create repressing beliefs in our subconscious mind.

The aim of Ho'oponopono is find out who we really are and see beyond all the judgements both internal and external and any shallow beliefs from others or ourselves.

So, in essence, what Ho'oponopono really does, is it searches for inner peace, and also transmutation of the past. It helps us find the divinity that lives within each of us, and it fixes errors, it cleans and brings light into us and around us.

It also helps us to re-connect, and it does that by cleaning our repressed beliefs, with our true self and the divinity.

T
he Huna Philosophy

Huna: - that which is difficult to see

Hu: - movement   Na: - calm

This philosophy was born around 5,000 years ago in Polynesia, and it encourages questioning and reflection within ourselves and others around us. It is an open technique based on the Universal truths.

The 14 Huna Principles

1. we create our own reality, through our beliefs, expectations, and fears.
2. We get that which we focus on.
3. We are responsible for our own experience.
4. Thoughts attract their equivalent

5. Life presents you the content of all your thoughts.
6. When you change your way of thinking, your life experience changes.
7. You are an unlimited being, everything is possible. You just need to believe it.
8. The present is the fruit of the past and the seed of the future.
9. The world is what you think it is. If you change your beliefs, the world around you changes too.
10. The energy flow to the place where your attention is directed.
11. Nothing happens that we haven't attracted first.
12. All power comes from within
13. We create exactly what is related to our vibration
14. Think about what you wish for. Thoughts are vibrations.

7 Huna principles which will change your life
- IKE: - the world is what you think it is
- KALA: - There are no limits, everything is possible
- MAKIA: - energy flows where the attention goes
- MANAWA: - now is the moment of power
- ALOHA: - to love is to be happy with
- MANA: - all power comes from within
- PONO: - effectiveness is the measure of truth

The Meaning of Aloha
- A: - AO – means light. We need to make sure we always have positive intentions, and our behaviour is pure and moves us towards the light.
- L: - LOKAHI – means Oneness. All is one. Support people who are on the path with us. Oneness means we must be PONO and ONE with everybody.
- O: - OIAIO – means Truth. Tell the truth. Many of us are too polite to tell the truth, and we don't participate completely in the process in the construction of our universe. Don't withhold your feelings, as this doesn't allow us to be one with the people around us.

- H: - HA'A HA'A:- means to be Humble. Let go of your ego. If you play the game of power, you will always have to know more than others. Let go of your ego... Share with others, remain humble.
- A: - ALOHA – means Absolute, True Love. don't think you are better than anyone else, don't make comparisons, judgements etc, because when you do, you separate yourself from true love.

To find ABSOLUTE TRUE LOVE, you need to be HUMBLE, and tell the TRUTH, which allows you to reach ONENESS with yourself and everyone around you, and this will guide you to the LIGHT.

I want to tell you a story about Dr Hew Len who was a student of Morrnah Simeona the creator of Self-I-Dentity through Ho'oponopono.

Between 1984 to 1987 he worked as a staff psychologist for Hawaii State Hospital where he oversaw a high security unit with male criminally insane patients. In 1987, the daily violence which once happened had virtually ceased, and these inmates were even going on off-site activities. The spirit and order in the unit was so greatly improved. According to Dr Hew Len he did not do any therapy or counselling with the patients, what he did do was practice Ho'oponopono daily that included accepting 100% responsibility for everything being experienced by HIM.

Dr Hew Len said "I didn't heal them; I healed part of myself that created them"

You are 100% responsible for everything! Everything and everywhere... that means the things you do wrong, personal successes etc., but also it means if someone somewhere else did something, and you become aware of it, YOU are 100% responsible for that!

"when you return back to your inner nature – to zero – everything becomes available to you effortlessly and you are being driven by inspiration from divinity and not petty ego" Joe Vitale

I would highly recommend getting the book 'Zero Limits' by Joe Vitale, which is a fantastic book.

So, how do we get to this magical state? It is achieved by a cleaning process which you do constantly. You clean yourself from all the subconscious garbage, the programs that run your life.

<u>The 4 healing words of Ho'oponopono</u>

The actual cleaning process consists of repetitions of these 4 wonderful phrases.

- I am sorry
- Please forgive me
- Thank you
- I love you

When you repeat these 4 phrases, the cleaning process just happens. You can clean relationships, people, places, life situations etc. When something comes into your awareness, you accept 100% responsibility for that thought and repeat the cleaning process.

You may ask the questions... How can you heal yourself and others by saying these 4 phrases? Why would repeating these 4 phrases affect anything or anybody out there?

The fact is, there isn't an out there... everything happens to you, in YOUR mind.

Everything you see and hear, every single person you meet, you experience in your mind. You only think it is out there, and you think that absolves you from responsibility.

But YOU are responsible for every single thing you think, and every single thing that comes to YOUR attention. Even things you hear about while watching the news, is YOUR responsibility. This may sound a little crazy to some, and harsh to others, but realizing this also means that you are also able to clear it, clean it, and through the use of these 4 phrases and forgiveness, change it.

When you are repeating these 4 phrases, you don't need anyone else to be there with you, you don't need anyone to hear you, and you can say the words in your head, because the power is in the feeling and the willingness of the universe to forgive and love. Remember we are all energy, and we are all one: -

1. I'm Sorry: - repentance – you are responsible for everything in your head, even when it is 'out there'. Once we realise, we cause our own reality, we feel a natural state of remorse. So, who are we asking? We ask ourselves, we are responsible for our problems, and our forgiveness.

2. Please forgive me: - ask forgiveness – it doesn't matter who you are asking, just ask please forgive me and mean it.

3. Thank You: - gratitude – again it doesn't matter who we thank, when you are offering gratitude, you are affecting your soul which is connected to the souls of all, of everyone. Thank yourself for the courage to change and learn. Thank the people who surround you.

4. I love you: - Love – say this often and say it to all who surround you. Remember now you have no enemies around you, there is only you! You can love everything with complete honesty, because you have released all the layers of pain, anger, remorse, guilt that kept you from love.

Ho'oponopono is a wonderful practice and therapeutic technique, which I use daily, and it brings you such peace and it can be such a powerful healing tool.

Chapter 21

Food as Medicine

Common nutrient deficiencies in men
- Magnesium: - if you are feeling weak, experiencing fatigue, low energy, anxiety, the chances are you might be deficient in magnesium. Other signs of magnesium deficiency include insomnia, infertility, depression, coldness in extremities, back pain, body odor, constipation, kidney stones and thyroid issues. Magnesium is so vital to the health of your body, and your body uses it in over 300 processes. Every single cell in the body needs it to function. We also need magnesium for healthy bones, teeth, joints, and muscles, cellular energy, to keep red blood cells healthy, and to sleep. If you have low magnesium levels you find it in raw cacao, salmon, dark leafy greens, nuts and seeds, molasses, dates and oatmeal.
- There are a lot of men who are deficient in Vitamin D3, this is known as the sunshine vitamin, and it can be produced in the boy with mild exposure to the sun or consumed in food or supplements. Vitamin D intake is important for the regulation of calcium an phosphorous absorption. It is also important for maintenance of healthy bones and teeth, and it can protect against multiple diseases and conditions, such as multiple sclerosis, Type 1 diabetes and cancer. Food sources for Vitamin D3 include fatty fish, raw milk and mushrooms
- Omega 3 fatty acids: - these are so important for their anti-inflammatory properties as well as protecting against cardiovascular disease, cancer, depression, Alzheimer's disease, arthritis and osteoporosis. They can also have lower triglycerides. Food sources which are good for Omega 3 fatty acids are cold water fish such as salmon, herring, sardines, walnuts, flaxseeds and grass-fed beef,

- A lot of men are not eating enough raw plant foods that contain live enzymes needed for digestion. They should eat more fresh fruits and vegetables. These foods will also contain the antioxidants that most men are deficient in as well. These can be found in green leafy vegetables, orange hued vegetables such as sweet potatoes and carrots, berries and citrus fruits

Common nutrient deficiencies in women
- Just the same as men, a lot of women are deficient in magnesium, and vitamin D3, which is the same as above.
- It is also common for women to be deficient in Iron, because of menstruation, and iron deficiency anemia is the most common form of anemia. This is a decrease in the number of red blood cells caused by too little iron. Without sufficient iron, your body can't produce enough Hemoglobin, which is a substance in red blood cells that makes it possible for them to carry oxygen to the body's tissues. As a result, the person may feel week, tired and irritable. You can find iron in Beef, spinach, liver, oysters, lentils and beans.
- Many women are also low in probiotics. This is due to contraceptive or birth control use. Birth control can cause systemic candida, which can really affect the gut health, and particularly the gut flora. The body needs probiotics for gut health, immune health, they also affect our moods, and they affect almost every system in the body when they are not in balance.
- Many women are also deficient in Vitamin B6, which is important for energy and red blood cell production, you can find B6 in meat, fish, lentils, poultry,
- Women also need healthy fats such as avocado, olive oil, coconut oi, flax il, raw nuts and seeds

The Immune system
A healthy immune system provides multiple response layers against aggressive environmental factors and the strength of these barriers are influenced by lifestyle choices that may deplete the bodies reserves, such as stress, processed foods, junk foods,

toxins, and lack of exercise. Replenishing nutrients that are essential to healthy immune function, as well as rest and relaxation. There are some natural remedies for boosting the immune system.

- Lemons and other citrus fruits contain Vitamin C, which breaks up Mucous and kills acidic poisons in the body
- Pineapple juice is high in Vitamin C, and it also contains bromelain, which is a natural anti-inflammatory agent and digestive enzyme that helps to break down proteins.
- Cayenne pepper contains capsaicin, which eases symptoms like nasal congestion, mucous, fever and body aches.
- Ginger: - drink this as a tea, as it has amazing immune boosting properties, and it also helps with nausea, motion sickness, digestion and inflammation.
- Healing bone broth: - drinking the bone broth made from grass fed, organic bones and organic vegetables is one of the easiest ways to get lots of digestible nutrients in your body when you are sick,
- Raw honey soothes coughs, aids digestion, and it is also anti-viral, anti-fungal and anti-bacterial.
- Coconut oil is anti-viral, anti-bacterial and anti-fungal
- Epsom salt can be used in a bath to draw out impurities, and this can help with stress, improve circulation and reduce inflammation.
- Turmeric contains curcumin, which has powerful anti-inflammatory and anti-viral properties.
- Echinacea can be used for boosting immunity, relieving pain, reducing inflammation and it has excellent anti-viral and antioxidant properties.
- Vitamin D3 is essential for its immune protecting properties
- Green tea is also excellent for boosting immunity due to the catechins found in the tea that prevent oxidation of the cells
- Garlic is truly wonderful for boosting immunity and fights infection with allicin, which is anti-microbial, anti-bacterial, and anti-viral.

- Onions are expectorants, which mean they loosen mucous that can cause a cough. They contain quercetin which reduces inflammation and onions are also anti-viral.
- Apple cider vinegar can cure a cough quicky by drinking a tablespoon mixed with honey and water.

- Fermented foods contain beneficial anti-biotics that keep your gut healthy and in turn keep your immune system functioning well. These include Kimchi, kombucha, sauerkraut and kefir.
- Licorice root is excellent for the immune system and especially for the throat and coughs
- Fermented cod liver oil is excellent to boost your levels of Vitamin A and D which are essential for a strong immune system.
- Bicarbonate soda balances the pH of the body, and allows the body to heal itself

Cancer prevention
We have discussed cancer at length in an earlier chapter, but i just wanted to touch on cancer prevention in this chapter, and the importance of boosting your body and preventing cancer with food. Cancer prevention is all about pH balance. Cancer can only occur in an acidic environment. Keeping your body in alkaline state slashes the inflammation and it can also help you lose weight as well.

When you eat too much acidic food, the body pulls minerals from your bones to balance the pH. Ideally in your diet you should be aiming for 70% alkaline and 30% acidic, and of course if you do have cancer the alkaline foods should be much higher. It is imperative that you try and avoid sugar, as sugar feeds cancer,

So, let's look at some acid forming foods and some alkaline forming foods

- acid forming foods: - alcohol, coffee, tea, soda, meats, chicken, pork, lamb, beef, bread, pasta, white rice, candy, sugar, ice cream, artificial sweeteners, eggs, peanuts, friend and processed foods, junk food.

- Alkaline forming foods: - green leafy vegetables, sweet potatoes, grains, sprouts, beans, whole grains, tomatoes, avocado, sea salt, raw nuts and seeds, flax oil, fresh herbs, lemon, most fruits, stevia.

So of course, if you currently have cancer, you really do NOT want to be having most of the foods on the acid forming, because they are feeding the cancer, or limiting as said above to 70-80% alkaline and some meat and fish etc., but you need to cut sugar out of your diet totally.

It is also good to get in the habit of testing your pH levels with litmus strips or pH strips, where you test it with your saliva in the morning and throughout the day. You need to be aiming for between 6.5 and 7.5 for both saliva and urine,

There are many foods and supplements that can help with cancer prevention. These include: -

- Cod liver oil, powdered greens, glutathione, Broccoli, Cauliflower, kale, cabbage, Brussel Sprouts, seaweed, warm lemon water, hormone free and antibiotic free animal products.

Digestion

Acid reflux otherwise known as GERD affects millions of people, but it is caused by low stomach acid, not too much. It is caused by the mal absorption of Vitamin B12 and Iron. 905 of people have low stomach acid, due to the inability to break down proteins. You can heal GERD naturally in just 3 weeks

- GERD tonic: - 1-2 tbsp apple cider vinegar and 16oz water. First thing in the morning when you wake up, mix the apple cider vinegar and water and drink. This should be done daily for 3 weeks for best results. This tonic can help your body to produce more hydrochloric acid on its own. It will also help alkalize your body at the same time.

Small intestinal Bacterial Overgrowth (SIBO) is another serious problem, and it is a chronic bacterial infection of the small intestine. The infection is of bacteria that normally live in the gastrointestinal tract, that have abnormally overgrown in a

location not meant for so many bacteria, the symptoms for this include: -
- Gas, bloating, diarrhea, abdominal pain, cramping, constipation, IBS, food intolerances, chronic illnesses such as fibromyalgia, chronic fatigue syndrome, diabetes, neuromuscular disorders, autoimmune diseases, B12 deficiency, as well as other vitamin, mineral and fat mal absorption.

There are several factors that contribute to the development of SIBO, the first being a lack of hydrochloric acid in the stomach. 90% of people have low stomach acid. Hydrochloric acid helps the body digest proteins, but it also helps to kill bacteria in the food that we eat and prevents them from colonizing in the small intestines. Another cause of SIBO is a malfunctioning ileocecal valve, this valve is in between the small and large intestine, and it is designed to prevent backflow.

There is a SIBO diet and natural remedies to help with this issue.
- Diet low in fructose avoid honey, apples, pears, peaches, mangoes, watermelon, coconut, dried fruits and fruit juices
- Limit fructans such as artichokes, asparagus, beets, Broccoli, Brussel Sprouts, cabbage, garlic, leeks, onions, lettuce and legumes.

Gut health

Although I have covered gut health in detail in a previous chapter, I want to run over a few pointers in this section. So, if you remember from the earlier chapter, Leaky gut is a condition where the junctions of the intestinal wall become overly impermeable and allow pathogenic substances and undigested food particles through to the bloodstream. This can cause immune responses, leading to food sensitivities and autoimmune conditions. It is caused by stress, overuse of antibiotics, over consumption of processed foods, candida overgrowth, Toxicity, dysbiosis in the gut and heavy metals. Symptoms of leaky gut include: -
- Bloating, gas, constipation, IBS, food sensitivities, acne, psoriasis, rosacea, eczema, depression, anxiety, fatigue, joint

pain, thyroid problems, infertility, inflammation and of course auto immune disorders.

it is important to remove the stress out of your lives, the processed foods, junk food, toxins, and replace the offenders with good healthy food, and also fermented foods such as kefir, kimchi, kombucha and sauerkraut. you need to repair your gut with healing supplements and good food. Foods for leaky gut include: -

- Non starchy vegetables, greens, berries, organic and grass-fed meat, bone broth, probiotic rich foods such as kimchi and kombucha.

The foods to avoid when you have gut problems and leaky gut are: -

- Bread, rice, pasta, barley, wheat, conventional dairy, oats, conventional meats which have been treated, beans and legumes, processed sugar, artificial colorings and flavorings, white potatoes, caffeine, fruit except berries.

There are also several supplements which are beneficial for leaky gut which include: -

- L-Glutamine, grass fed gelatin, digestive enzymes, probiotics (50-`100 billion organisms), saccharomyces Boulardi, aloe vera, Deglycyrrhizinated licorice (DGL) and omega 3 fatty acids

Hormonal health

Some of the most common side effects of hormone imbalance are infertility, weight gain, depression, fatigue, insomnia, low libido, hair loss etc. Your organs and glands such as your thyroids, adrenals, pituitary, ovaries, testicles etc. regulate most of your hormone production. If your hormones become even slightly imbalanced, it can cause major health issues such as hypothyroidism, PMS, PCOS, Infertility, menopause symptoms, endometriosis, low testosterone, impotence.

There are several things that you can do to start healing your hormones and start to regain balance within your body.

- Include more healthy fats such as coconut oil, avocado and grass-fed butter in your diet, as these are essential fats and

building blocks for hormone production, they also speed up your metabolism.
- The omega 3/6 ratio should be 1:1, instead of the typical 1:20. Stay away from oils high omega 6 such as sunflower oil, corn, soyabean, cottonseed etc. These are all inflammatory oils. You need more omega 3 fats such as fish, flax seeds, chia seeds, walnuts and grass-fed animal products.
- Adaptogens are herbs that protect hormone balance, and these include ashwagandha and holy basil.
- You need to heal the gut, eliminate toxins and exercise more. And it is important to get more sleep.
- Vitamin D3 is so important for healthy hormone production, and you should limit your caffeine intake as it elevates your cortisol levels and lowers thyroid hormones and wreaks havoc throughout the body.
- Get off birth control, as this is hormone therapy which raises estrogen levels to such dangerous levels.
- Reduce your carbs and increase your fats. Eating a variety of foods with short, medium and long chain fatty acids will keep your hormones in check. Some of the best include coconut oil, avocados, sprouted nuts, grass fed butter and salmon.
- Adaptogen herbs are healing plants that promote hormone balance and protect the body from a wide range of diseases.
- Herbs such as ashwagandha, Rhodiola, Ginseng, Holy Basil, Licorice Root enhance hormone balance by improving thyroid function, lowering cholesterol, reducing anxiety and depression, reducing brain cell degeneration, stabilizing blood sugar and supporting adrenal glands.

What you do need to do if you can, is to use different kind of birth control than the pill. Why? The Birth control pill is a synthetic hormone that raises estrogen to dangerous levels. It has been linked to: -
- increased risk of breast cancer,
- increased risk of blood clotting and stroke

- Migraines, increased blood pressure, weight gain, mood changes, irregular bleeding and spotting, benign liver tumors and breast tenderness.

Thyroid health

The thyroid gland is a small gland located on the front of the neck. It regulates our metabolism, keeps us at a healthy weight, mood balance, and it aids in sleep and digestion. Hypothyroidism is an underactive thyroid and symptoms feeling tired, fatigue, mental fog, thinning hair, dry skin, puffy eyes, and feeling cold a lot of the time. Hyperthyroidism is the opposite and overactive thyroid, this is where it releases too much thyroid hormone, and it can cause symptoms like nervousness, anxiety, insomnia, racing heart, and basically the functions in the body tend to speed up. Some causes of thyroid dysfunction include: -

- Mercury and copper toxicity, water fluoridation, gluten/dairy/soy in the diet, problems of conversion in the liver, zinc deficiency, selenium deficiency, and infections in the body.

There are three halogens that cause thyroid dysfunction. Chlorine, bromine and fluoride. Chlorine is found in water and swimming pools etc., Bromine is found in baked goods, soda, plastic. Fluoride is found tap water, toothpaste, and other products, and what they do is compete for iodine in the body, and block it, therefore affecting thyroid function. You need to get a water filter for your shower and taps. Did you know that every shower you have, gives you the equivalent of 8 glasses of drinking water.

There are many healing foods for hypothyroidism.

- Stay away from gluten. It is overly acidic, genetically modified devoid of nutrients and causes immune antibody production.
- Always eat goitrogen foods cooked and not raw such as cabbage, broccoli, cauliflower, Brussel Sprouts, Kale, Bok Choy and watercress. Eat high iodine foods such as kelp, flakes, artichokes, pineapples, onions
- Selenium helps with the conversion of T4 to T3 so foods like shellfish, Brazil nuts, mushrooms, garlic and eggs

- Omega 3 fatty acid foods such as cold-water fish, chia seeds, walnuts, flaxseeds, leafy greens
- High copper foods such as beef, liver, clams, cashews
- High iron foods such as grass-fed beef, black beans,
- High zinc foods such as oysters, meat, poultry, beans, egg yolks, and pumpkin seeds.
- 2-3 tbsps. coconut oil daily.
- Bone broth daily.

Did you know that women on long term thyroid hormone replacement medication are 50% more susceptible to breast cancer due to an iodine deficiency? Iodine has the highest concentration in the thyroid, then the ovaries and then breast tissue. It is very important to get more iodine through kelp and other seaweeds and NOT table salt. You can get kelp granules to spread on food and in smoothies etc.

Simple thyroid testing from home

There is a simple accurate thyroid test that you can do from home.

- Take your temperature every morning before getting out of bed, for 5 days, do not get up, brush teeth or drink. Just lie there and take temperature. Then average the temperatures. Using a mercury thermometer is best.
- Normal range is 97.8 to 98.2. above that can be an infection or hyperthyroid,
- 97.5 to 97.7 can be a sluggish thyroid
- 97.4 and below is underactive or hypothyroid.

Most doctors just test TSH, but this is not enough information. You should also ask your doctor to test you for T4, T3, reverse T4, reverse T3, TPO, and TAA for antibodies. You need at look at the whole picture.

Adrenal fatigue

Adrenal fatigue is a depleted stress hormone state of chronic exhaustion, where the vitality is low, the person may feel depressed, dark circles under the eyes, like a tired but wired feeling. Stress wreaks havoc on the adrenals. You may look and act relatively normal with adrenal fatigue and may not have any obvious signs of physical illness, yet you may feel just generally feel unwell and like a grey feeling. Poor adrenal function leads to poor thyroid function by telling the body to make more of reverse T3 instead of active T3. You need more of the active T3 to get into the cells for better cellular energy.

Adrenal fatigue can also cause food sensitivities and inflammation due to less natural anti-inflammatories being produced.

We already know stress wreaks havoc on the adrenals, and these types of stress can come from external stressors such as: - death of a loved one, loss of job, chronic health issues, divorce, getting married, work pressure, emotional issues such as anger, grief, depression, anxiety, and also trauma and traumatic events.

Internal stressors can come from blood sugar imbalances, infections, food sensitivities, leaky gut, heavy metals, toxicity, and mold in the environment.

So how do we start healing adrenal fatigue. Well, there are many foods that can help strengthen the adrenal glands.

- Eat a balanced breakfast after waking up in the morning, which should include protein and fats. Eggs, whole grain toast, avocado, protein bar, full fat yoghurt,
- Avoid coffee and sugar, this leads to increased cortisol production and adrenal overdrive.
- Use pink Himalayan salt to help raise blood pressure
- Keep blood sugars balanced. Eat diet high in protein and fats.

There are also several adrenal supplements which can help boost the adrenal function. These include: -

- B Vitamins for energy, magnesium, adaptogens such as ashwagandha, rhodiola, and Holy Basil, Vitamin C and Fish Oil for fatty acids.

Healing your heart

When there is free radical activity from outside it creates inflammation in the body. LDL cholesterol becomes oxidized, and plaques build in the interior walls. This creates a bottleneck condition called atherosclerosis. This can result in heart attacks and strokes.

One in four Americans now take cholesterol lowering drugs known as statins. These are for the prevention of heart attacks and strokes. The problem is that the benefits for them preventing heart attacks and strokes is highly questionable, they also come with many side effects including diabetes, liver damage, memory problems, muscle weakness and much more.

Let's get this straight... High cholesterol is NOT the cause of heart disease. It is in fact essential for good health as is carries out essential functions within your cell membranes and is crucial for proper brain function and production of steroid hormones.

The real cause of heart disease is related to damage inflicted on the INSIDE wall of your arteries, and the primary culprit of this is sugar, which causes plaque formation and thickening of the artery wall.

Your body needs cholesterol as it is important in the production of cell membranes, hormones, Vitamin D, and bile acids that help you digest fat.

Foods for good heart health include the following: -

- Dark leafy greens to help detox the blood stream including collards, spinach, Broccoli, kale
- Garlic for its powerful anti-fungal, anti-bacterial and anti- parasitic properties
- Green tea and dandelion tea are excellent for liver support
- Ginger is good for helping balance blood viscosity
- Turmeric is good to reduce inflammation
- Olive oil, hemp oil, flax oil, salmon, and sardines which increase unsaturated fats
- Fiber rich foods like beans, peas, and legumes, which are great for their complex carbohydrate that stabilize blood sugar
- Walnut help regulate blood sugar and support omega 3 fatty acids.
- Antioxidant foods such as acai berry, raw cacao, blueberries, pomegranates, prunes, kale, Brussel Sprouts, red bell peppers

- Onions, leeks and green onions contain sulfur compounds to maintain platelet aggregation.

There are also some good supplements and these include; Fish Oil (omega3), COQ10, garlic, red rice yeast, Niacin (B3), Vitamin D, magnesium, Natto H, Hawthorn Berry.

Liver health

Your liver is responsible for over 500 functions. It regenerates every 40 days when you look after it and feed it the right medicine. When you are having headaches, migraines, chronic fatigue, circles under your eyes, hormonal imbalances and feeling nauseous, these are all signs that you need to detox and support your liver.

Foods for your liver are essential to keep your body's powerhouse functioning optimally. When you have a healthy liver, it plays a key role in helping digestive issues, gas bloating constipation. it also regulates blood sugar levels, and it can lead to many inflammatory diseases such as diabetes, arthritis, high blood pressure and autoimmune diseases. When your liver is not in a healthy state, you may suffer from hormone imbalances, which can cause headaches, mood swings and depression.

When you are trying to nourish and heal your liver, the first thing you need to do is cut out that sugar, avoid sugar, trans fats, and alcohol which are all toxic substances that your liver has to work hard to neutralize.

Vegetable such as Kale, Brussel Sprouts and cabbage are powerful vegetables that contain high levels of Sulphur, which will support your liver in detoxification, triggering it to remove free radicals and other toxic chemicals.

Dandelion greens are the best food for the liver. One of dandelion's chemical components tarsasin, is believed to stimulate the digestive organs and trigger the liver and gallbladder to release bile, which supports digestion and fat absorption.

There are also super-antioxidants such as acai berries and turmeric that can reverse inflammation and help the liver regenerate itself.

Cruciferous vegetables such as cabbage, cauliflower, Broccoli, Bok Choy contain vital nutrients and flavonoids to help your liver neutralize chemicals, pesticides and drugs,

Garlic contains an active compound called, allicin, which is critical for liver detoxification. It also helps your body rid itself of mercury, certain food additives, and estrogen. Onions, shallots and leeks are all relatives of garlic and support your liver in the production of glutathione which neutralizes free radicals.

Eggs provide some of the highest quality protein containing all eight essential amino acids, cholesterol and the essential nutrient choline. And this helps detoxifying heavy metals.

Medicinal mushrooms such as maitake, shitake and reishi are all thought to provide nutrients that nourish your immune system, they help to neutralize free radicals whilst at the same time boost antioxidant activity.

Gallbladder

The body produces bile to break down fat. It is the liver that produces the bile, and the gallbladder stores it. When you are eating fats, the gallbladder releases bile to help emulsify the fats and break them down. If you have a sluggish gallbladder, you should reduce your fat intake, and you need to consume short chain fatty acids instead of long chain fatty acids. Coconut oil, ghee, milk avocado and grapeseed oil are all short-term fatty acids. You should eat a lot of vegetables and fruits and lean organic meat, probiotic rich foods and sprouted nuts and grains to help with your gallbladder health.

There are some very good supplements for gallbladder health including Lipase, probiotics, milk thistle, turmeric and bile salts.

Chronic pain

Just remember medication never heals pain it just masks the pain. Reducing processed inflammatory foods and increase whole foods for natural relief.

Cherries are good for reducing pain, as they contain anthocyanins, powerful antioxidants that reduce inflammation. Anthocyanins give them their red hue. They inhibit pain enzymes just like aspirin, naproxen, and other non-steroid anti-inflammatories. They are great for relieving arthritic pain.

Ginger relieves arthritis, migraines and sore muscle pain. It is a powerful anti-inflammatory and stomach soother.

Cranberry juice prevents ulcers by preventing H. Pylori from adhering to the stomach lining. It can also eliminate infection on its own.

Omega 3 fatty acids found in fish, salmon, herring, mackerel, are good for healing chronic pain, they can relieve back, neck, and joint pain. Omega 3's improves blood flow and reduce inflammation in blood vessels and nerves.

Turmeric can heal achy joints and can relieve pain with its anti-inflammatory properties. It also promotes healthy nerve cell function, and protects the body from tissue destruction and joint inflammation,

Hot peppers can relieve arthritis pain. They contain capsaicin which stimulates nerve endings and depletes a chemical that relays pain signals.

Chapter 22

Herbalism, superfoods and nutrition

This section expands a little on the previous chapter and talks about herbs and superfoods.

So, what is a superfood? Superfoods are the foods that are packed with essential vitamins, Vitamins and can be described as nutrient rich dietary foods that have an extraordinarily high concentration of essential vitamins and minerals, antioxidants that can significantly benefit your health,

These foods support your immune system and support your overall well-being.

- Avocado: - rich in heart-healthy monounsaturated fats that can reduce the risk of heart disease and stroke. The avocado is an abundant source of potassium. Avocados are low in carbs and high in fat, healthy fats. Over 70% of their fat is good fat linked to healthier cholesterol levels and a reduced risk of heart disease. Avocados are good for blood pressure, anti-inflammation, and are also good for your blood sugars.
- Beets: - rich in nutrients, and they are also packed with essential vitamins and minerals. They are an excellent source of folate, which protects cell division and the formation of DNA. Beets also contain significant amounts of Vitamin C, potassium, manganese, and Vitamin B6. Beets promote a feeling of fulness, and it is also a source of dietary fiber, both soluble and insoluble. Beets can help regulate blood sugar levels, and they are rich in antioxidants particularly Betalains, have been studied for their potential anti-inflammatory and detoxifying properties. Beets also have nitrates which help dilate blood vessels, leading to improved blood flow. The nitrates have also been shown to

improve athletic performance by improving oxygen utilization in muscles. The nitrates in beets may also help with cognitive function by increasing blood flow to the brain. Beets can also support liver function, and detoxification processes due to the betalain.

- Berries: - berries including blueberries, cranberries, goji berries, raspberries, strawberries etc. are considered superfoods due to their high concentration of flavonoids in berries. Flavonoids are antioxidants. They combat oxidative stress and inflammation.
- Chia seeds: - Chia seeds have a very high nutritional profile. They are rich in fiber, antioxidants, protein, and vitamins, The nutrients found in chia seeds play a pivotal role in promoting heart health, enhancing bone strength, and managing blood sugar levels among other benefits. Chia seeds also contain calcium, magnesium, iron, phosphorus, zinc, Vitamin B1, and Vitamin B3. Chia seeds also contain quercetin.
- Cinnamon: - Cinnamon contains potent antioxidants and also anti-inflammatory compounds which can help combat oxidative stress and also inflammation in the body, which reduces the risk of chronic diseases and supports overall well-being. It is excellent at regulating blood sugar levels, and it may also improve insulin sensitivity. It has also been linked to lowering LDL (bad cholesterol) levels in the blood.
- Dark leafy greens: - Vegetables such as kale, spinach, Swiss chard, romaine lettuce, and argula, are all abundant in essential vitamins, which include Vitamin A, C, E, and also minerals and antioxidants. They are also rich in Vitamin K, and have potential to help with cancer, support bone health, and enhancing heart health thanks to high levels of folate. They also regulate blood clotting and help from inflammatory diseases. They may also help with age related cognitive decline.
- Green tea: - green tea has high chlorophyll levels. Green tea is rich in polyphenols which is a micro-nutrient with potent antioxidant properties.
- Lentils: - they are exceptionally rich in essential nutrients, and they provide fiber, vitamins, minerals, protein.

Lentils are full of fiber, potassium and folate and iron. They are an excellent source of plant-based protein. The protein content supports muscle health, tissue repair, and feelings of fullness.

- Salmon has a high content of Omega 3 Fatty acids. Including EPA and DHA, Salmon has high quality protein, minerals, and Vitamin D, Vitamin B12, selenium, and potassium. The pink or reddish colour is due to a potent antioxidant called ester xanthine, this antioxidant helps protect cells from damage caused by free radicals, reducing the risk chronic diseases.
- Yoghurt and Kefir: - these are fermented dairy products, that are considered super foods because of their probiotic content, and they have potential cancer fighting properties. They are also excellent sources of calcium, and protein.
- Dark chocolate: - dark chocolate is good for your health in many ways. Dark chocolate is packed with flavonoids and polyphenols. These antioxidants protect against oxidative stress and also contribute to heart health and reduced risk of chronic illness. Dark chocolate also contains mood-enhancing compounds such as phenylethylamine and serotonin precursors.

Superfoods and herbs
- Soursop (graviola): - this is a sizeable heart shaped fruit which thrives in tropical areas. It is green on the outside and has a creamy interior which is perfect for beverages. The outer skin is inedible, but the inner flesh and the leaves have incredible health benefits. The biggest potential benefit it has is against cancer and defeating cancer cells. It is 10,000 ties more effective than chemotherapy, as discussed in the cancer section. Traditional remedies incorporate the leaves, the roots, the bark and the seeds to harness the fruits therapeutic powers. Soursop leaves can also be used effectively for skin problems such as eczema and acne. Soursop also supports the immune system, insomnia relief, and helps with arthritis, gout and diabetes,
- Moringa Oleifera: - this is one of the planets most nutritious trees, and its leaves are comprised of medicinal therapeutic properties. It has 18 of the 29 amino acids, which includes all of the nine essential amino acids. It has 46

antioxidants, and also 36 anti-inflammatory properties. The Moringa tree is often called the tree of life, and every part of it, from the leaves to the pods are eaten and utilized. There are over 90 different vitamins and minerals. The moringa naturally reduces blood pressure, lowers the risk of cancer, reduces post-meal glucose levels in type 2 diabetes, gastric ulcer relief, and it is also a mood enhancer. It also helps with mental clarity due to the zinc and iron content. The Moringa also helps to promote weight loss by suppressing your appetite, boosts energy levels. The vitamins included are Vitamin A, B1, B2, B3, B6, C, and E. The Moringa Seeds are used for various things, such as enhancing sex drive, antibiotic and anti-inflammatory properties, gout, cramp, STD's.

- Organic Maca Powder: - Maca is a root belonging to the radish family, it is normally available in powder form. It is grown in the Peruvian mountains and is called Peruvian ginseng, but it is not ginseng. The maca root comes in 3 different forms, yellow, black and red. The yellow maca is known as a libido enhancer and sometimes called natural Viagra. You can use this in whole or powder form, in salad dressings, cereals, smoothies etc. It is rich in vitamin B, C, E, calcium, zinc, iron, magnesium, phosphorous and amino acids.

In women's health it helps to alleviate menstrual issues, menopausal symptoms, cramps, body pain, hot flashes, anxiety, mood swings and also depression. The black maca is actually renowned for increasing sperm count, and helps with stress, it is a natural anti-depressant, and it helps build muscle naturally. Red Macca helps enhance health, mood, reduces stress and also strengthens bones. It is also beneficial for prostate health in men.

- Ashwagandha: - Ashwagandha is also known as winter cherry, and it belongs to the nightshade family. Both the roots and the berries are used to create an herbal powder. It is used for a wide range of issues. It serves as an adaptogen controlling the body's response to stress and environmental changes. So, it aids in coping with external stressors. It is also used as a general tonic, as it contains chemicals that may help calm the brain, reduce inflammation and lower blood pressure. It also helps the immune system, improve cognitive function, reduce pain and inflammation and combat the effects of ageing. Ashwagandha has so many health benefits which include managing chronic liver disease, menstrual issues, asthma, arthritis, addressing bronchitis, promoting production of red blood cells, combatting tumors, addressing skin conditions and so much more.

- Mango Leaves: - the leaves contain Vitamin A, B, C, flavonoids, phenol. They have a rich nutritional profile including tannins, alkaloids, glycosides, steroids, saponins. These leaves possess anti-microbial properties making them effective against bacteria, viruses and fungi. Mango leaves have been known to help treat diabetes, as they contain tannins which aids in addressing the early stages of diabetes by reducing hyperglycemia. Mango leaves can also help with vascular diseases, lowering blood pressure, relieving anxiety, and it can also help with kidney and gallstones. Mango leaves can also be beneficial for your respiratory health problems, such as colds, bronchitis, and asthma.

- Cerasee:- (bitter lemon) it is a bitter herb, and is renowned for its blood purification and detoxifying properties. Cerasee contains essential nutrients and vitamins such as A, B1, B3, B9, C, alongside with choline, lutein, calcium, iron, potassium, phosphorous, zinc and dietary fiber. Cerasee can also help with a variety of different problems including skin problems, infertility, urinary tract infections, menstrual pains, hypertension, constipation, diabetes, abdominal pain, it can also be used against scabies and ringworm. It has also showed promised in treating conditions such as psoriasis and eczema. The leaves are rich in beneficial antioxidants, including catechin (phytochemical) and gallic acid, which boost the immune system and protect against free radical damage.

- Lemon Grass (Fever grass): - this is unique plant which offers many health benefits, The health benefits can include lower blood pressure, reduced inflammation, protects against cancer, fights heart problems, itchy skin, gout, liver inflammation, reduces swelling. It also has anti-bacterial and anti-fungal properties

- Sea moss (Irish Moss): - sea moss is a general term for red algae which is a plant with over 6.000 species. The organic Irish Sea moss is a remarkable species of red algae, a type of seaweed that thrives in cold waters. It can vary in colour ranging from greenish yellow to deep purple or purplish brown. It has a high vitamin and mineral content which is perfect for replenishing the body. Irish moss is also said to be an aphrodisiac and remedy male impotence. It is also comprised of nearly 10% protein, which is about 15% mineral matter. It contains 92 essential minerals out of the 102 that compose of the human body. It has calcium, magnesium, folate, sodium, iodine, sulfur, potassium, vitamins A, B,C,D,E,F and K.

The Irish Moss can help with many health issues including bladder disorders, bronchitis, bad breath. It can also be used to address skin problems like dryness, eczema, rashes and sunburn. It is also known for helping coughs, colds, and regulating bowel movements. It can also accelerate recovery from joint injuries, strengthens connective tissues and acts as a natural inflammatory.

- Spirulina: - this is a naturally occurring algae that has survived for approximately 3.5 billion years. Spirulina is nutritionally complete and surpasses even soya beans and quinoa combined. It is an excellent natural source of iodine, and it also contains the same amount of phosphorus, magnesium and calcium as milk. Spirulina is also a rich source of vitamins and mineral which include Vit K, potassium pantothenic acid, which is B5, B1, B2, B3, copper, iron, and manganese, it is also rich in omega 3 acids. It also has omega 6 and 9. It contains over 26 times the calcium found in milk. Some of the benefits from eating spirulina are it can aid in combatting candida, cancer prevention, blood pressure regulation, cholesterol management, stroke prevention, body detoxifying, immune enhancing,.

- Red clover: - red clover contains substances called isoflavones, which are compounds that are similar to estrogen. Red clover can help with menopause symptoms, osteoporosis, asthma, whooping cough, high cholesterol levels. The isoflavones which undergo conversion within the body, which are phytoestrogens, and they are similar to estrogen. Women can turn

to red clover to ease menopausal symptoms such as hot flashes, breast pain.
- Nettles: - Yes, Nettles… Nettles are high in Vitamin K, which is important for healthy blood clotting. Nettles are also a good source for Vitamin A, Calcium, magnesium, fibre, iron, potassium, and they are rich in antioxidants, support bone health, help balance sugar levels, skin healing properties, and can help prevent some cancers.

Chapter 23

Lifestyle medicine

As I have said on a few occasions in this book, most of our chronic diseases are preventable, and in many cases reversible when we address the underlying cause. Conventional medicine ignores the underlying causes and makes very little attempt to reverse or prevent these diseases, and unfortunately instead focuses on the long-term management of these diseases, which of course benefits big pharmaceutical companies.

There are six pillars to lifestyle medicine, which show the way as a whole in taking back control of your health and wellbeing. The pillars of lifestyle medicine represent key areas which need to be focused on, and when you do this, it can have a profound impact on a person's overall health and wellbeing,

The six pillars are: - Whole food plant-based nutrition, Physical activity, Avoidance of risky substances, Restorative sleep, Stress management, social connections. These six pillars serve as a framework where individuals can address and optimize the lifestyle factors that contribute to health. Now in this book I don't want to go into details about lifestyle medicine and the 6 pillars, as I am sure a lot as been covered in others of the book.

It's is all well and good having all the information in this book at your side, and another 100 books about how you can change your lifestyle to become heathier, fitter, less stressed and dis-ease free, but are you ready to make the changes in your life to reverse your diabetes, or make your gut health better, or deal with your autoimmune issues, adrenal fatigue or cancer? Why are you going to succeed? Why do you want to succeed? Have you been honest about your lifestyle, what you are eating, your stress levels, and how all this affects you and your health.

Your genetics DO NOT control your health, you control your health and your future. It is down to you whether you want to be fit and healthy, or unfit and full of inflammation, and dis-ease.

What is your story that you have created as regards to your health and why you are where you are RIGHT NOW?

I want you to ask yourself why you want to change, and how you are going to get that drive to do something at maximum level to change your life. What are your reasons for changing your lifestyle and your lack of exercise, or stress levels? You already know that fast food restaurants, takeaways, processed foods, carbohydrates and sugars are inflaming your body, putting your immune system under so much pressure, and causing health issues, illness, dysbiosis and dis-ease in your body, or if not now, you know that the small symptoms you are getting now, means that your body is under pressure,

So, what are your reasons for change? Do you have children? Do you want to do more things in your life and more adventures and see more things? Do you want to claim back your life and health? Blaming your health and where you are right now on your genes is neither true nor real.

You know now that your life is in your hands. Epigenetics proves that it is not in the hands of your genes. or your ancestors, but your health and your life, and your future is in your hands. So, it really is down to you and whether you want to keep putting your body under pressure, or you want to take your life and health back.

Don't listen to conventional medicine, or the doctor who says you have weeks or months to live, that's a nocebo effect, and if you believe that, and what they say, then you will have weeks or months to live. They talk absolute rubbish, and they don't have a crystal ball, and they don't have all the answers, nobody does! But what you do have is the ability to change things in your life, if you change the foods that you eat, the toxins you put in your body, and how you react to stress.

the rules of clean eating

1. The 80/20 rule: - 70/30) 80% of your food should be green, healthy vegetables, at its most natural state. The 20-30% is the meat, complex carbs, fats.

2. Eat organic: - organic without GMO modified foods, additives and pesticide free

3. Animal proteins: - choose very carefully, grass fed, organic, free roaming, no anti-biotics, no hormones. Stay away from corn fed.

4. Water rich foods: - blueberries, vegetables, drink lots of water, fruits.

5. Avoid processed foods: - the burger, sausages, packaged foods, bacon, hot dogs, your typical fast-food restaurants.

6. Avoid processed sugar, salt, preservatives & dye: -

Protein

Protein is the main component of a person's muscles, bones, skin, organs, hormones and manes up a significant part of the body. It is also an integral nutrient that the body need to create and also repair your cells. The reason why protein is so important is because it contains amino-acids, and they are the building blocks of the body. There are 2 types of amino acids: -

1. Non-essential: - and this means that these amino acids can be made inside the body

2. Essential: - this means that these must be consumed from outside sources.

There are 9 essential amino acids which are Histidine, isoleucine, leucine, lysine, methionine, phenylalanine, threonine, valine and tryptophan.

So how much protein do you think you need each day? Well, this varies by someone's age, gender, physical stress on the body and other bio-individual factors. For a general rule of thumb, it should be 335% - 50% of your body weight in grams. The problem is too much protein can produce excess nitrogen in the body creating fatigue.

Fat

Fat makes you fat... that is false and so misleading, because fat does NOT make you fat... Newsflash, it's the carbohydrates and sugars that make you fat.

And this doesn't mean that you should eat fats all the time like bacon, meats, etc., and follow the keto diet, because this will NOT make you healthy. It may make you lose weight, but in the long run it is NOT healthy for you.

Ok, so basic fat lesson, fats are basically three molecules which are joined together, called triglycerides (fatty acid combined with glycerol). Fat is essential for the ability to sustain life, and fats are essential for body processes.

There are two types if fat
1. Saturated: - solid at room temperature, butters, etc
2. Unsaturated: - liquid at room temperature, oils etc.

The bad fats are Trans fats, because they are high in hydrogen, because it is added to extend shelf-life. They are bad for you. The fries, chips, crisps, pepperoni, processed foods, vegetable oils etc. get the trans fats out of your life totally. The worst types are hydrogenated cooking oils, commercial fried foods, cakes, cookies, crusts, margarine, soybean oil, and most pre-packaged foods.

Saturated fats are tightly packed molecules with no double bonds between them, and they are generally solid at room temperature, and these include burgers, fries, etc., fatty red meat and other animal products, dairy are also saturated. Unsaturated fats are loosely packed with double bonds, liquid at room temperature, reported to be essential for cognitive health.

1. Eliminate all trans fats
2. Choose olive oil, coconut oils, avocado oils over other oils
3. Avoid any vegetable of hydrogenated oils at all costs
4. Avoid dairy
5. Limit fat from animal protein except cold water fish which is loaded with omega.
6. Avocados are an excellent source of healthy fat.

Acid versus alkaline

Our blood Ph is supposed to stay at 7.35 to 7.45to stay in the healthy range. Our bodies self-regulate this, but if your body is in more of acidic state then the body needs to regulate by taking calcium away from bone and other sources. So this is why a more alkaline diet is better for you and your body, as your body does not need to work as hard to keep it in homeostasis.

Symptoms that your body could be more acidic than alkaline could be fatigue, confusion, shortness of breath, headache, rapid breathing, acidic tastes in your mouth.

Acidic lifestyle

Too much coffee intake, fast food drive through meals, processed and cooked foods, stress, alcohol and tobacco consumption, polluted environment, harsh cleaning, body care and airborne chemicals... this life will eventually lead to dysbiosis, health problems, inflammation and dis-ease.

Alkaline lifestyle

Lots of raw clean organic fruits and vegetables, clear pure alkaline water, fresh clean air and environment, stress reducing activities, herbal teas or small amounts of organic lower acid coffee, no processed foods or GMO type products, cleaning, bathing and other products free of harsh chemicals and toxins... this is where your health gets better, healthier, homeostasis,

Fasting

There are different forms of fasting and these include 24 hours fast, 48 hours fast, 72 hours fast, intermittent fasting, alternating fasting, water fast, 500 calorie fast, keto fast

The full day fasts which could be for 1,2 o3 3 days are where you consume no food at all, and drink only water, lemon water, black coffee and herbal teas. The good side of the full day fasting is that it allows for digestive rest, it gives your body the chance to eliminate toxins, and it has also been shown to eliminate amyloid proteins that have been linked to Alzheimer's and dementia. It keeps your blood and insulin levels stable, lowers your cholesterol as well as giving rest to your adrenals.

With the intermittent fasting there are times when you are fasting and small windows where you can eat through the day. Popular intermittent fasting times are 16:8, 18:6, and 20:4. So, for instance in a 18:6 fast, you would fast let's say from 6pm at night, skip breakfast in the morning, and start eating at 12pm until 6pm every day, or on days you decide to fast.

So, the advantages of fasting include digestive rest and elimination, insulin resistance and sugar regulation, it helps to create more stem cells which reflect ageing, clearer thinking, weight management, and cell autophagy where your body eats up the abnormal cells, the toxins, the waste in your body.

"when you look at yourself, you are not a single entity, but you are a community of 50 trillion cells. Every cell is intelligent, but when they are in a community, they give up their personal intelligence, and respond to the central voice, and if the central voice says to die, the cells will die. The central voice is THE MIND. There are signals from the environment, both the internal and external environment, and the function of the brain is to receive the signals, and then interpret those signals and then send the information to the cells to control the behaviour and the genetics" Dr Bruce Lipton

Exercise and fitness

So, what are the benefits of exercise?

1. Healthy heart and lungs\;- Your heart is a muscle and obviously responds to exercise. When you exercise your lungs, you transmit more oxygen to your body. Exercise opens arteries to deliver more oxygen to the cells which in turn lowers blood pressure.

2. Stronger muscles and bones: - when you exercise you make small micro tears in the muscle which then when they heal build more muscle hence making you stronger.

3. Elevated emotion and reduced stress: - exercise stimulates hormones called endorphins, which are the body's happy chemicals, and at the same time you are sweating out toxins, delivering more oxygen to your brain and body and it satisfies our emotional need to be productive.

4. Better sleep: - exercise helps promote sleep and reduce stress.

5. Positive body image: - A healthy body image of yourself can help with self-confidence, depression, anxiety and other mental health issues.

6. Balanced hormone, sugar and energy levels: - exercise has been linked to ore balanced hormones, and it has also been shown to reduce blood sugar levels, balancing cholesterol levels, and it stimulates the production of ore blood vessels through the process if vascularization.

There are different types of exercise which you could do to get yourself going and changing your life around such as cardio, strength, endurance, cross/interval training, impact, and stretching /yoga.

Cardio
Cardio is good of course for cardio/pulmonary health, it increases endurance, and it can burn fat, increases blood flow and elevates mood.

Strength training
This type of training increases muscle growth which stimulates fat metabolism, it supports the skeletal system and prevents atrophy, creates definition and balance of the body, stimulates 'feel good' hormones, and allows for vascularization.

Cross / interval
Cross interval training builds both types of muscle, it is very effective for weight loss and general balanced fitness.

Sleep
I think this is the time in the book that we cover sleep again, as it is an area where people often neglect, or struggle with if you have insomnia. So, what is sleep and what happens when we sleep? We have covered this in more detail in the book already, and this is to just reiterate how important sleep is when it comes to detoxing your body and getting your health and life back on track.

Some people may think that sleep is just where the mind and body and just stop and shut down for a while and this isn't true. When your eyes close, the work in your body begins, and so many things happen. This is where the brain starts indexing those memories, the flushing of the brain fluids, the cell regeneration. It's where the liver starts pulling toxins from the blood, and your cells start to regenerate and repair themselves and any dead or dying cells are eliminated.

Breathing
Breathing and breathwork is so important not only for your health and optimal oxygen intake but also to help alleviate health issues.

We can live months without food... we can live weeks without water... but only minutes without air.

Breathing is the exchange of oxygen for carbon monoxide. Oxygen is necessary for optimal cell function. Carbon dioxide is the waste product that needs to come out.

Nose breathing is optimal, in through nose out through nose, this is because the nose is equipped with cilia that filter the air, this also warms the air prior to hitting your lungs. On the exhale it also clears trapped pathogens from the nasal passages.

Mouth breathing has no filter allowing pathogens, dust, molds etc. to enter directly into the lungs, also in colder climates the air is not warmed as well, this can trigger asthmatic response. There are many types of different breathwork techniques, which you can learn by going to classes, and the different benefits each of these types of breath techniques have on the body. You can learn these techniques by going to breathwork classes, or video tutorials, The Viking Buddha do offer classes in breathwork meditation, Qi Gong and mindfulness, and 14-day full detox retreats. Visit www.thevikingbuddha.co.uk

Chapter 24

Hypnosis

Two of the biggest causes of ill health and disease are stress and trauma. In addition to the blockages in your body caused by what you eat, what toxins are put into your body, and how you treat your body, there are blockages in your body and mind which are caused by stress and trauma and the past which you have not let go.

To become fully healthy and well and living your best life which you were meant to live, you need to manage stress in your life better, and cortisol levels, and this can be helped with things like mindfulness, breathwork, yoga, meditation and getting out into nature. The trauma, phobias, fears, addictions and habits are a little more difficult to deal with,

Now, I have called this chapter hypnosis, and I have done this for a reason. I have been lucky enough to be trained as a clinical hypnotherapist many years ago, but in addition to this I trained to become an hypnotist. I spent quite a bit of time training with top celebrity and international hypnotists, and I have had the pleasure and honour to train with Jonathon Chase, Jonathon Royle, Andrew Newton, and learnt so much from these guys as well other top hypnotists such as Karl Smith, Freddie Jacquin and a few other top hypnotists.

There are unfortunately a lot of what they called script-no-therapists out there, where people haven't had the best experiences or most successful experiences. On top of this, one of the first questions I always get asked is 'are you going to make me run round like a chicken', which of course the answer is 'no', because even the stage hypnotists can't make you do that. Nobody can make you do that. What does happen is a very clever process which allows the people who are more susceptible to hypnosis and are willing to be more open to suggestions and quite honestly in some ways want to be on that stage. This leads to people being hypnotized and doing silly things on stage. It is basically that fine line of what you would be prepared to do on stage as you are more relaxed and open, to what you would normally be prepared to do. If you weren't happy believe me, you would just wake up.

With regards to hypnosis and the power to deal with trauma and other issues such as phobias, fears, addictions, habits, smoking, weight loss etc., hypnosis is very powerful, as it is dealing with your subconscious mind where all YOUR phobias, fears, trauma etc. are all stored.

Ok, I am going to leave hypnosis there, for a moment, as we look at your normal talk therapies. The counselling, CBT, DBT, REBT, Psychotherapy etc. Over the years I have added more and more of these to my repertoire so to speak, to be able to help as many people as I can, and they all have their place in helping people. Unfortunately, CBT, DBT and counselling are the 'go to therapies' for the NHS, because as we have discussed in this book conventional medicine loves to put plasters on problems. You have some pain; they give you medicine. You are out of breath; they give you a spray. Unfortunately, the same is for psychological problems or trauma etc., the give you coping skills to dampen down the symptoms. But what about dealing with the actual cause?

Someone who has been abused, or has trauma / PTSD, or phobia etc., will not be 'cured' from counselling, or CBT! Why? Because the trauma you have, or other serious issues, are locked away in your subconscious mind, and your talk therapies deal with your conscious mind, so with the best will in the world, the best outcome you are going to get from CBT/DBT, or counselling is learning coping skills to deal with your trauma.

They give you a plaster, and help you to try and cope with your trauma, and in some cases, it makes you feel worse. This I know, because many who have come to myself for Hypnosis for trauma have tried talk therapies and when asked did it help, not really, because the trauma is still there.

I think one of my biggest worries about the wanting to dampen down the symptoms and not deal with what is causing the symptoms in the first place, came once when I was doing a shift as a support worker at a Mental Health Hospital. I was looking after this particular person, and 3 people came into the room, a MH practitioner, and 2 psychiatrists, and as they started to talk to this patient, they kept overlooking the fact that she wanted to end her life, and when they asked how they could help her, she must have mentioned she wanted trauma therapy at least 4 times. They ignored that, and went back onto increasing her medication, which again is the plaster over the problems. Block the symptoms rather than dealing with the actual issue.... Trauma!

Another thing that worries me quite a bit, is when therapists or counsellors put trauma in a box, and that textbook, 'ah you have trauma so you must be feeling this way' and this is how we deal with this trauma you have'. Seriously? Everybody's trauma is different, people deal with their trauma, and stress differently and see if differently, so you cannot put in a box how someone is actually feeling, because everyone is different.

Talk therapies, CBT, DBT, are excellent in many areas and general counselling, relationships, bereavement, group therapy, and many other areas, but the simple fact is that if you want to get rid of trauma or phobias etc., you must access the subconscious mind to do this. Now there are a few different models now which kind of do this with NLP, EMDR, IEMT, Brain spotting, Magnetic Recode which are all great, and again I myself have added some of these to what I do, but for me, as a hypnotist, the best stand out therapy by far is hypnosis.

Psychoanalysis	Cognitive Behaviour Therapy	Hypnotherapy
38% Recover after 600 Sessions	72% Recover after 22 Sessions	93% Recover after 6 Sessions

So, what is hypnosis?

Hypnosis is a deep state of relaxation, or a heightened state of awareness. Have you ever been driving along, and you get to your destination and think how did I get here, as if you are on autopilot, that's kind of hypnosis, a light trance, much the same as watching tv and getting engrossed in it.

As a hypnotist, we guide you into that trance like state, and deepen the state if we have to, where you will feel relaxed, you will be able to hear everything around you, but you are focused on the therapist's voice. The client is doing the work inside, the hypnotist is the catalyst for the change. So yes, hypnosis is powerful and has incredible results, and it is the power of the words said by the hypnotist, and how the client uses those words which helps release trauma, get rid of phobias, pain, and help s people lose weight and stop smoking,

Can everybody be hypnotized? Most people can be hypnotized, and some go deeper naturally. Of course, part of being able to be hypnotized is being able to relax and visualization is very beneficial. So, if someone's mind is all over the place, and its none stop thinking, or someone has psychosis or can't relax, then they are probably some of the few people who will struggle with hypnosis, and then cognitive therapies will be used to help cope with issues, but most people can be hypnotized,

But I also think this is where a note of caution comes in also. I have had people come to me for hypnosis session, and the first question I ask, have you been hypnotized before, and on a few occasions, they have said yes, and it didn't work. When I ask what the hypnotherapist did, they say, 'well I laid on the couch, and they just talked to me for an hour, saying you will go down escalator to a beach etc. (what if they hate escalators and beaches) and they didn't feel anything and of course no change was made.

Hypnosis is powerful, it works on most occasions, it can change lives. Hypnosis is very powerful, it can be done in 10 or 15 minutes for a phobia using something like 'the arrow technique' or trauma release which is incredibly effective, and the client is being led to release his or her trauma, and any other negative emotions. If you want to get your life back, and heal your mind, body and spirit, it is essential you start handling your stress much better, with mindfulness techniques, and it is so important that you deal with the issues holding you back, whether it be trauma, abuse, bereavement, addiction, and also forgiveness, let it all go, because they are all causing your body to be full of toxins, and causing blockages with are causing inflammation and dis-ease.

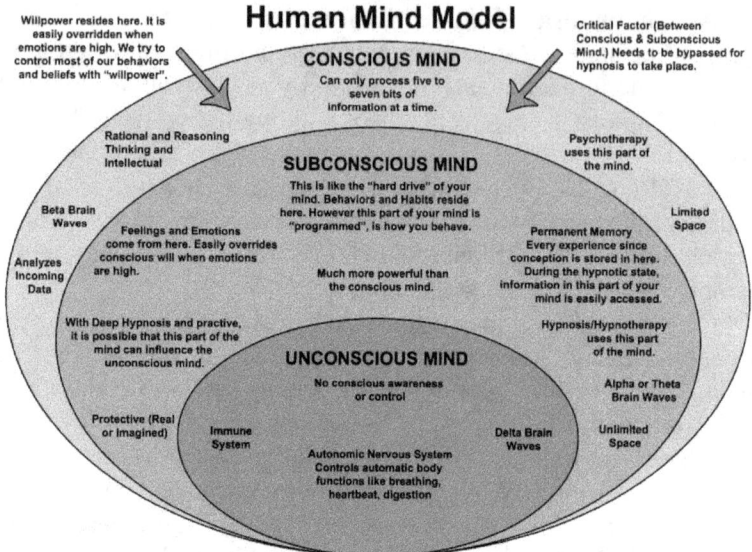

This has been a very short chapter on Hypnosis, as I have another book which I will be publishing at some point in early 2026 called the Truth about Hypnosis, which goes further into depth about all things Hypnosis, and this was just a chapter to say if you want rid of trauma, phobias, and other issues go and see a reputable hypnotist, and allow your mind to become free of any issues holding you back in life.

Chapter 25

Regenerative full detox

In this chapter I would very much like to go through a regenerative detox, and it may seem again like I may repeat a few things throughout the book, but this is good, because the more I can hit home points about inflammation, free radicals, the need to detox and reclaim your health, the more it will sink in about all the pieces fit together like a jigsaw

DIS-EASE
I would like for you to look at that word again. Dis-ease when broken down means our body is not at ease with itself, it is quite the opposite, it is in dis-ease. Disease is where we are feeling either physically or emotionally out of balance. Our body is talking to us through this dis-ease. Your body is trying to tell you that something different is needed and that it is under pressure.

When we start labelling diseases, it becomes detrimental, because you are accepting that disease as your own, and it can lock someone into feeling that they have this outside problem on them and there is nowhere to go. A disease is a set of symptoms that actually varies from person to person, and this varies due to what the imbalance is in the body. Your body is trying to tell you through symptoms, that it is out of balance, and organs are under pressure, and it needs to heal, and it is crying out for you to change your lifestyle emotionally and physically.

Power = V – O   Power = Vitality – obstructions

The formula above is so important. It means that we have the power within us, it is inherent to us, and it knows how to heal. When you remove what is obstructing your internal power to your healing, to your vitality, and when we remove all that is obstructing it physically and emotionally, then you WILL HEAL. Any health issue WILL heal when we remove the obstructions.

What we need to do to remove those obstructions, is to listen to what the body is telling us, because the symptoms are signs that there is an obstruction to the flow of vitality, it is that simple.

When we ignore these signs, then the symptoms go deeper, the illness becomes more chronic, and at a certain point we struggle to turn things around.

There are three root causes of disease.

1. Genetic weakness: - when someone who has an health issue and they relate to what they have as genetic, they have an attitude of disempowerment, a feeling of this is the way it is, and basically there is nothing they can do about it. This is so wrong and untrue. Remember the epigenetics chapter. You are your destiny, just because your parent may have had it, and you may even be predisposed to it, it does not mean you will get it, that is up to you. Remember when we talked about the epigenome, and your intelligent cells? Genetics do not, or should not be a factor, because you quite simply have the control. With epigenetics we can pass on new genes that have happened in our lives to our descendants, through epigenetics.

2. Toxicity: - we are having dis-ease because we are trying to get rid of dis- ease symptoms that we are experiencing, and our body is trying to get rid of toxins that we have taken in from outside, whether it be air pollution, food, water, etc. when we add additives to our foods these are toxins, when we breathe in chemicals, pollution, pesticides, cosmetics are all toxins,

3. Over acidity: - Anything that you take into your body that generates acidity in the body, this refers to the food that you put into your body. If you are constantly putting acidic foods into your body, the this is going to affect the pH of the blood in your body, and over time your body will start to have symptoms due to being out of balanced due to way too many acidic foods in your diet. Acid causes tissue weakness in your body. Your body needs to be in that alkaline state around 7.35 to 7.45 ph.

When we are referring to healing, we are talking about the lymphatic system of the body. The lymphatic system comprises of about 75% of your body fluids. The other 25% of your body fluids is blood. The blood is what nourishes the cells, brings nutrients around your body. The lymph fluids are responsible for removing all the waste in your body from all of the metabolic processes that go on in your body.

We need foods that are going to promote the movement of fluids within our body, and the best foods are the most water rich fruits and vegetables. For us to remove acid waste it is important to eat fruits and vegetables and cut down on proteins and other foods for a short time during detoxification. During a detox we need to go into a cleansing process. Protein and fats are building foods, and during a detox we are in a cleansing process. So, it is about eating fruits and vegetables and for a short period cutting down the fats and proteins and of course carbs.

There are three different detox levels.

Beginner level / Level 1
Breakfast: - start with smoothie, or fruits.
Mid-morning snack: - smoothie or fruit
Lunch: - vegetable salad or cooked vegetables
Afternoon snack: - juice, fruit or vegetables
Dinner: - protein & vegetable and fruits

Deeper level / Level 2
Breakfast: - smoothie or fruit
Mid-morning snack: - smoothie or fruit
Lunch: - smoothie or fruit or veggie salad
Afternoon snack: - juice, fruit or vegetables
Dinner: - vegetable salad or cooked vegetables

Advanced level/ L3
Breakfast: - juice, smoothie or fruit
Min-morning snack; - fresh juice, smoothie or fruit
Lunch: - smoothie or fruit
Afternoon snack: - fresh juice or fruit
Dinner: - smoothie or fruit

The length of the detox would vary for different people. With the Viking Buddha Retreat, which is 14 days, the actual detox period is 10 days. Within this detox retreat which we run, you would also be doing meditation, breathwork, yoga, Qi Gong, and other sessions.

If you are doing this detox, it is an individual detox, and depends on if you are experiencing symptoms, but 3-day detox, 5-day, 7 day or 10 day detox is very good for your body and detoxing your system.

The kind of symptoms that you might experience are tiredness, and signs that your body is getting rid, body odor, cold type symptoms, mucus, headaches, etc., and these are all normal symptoms, and much of this is your body detoxing from toxins etc.

Conclusion

Well, Firstly, thank you for investing in this book, and I hope you managed to get a lot from the book. There are a lot of different chapters in the book, focusing on different issues from the autoimmune solution to adrenal fatigue, to the hormones, to menopause, and there are a lot of different bits of advice which help with different issues. Each section has invaluable information about trying to get your body back healthy, and trying to heal your body from each condition, which you can refer back to and make your own plans going forward that work for you.

But on a general note, there are things that you can do which can start to regain your health and life back. Stop eating processed foods, reduce your carbohydrates, gluten, dairy. You can start looking at the chemicals in the shampoos, soaps, cleaning products which are toxic. Start reading of the foods that you do buy, and start eating non-GMO, organic fresh fruit and vegetables. Start looking at your life, the stress, exercise, the trauma or past issues which haven't been resolved.

Rather than looking at having disease, or illness, look at your symptoms, and why you have those symptoms. When you start looking at your lifestyle, and ger rid of the toxins, bad food, and the stress, you will find yourself regaining your health, the blockages will start to disappear and those symptoms which you have been experiencing will disappear.

When you get chance, look at all your medications that you are on, and then look at all the potential side effects that each medication has, and if you are on 3 or more different medications, how many symptoms that synthetic toxic medication is causing your body to have, why? Because you don't care enough about your health and what you are doing to it right now.

Ultimately, it isn't the doctor, or the fast-food takeaway, or the corner shop, or anybody else's fault that your body is under pressure, or you are sick and ill., It is your fault. They are not forcing you to drink alcohol, or smoke, or eat processed junk food, or that takeaway, and in the Doctor's defence he is helping by helping take away the symptoms, but those symptoms are only going to get worse, because the symptoms are just a way of your body telling you that it is under pressure. Your body is only going to get more blockages, and become more toxic, until it doesn't matter what medication they give you as your body is full of disease.

It is down to you, to take stock of your life, where you are now, and what needs to change to make you feel healthier and live the life you should be living.

This book has never been about having a go at conventional medicine, and certainly not about having a go at doctors, nurses and other healthcare staff, quite the opposite, as I have the utmost respect for every single person who work in hospitals and the care industry, who give amazing care to their patients, and are in many wards in many hospitals, overworked and understaffed. It is having a go at the Big Pharma companies who make millions out of people being ill, and the people in the conventional medicine field who want to hide the symptoms and not get down to the real cause of the disease, and the ones who still think using toxic drugs like chemotherapy actually heal people. It doesn't. And I do believe that if alternative medicine and conventional medicine joined together with all the testing, and the lifesaving doctors and nurses, and along with cutting out the fast foods, the processed foods, and toxins, and dealing with mental health and trauma etc. better instead of just the symptoms, and working towards healing people, then miracles can truly happen.

While it is still more important to look at the symptoms and not the causes of those symptoms, and mask the symptoms with drugs, then people will continue to become more and more ill, suffering and dying from conditions that are reversible. Big Pharma companies don't want people to be well, as they have customers for life. There is a cure for everything on this earth, whether it be from therapies to the food we eat, or around us in nature with plants etc.

It is down to the individuals, and I am sure people will still choose the road of toxins, alcohol, smoking fast food and takeaways, and that is unfortunate, and there will always be conventional medicine for them to mask their symptoms as they get sicker and sicker.

But for the ones who really want to change, and get healthier, and become fit and get their lives back, then this is the start of a new exciting healthy life starting today.

On the following pages you will find more information about the Viking Buddha and our therapy sessions available both in person and online, and the retreats and workshops coming soon

Namaste

The Viking Buddha

The Viking Buddha Mind Management Detox Therapy sessions

The Viking Buddha, aka David, has been a qualified hypnotist since 2004, he is now a master hypnotist, and is also trained in EMDR / IEMT / NLP and cognitive therapies such as CBT/DBT/REBT/ Solution Focused Brief Therapy / Gestalt Therapy and various other models.

He is also a qualified Stress Management Consultant, Mental Health & Wellness Practitioner, and Trauma Specialist.

He particular interests are Trauma and Past Life Regression therapy.

He is available for face-to-face sessions in the UK, and also online sessions UK and internationally for any issues including Trauma, Smoking Cessation, Weight Loss, Fears & Phobias, Pain Management, Habits and Addictions, general health issues, mental health problems, Confidence, Peak Performance and many other issues.

You can contact him directly on +44 0330 043 3203 or email on the vikingbuddha@yahoo.com

Website .www.thevikingbuddha.co.uk

The Viking Buddha Full Body Detox Therapy sessions

In addition to being qualified as a Mind Management Specialist and Master Hypnotist, The Viking Buddha, aka David, has also studied in different Holistic Alternative Medicine approaches to full body health

Following the passing of his father in 2010 due to Cancer, David devoted a lot of study time to Cancer and other diseases and why the body becomes inflamed and starts to get blockages which ultimately lead to illness and disease. He also worked for the NHS for 9 years in general medicine and support,

Over the past 15 years he has studied intensively for thousands of hours and trained in many different areas of alternative medicine and different areas including the natural cancer protocol, Hormone imbalances, Type 2 Diabetes Reversal, Insulin Resistance, Gut-Brain Axis, Hypothyroidism, Skin problems, Menopause, Lifestyle Medicine, Precision Health, regenerative health detox, healthy eating, body inflammation, adrenal fatigue, gut health and much more.

His passion is Epigenetics, Neuroplasticity and Quantum Embodiment.

With the full body and Mind detox sessions, you can work with David as Your coach to change your lifestyle, diet, toxin eradication, food as medicine for your body, and work on all aspects of your life from your mind and trauma, stress, and other issues holding you back, to your physical body and insulin resistance, diabetes, cancer, menopause, gut dysbiosis, adrenal fatigue and other issues by looking at your lifestyle, trauma and issues from the past, your lifestyle choices, and also working with law of attraction and life coaching to get you back on track and living the life you should be living,

Sessions are available face to face in the UK and online video sessions

To have a chat about sessions and how we can help email David on thevikingbuddha@yahoo.com

You can contact him directly on +44 0330 043 3203

Website www.thevikingbuddha.co.uk

The Viking Buddha Workshops

The Viking buddha workshops are coming soon the UK and in 2026 onwards to the USA and beyond.

1 Day Mental Health Workshop

This workshop is a 1-day workshop which is for people struggling with mental health, and also for family and friends of people struggling with their mental health. It is also ideal for companies who want their staff to become more aware of Mental Health Issues and how to support staff.

2 Day 'Radical Wellness Workshop

This workshop is based on this book but a little more in-depth over the 2 days, with a lot more questions as to attendees lifestyle and deeper look into how to change the negatives and look at how to clear blockages and inflammation, with hypnosis sessions for trauma and other issues, and also dealing with stress as well as the nutritional side, It also includes breathwork and meditation sessions to help heal the mind body and spirit.

3 days 'The Awakening' Workshop

this workshop is based on his first book called the 'awakening' which was published in July 2024.

In this Workshop you learn about stress, Mental health, epigenetics, neuroplasticity, Your Ikigai, Life Coaching, Law of Attraction, Ho'oponopono, and the Millionaire Mindset and much more.

It is a fantastic workshop which focuses on how to get the most out of your life, and your positive attitude and includes manifesting, vision boards and much more

If you are a company wishing to book any of these workshops for your employees, please contact The Viking Buddha on 0330 043 3203 or email thevikingbuddha@yahoo.com

If you want to book on one of the workshops coming to a town / city near you from autumn 2025 onwards please check on the website www.thevikingbuddha.co.uk

or email thevikingbuddha@yahoo.com or contact 0330 043 3203 for more details.

The Viking Buddha Retreats

The Viking Buddha wants to be able to reach as many people as possible and change as many people's lives as possible.

From 2026, the Viking Buddha has plans to hold retreats in the UK, the USA and Nepal. The retreats in the UK will be near the Lake District and Wales. The Retreats in Nepal with be in Kathmandu and also Pokhara. The retreats in the USA will be in Los Angeles and Texas

14-day Full detox retreat
This retreat is a 14-day retreat which will be a full detox vegetarian retreat for 10 days out of the 14 days, It will include dark silent reflective sessions, meditation, breathwork, Qi gong, yoga, sound healing, and also seminars on things discussed in this book. There will be therapy sessions and other activities over the 14 days and changing your lifestyle. In the following of retreats like dark retreats, phones or gadgets will NOT be allowed, as it is a full detox retreat, which means getting away from the world you currently live in and going back to basics. You will also have 2 excursions out, one before and one at the end of the retreat, and also a celebration on the last night of the retreat.

This retreat will be run in the UK, Nepal and USA at a retreat centre

10-day chill and relax retreat
This retreat is actually for the ones who do want to change their lifestyles and learn about how to live that healthy lifestyle and how to de-stress and get rid of psychological issues. There will be seminars daily, as well as meditation, breathwork, qigong, yoga, and therapy sessions. This retreat is more relaxed. This again will be run in the UK, Nepal and USA in a hotel and conference environment.

Walk & Talk Therapy Mountains for the Mind Challenges

These are for the more adventurous amongst you, who want to incorporate therapy and learning with walking and challenges. These range from 2-day challenges in Snowdonia Wales and Scotland. To the 7-day challenge in the lake district, to 9 day west highland way challenge. In Nepal this includes many different challenges from 7 days to 18 days, including Everest Base Camp. In the USA this includes 10 day walk & talk therapy challenges where you will be walking different routes in LA or Texas.

If any companies want to book any of these retreats or challenges

contact the Viking buddha on 0330 043 3203 thevikingbuddha@yahoo.com

If anyone is interested in any of the challenges or retreats, please contact the Viking buddha to register interest and when there are enough people interested in the various retreats / challenges these will be booked. Otherwise keep a look out on the website www.thevikingbuddha.co.uk

The Viking Buddha Motivational Speaker

The Viking Buddha is available as a motivational Speaker for conferences, events, seminars, and shows. He is available for a 90-minute motivational speech, or he also has his very own show

Life motivational Show

This is a 2 hour show which is fully interactive show which covers mental health, stress, bullying, abuse, homelessness, family, parenting, life coaching, law of attraction and much more. It has audience participation and one or two demonstrations including hypnosis. It is available to book for hotels, conferences, and other events, and there will also be some shows coming out across the UK from 2026 onwards.

Community centre

David is also running 2 day community centre events, where you can book him, and he will be running 90 minute workshops throughout the 1 days on the following:- elderly resident meet & Greets, Badass Women Domestic abuse workshop (3 hours over 2 days), mental health awareness, bullyproof program, natural cancer program, substance abuse, gut-brain axis, epigenetics, truth about hypnosis, auto immune solution and the LIFE motivational show

If you want to book The Viking Buddha for any of the above events, or you are a community centre who wants to run the 2 day event please contact 0330 0432 3203 thevikingbuddha@yahoo.com
Website:- www.thevikingbuddha.co.uk

The Viking Buddha Corporate

The Viking Buddha and his team can come into your company and offer any of the Workshops for your employees, including the Mental Health Workshop, and the 2-day workshops. We can also offer any of the Walk & Talk Therapy Sessions and challenges for team building.

Employee Holistic Health & Wellness Program

The Viking Buddha is available to come and do 2 half day sessions or 1 full day session per week, working with your employees with the Health & Wellness Program, which includes Mental Health Support, Stress Management, Trauma Therapy, 1 to 1 therapy, Walk & Talk Therapy, and also Precision Health and Lifestyle Medicine.

1 Day Employee Mountains for the Mind challenges

This could be a 1 day or 2-day challenge depending on the location and difficulty of the challenge, it is based in the UK, where the attendees will be challenging themselves both mentally and physically walking up one of our incredible mountains in the UK. These include Snowdon, Ben Nevis, Pen Y Fan, Scafell Pike and many more, under the guidance of a mountain leader, and where you are able to talk to therapists on the way up and down about any issues, problems or general questions in life.

Philosopher's Stone Long Weekend Wild Camp Challenge

This is very much a team building weekend, in the middle of nowhere, from Friday evening to Sunday evening, where you will be camping out wild, with Bell tents, and lots of challenges throughout the day, and evenings sat around the campfire telling stories and getting to know your colleagues better. There is a reason it is called the Philosopher's Stone, which will all be revealed in due course. There will be a therapist on hand to talk to employees, and 1 to 1 sessions, as well as group activities.

The Kaizen Employee Awards

Now we all know about Kaizen and implementing small and continuous improvements to businesses and other areas of Kaizen. David is a certified Kaizen Event Specialist, but what we wanted to do for companies, or more specifically for employees, is to hold 3 awards every year for employers to reward the employees who they feel have contributed to improving things within their company the most over a 12-month period. So, for an employee who comes in 3rd it would be the bronze award and a 3-day long weekend in a top hotel resort in the UK. For an employee in 2nd place, this would be a silver award and a 5-day trip to a top hotel resort in Europe with an awards ceremony. And in 1st place, an 8-day trip to a top hotel resort in the amazing city of Los Angeles USA. These events will happen twice a year. Just imagine how much a reward for the top 3 employees to be rewarded with a trip to a top hotel.

The Corporate Retreat

This is an 8 day corporate retreat, for managers, executives, directors, where there will be stress management, mindfulness sessions, and also sessions with a therapist if needed, and also seminars on Law of Attraction, Millionaire Mindset, Mental Health support for employees, Kaizen, and plenty of time for relaxing and seeing the sights

If your company is interested in any of the above,

please contact the Viking Buddha on 0330 043 3203 thevikingbuddha@yahoo.com

www,thevikingbuddha.co.uk

The Viking Buddha Books

The Viking Buddha is so excited to have finally released this book which is his 2nd book, the first book was released in July 2024, called 'The Awakening', and he is so proud to have both of these books out there and hopefully they bring change to many people over the months and years to come. Over the next coming 12 months or so, The Viking Buddha is planning to publish several other books, so please keep an eye out for new titles coming out in the future including,

- Your Fight is our Fight: - this is a book about Mental Health, specifically aimed at families, loved ones, friends who are supporting someone with Mental Health problems.
- A Life Less Ordinary: - This book is an autobiography / life coaching book, based on The Viking Buddha's life, the ups and downs, and trials and triumphs, and tips on how to get the best out of life,
- The Viking Way: - this book is very much a book about Norse Mythology and what the Gods teach us about their flaws and strengths and how to transfer this into modern ay life. It also takes a deeper look into the Scandinavian ways of life in Hygge, Friluftsliv, Lagom, Sisu. Kalsarikanni

The Viking Buddha 3 day tour

The Viking Buddha tour is a 3-day tour, which is available internationally which includes
- Day 1: - The Viking Buddha full day Workshop
- Day 2: - The Viking Buddha full day workshop
- Day 3: - The Viking Buddha full day workshop
- The 2 hour 'LIFE' live Motivational Show
- Book signing event

If anyone would like to book the tour please contact the Viking buddha on +44 0330 043 3203

thevikingbuddha@yahoo.com
www.thevikingbuddha.co.uk

www.ingramcontent.com/pod-product-compliance
Lightning Source LLC
Chambersburg PA
CBHW070457120526
44590CB00013B/675